"Industry and Virtue Joined"
Schoolgirl Needlework of Northern New England

"Industry and Virtue Joined"
Schoolgirl Needlework of Northern New England

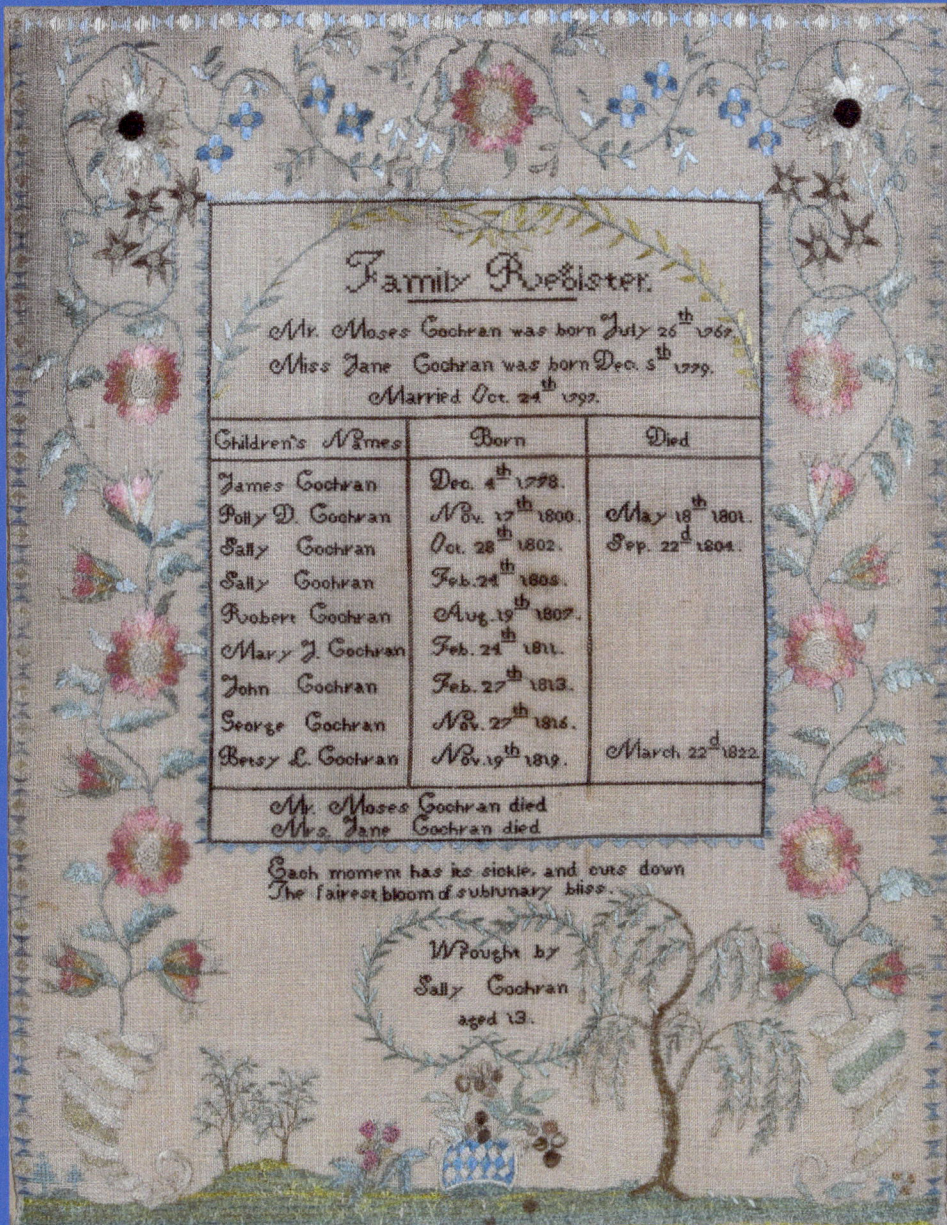

Tara Vose Raiselis

Leslie L. Rounds

Saco Museum

Saco, Maine

"Industry and Virtue Joined": Schoolgirl Needlework of Northern New England
ISBN 978-1-62137750-4

Published by Virtualbookworm.com Publishing Inc.
P.O. Box 9949
College Station, TX 77842
www.Virtualbookworm.com

This catalogue was published in conjunction with the exhibition
"Industry and Virtue Joined": Schoolgirl Needlework of Northern New England,"
organized by the Dyer Library and Saco Museum
and presented at the Saco Museum from May 9 through October 4, 2015.

Written by Tara Vose Raiselis and Leslie L. Rounds
Printed by Virtualbookworm.com Publishing

Contents

Oft as thine eye shall fondly trace
Those few lines I here exact
Whate'er the time, where'er the Place
Remember me my Friends

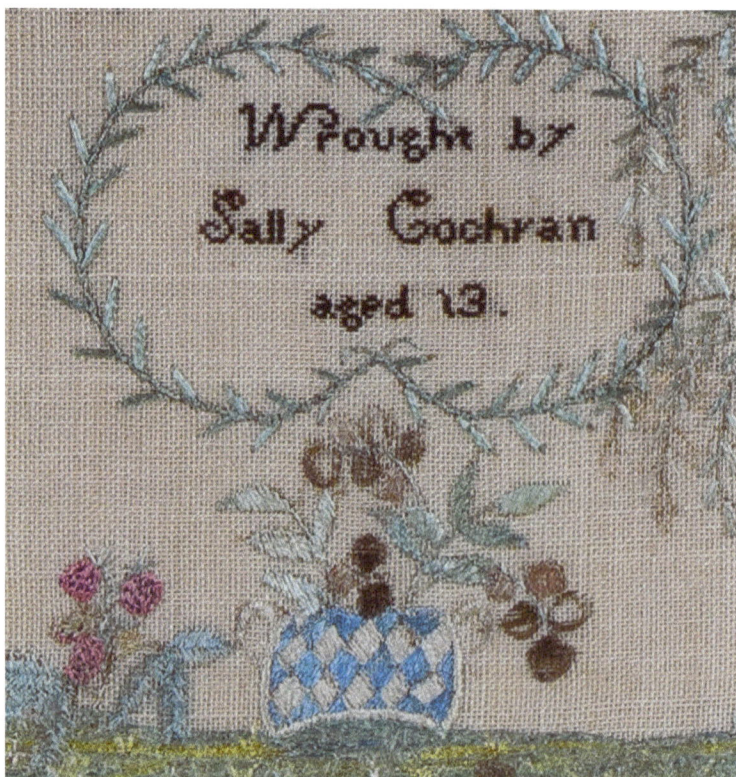

Acknowledgements

We wish to dedicate this book to our families, who have patiently listened to myriad, often tragic tales of sampler makers for just about two years now, as we worked on both the exhibition and this catalog. We thank them fervently for all their loving support and encouragement.

Many people have contributed to this effort. While we hope to name them all here, please forgive us if we inadvertently left someone out.

For providing major funding for this publication, thank you to Stephen and Julia Roberts. You've made this possible!

For assistance with research on the sampler makers and their teachers, Jill Jakeman was always willing to come through when we simply ran out of time to pursue some obscure clue.

Thank you to all the museums, historical societies, and private collectors who made access to their collections and knowledge so easy, but especially to Dan and Marty Campanelli, Glee Krueger and her family, Joanne Harvey, Sharon Lipton, Andrew Garthwaite, Henry Callan, and Sue and Dexter Pond for going above and beyond.

For wisdom, advice, and some key research, thank you to Lynne Anderson and Sheryl De Jong.

To staff members Carolyn Roy and Zoe Thomas, thank you for being there for every little thing!

Thank you again and again to Betty Ring, Ethel Stanwood Bolton, Eva Johnston Coe, and Glee Krueger. We stand on the shoulders of giants like these ladies when we undertake a project of this nature.

To the Dyer Library and Saco Museum Board of Trustees, thank you for your enthusiastic support and pride in the result.

Finally, we thank the sampler makers. Two hundred years ago, they patiently sat and stitched when their young bodies surely itched to do something a bit less tedious. Their perseverance and the wise guidance of their talented teachers led to the creation of this glorious and treasured body of work.

Tara Vose Raiselis and Leslie L. Rounds

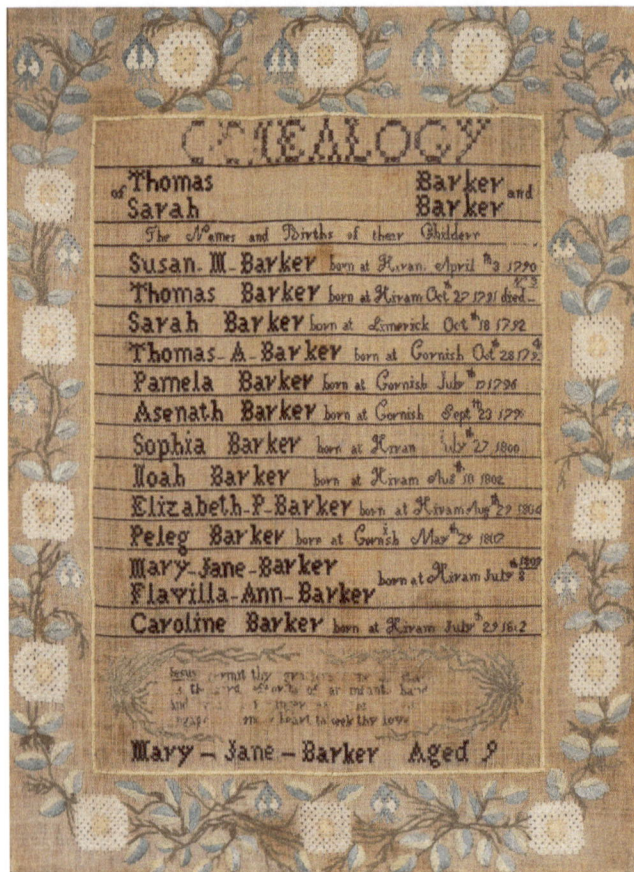

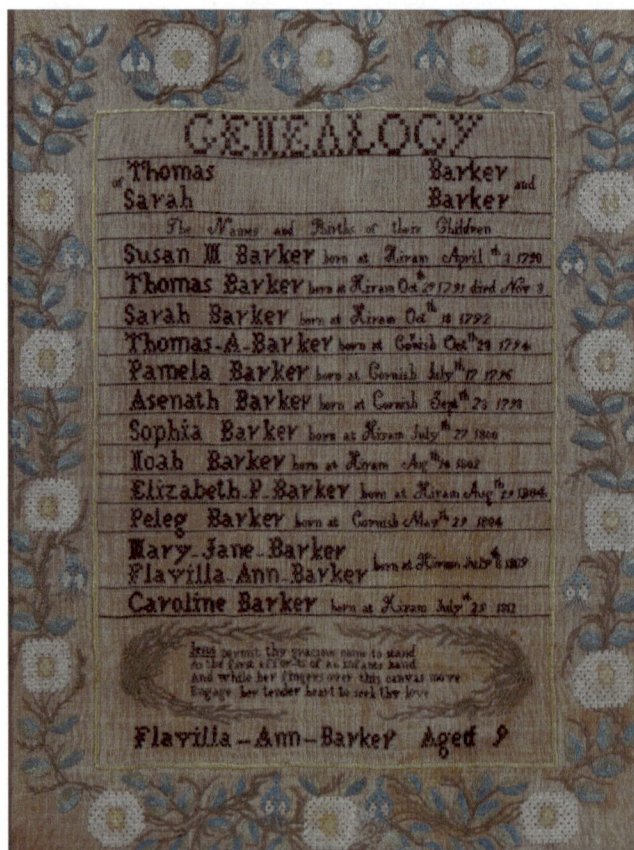

Introduction

Mary Jane Barker was among the youngest of the children of Thomas Barker and his wife, Sarah Ayer. The couple began their married lives in Hiram, Maine but by the time that Mary Jane and her twin sister Flavilla stitched their nearly identical samplers, Thomas had moved the family to Portland where he was operating a "public" or tavern. The twins' samplers feature queen stitch rose borders that had been immensely popular, even iconic, on Portland samplers for almost the last two decades, but were now becoming less stylish. Their roses are joined together by stretches of closely spaced leaves and their verses are surrounded by seaweed-like, olive green vines that are unlike any others on known Portland samplers.

The girls were just nine when they stitched their elaborate and informative needlework. Within a short time after they were done, Thomas Barker died. The loss of the breadwinner was a huge emotional—and economic—blow to a family of the period. Although his elder sons would take over the tavern, financial resources were likely uncertain, so, in 1825, when Timothy Eastman arrived in Portland, he must have seemed like a wonderful "catch." He had been born on January 17, 1798 in East Kingston, New Hampshire, educated at Dartmouth College and now was an apprentice physician. He was nearly twenty-eight to Mary Jane's barely sixteen when they were married on October 18, 1825. Not long afterward, Mary Jane and Flavilla—and quite likely their samplers as well—parted company. Timothy and Mary Jane moved to far off and very rural Canaan, Maine, near Skowhegan. Flavilla remained in Portland. In the first seven years of her marriage, young Mary Jane gave birth to five children, a frequency of child bearing that was unusual even in that era of large families.

Perhaps economic opportunities were not all that he had hoped for, or maybe Timothy had an urge to explore. For whatever the reason, in 1835 he packed up his very young family for the journey of a lifetime. They took the just-developing railroads across New England, filling in the gaps between lines by stagecoach. The 363-mile long Erie Canal had been completed ten years previously. They traveled up it from Albany, New York to the shore of Lake Erie. They sailed the full length of the Great Lake to Detroit. There they boarded a stagecoach and rode it as far as it went. Finally, their last mode of transportation was by canoe to the log cabin that would be their new home in the wilderness of western Michigan. Their oldest child was nine and their youngest a lively toddler not yet three years old. What Mary Jane felt about all of this is unknown. Many young wives made similar journeys and most found the separation from their birth families to be wrenching.

Although a gap of almost seven years went by with no recorded births, this may just signify a series of failed pregnancies. In 1842, less than a year after their cabin burned to the ground in the dead of winter, Mary Jane began to bear more children, giving birth in 1842, 1844, 1846, and 1848. She died at the age of just forty-three on April 7, 1853. Timothy, who was active in local politics and so well known that their now-village was renamed Eastmanville, made do until 1859, when he married Mary Jane and Flavilla's elder sister, Sophia, who was already twice widowed. Mary Jane's sampler was lovingly passed down through her children and grandchildren.

In 1921, when Ethel Stanwood Bolton and Eva Johnston Coe were assembling the list of samplers that would appear in the groundbreaking *American Samplers*, one of the contributors was the elderly Mrs. Jesse B. Thomas, who described Mary Jane's sampler at length. In addition to reporting the genealogical information and telling of "an odd cluster stitch," she reported a bit of family lore that had accompanied the needlework: "Mary Jane went to Mme. Niel's School in Portland with Henry W. Longfellow, hand in hand. They were playmates and near neighbors." Because of that information that linked a sampler to a school that I was researching—that of Rachel Hall Neal—at the time of our first exhibition, "I My Needle Ply with Skill," I became determined to try to track down Mary Jane's sampler. Surprisingly, and with the marvelous, revolutionary aid of the internet, I was partially successful. I found that it had been sold at auction in 2000 by Butterfields in San Francisco. Further work finally led to me to a copy of the auction catalog along with a photo of the sampler. It was shortly thereafter that I, quite by accident, discovered that the Androscoggin Historical Society owned the mate, the sampler stitched by Flavilla Barker.

Flavilla traveled a different route in life than her twin. She married James Mason Williams of Taunton, Massachusetts. He was the son of Joshua Williams and his wife, Frances. Born in 1802, he, too, was a somewhat older man than his young bride. When they were married on November 21, 1826, (when Flavilla was only seventeen), he had been living in Dixfield, Maine, where they resided for the first several years of their marriage. They later relocated back to his hometown, as she became the mother of three sons and two daughters, two of whom died in early childhood. James was a successful Taunton merchant when he was enumerated on the 1850 census, but things were about to go very badly for the Williams family. By the 1855 state census that Massachusetts conducted, James was living with only his son Seth in Taunton. No record could be found for any of the other Williams family members then or in 1860, but the 1865 Massachusetts census found Flavilla living in a boarding house in Worcester. By 1870, she was an inmate of the large Northampton State Hospital, described as "keeping house" but "insane." Flavilla was reunited with her husband and two of her children when she died on January 15, 1882, and was buried alongside them in Taunton. Virgil Williams, who was born during their time in Dixfield, later married a young woman from Maine. They relocated to California where he worked as an artist. When his wife, Dora, died in 1915, she was buried in Androscoggin County, Maine. It seems possible that her Maine connection was the reason that Flavilla's sampler returned to the state where it was made, and was donated to the Androscoggin Historical Society; their records for the donation are uncertain, however.

Since Henry Wadsworth Longfellow's education is a matter of historical record, and because it was in the school of Abigail Fellows, it seems most probable that the Barker twins were also among her students. Widowed at a fairly young age, (a common situation among the preceptresses of female academies), she operated a long-lasting but rarely mentioned academy in Portland. Her husband was a mariner and died in Havana in 1806. A son of theirs may also have died there about fifteen years later, which might have been the reason that she visited Havana in 1820. Although records are uncertain, she probably died while there. Henry Wadsworth Longfellow was born February 27, 1807, making him just a couple of years older than the Barker twins. He was said to have attended Mrs. Fellows' school at a very young age, perhaps when he was about four, several years before the Barker girls worked their samplers.

When we advertised in *Maine Antiques Digest* that we were seeking northern New England samplers for "Industry and Virtue Joined," we were contacted by the new owners of Mary Jane Barker's sampler, Pamela and Alan Kirby, who generously offered to loan it for the exhibition. Since it is very likely that the samplers parted company in 1825, when Mary Jane was married, that would mean that 190 years have passed since the last time these two works hung side by side. And so, these samplers manage to incorporate many of the myriad fascinating themes that schoolgirl needlework of the late eighteenth and early nineteenth centuries encompass. The samplers provide a detailed and accurate look at the genealogy of a family, as many northern New England samplers do. They provide hints to a rich and deeply complex tale of the life journeys of two women of the period: to a settler's travels to a new land, to the challenges of large families, to the consequences of mental illness in the 1800s, to the interconnectedness of siblings even in the face of scattered families, and to the resourcefulness of widows and young unmarried women of the Federal era. They tell us about the survival of textiles over two centuries, and in the case of Mary Jane, raise the intriguing image of her rescuing her treasured sampler off the wall of her burning cabin.

Finally, and most importantly, they tell us about the creativity of a generation of women in a time when expectations for females were sharply constrained. They remind us of the hopefulness of children who surely must have dreamed big dreams as they patiently worked stitch after tiny stitch over hours and hours of time, in summer heat or bitter winter cold. It has been a great joy for us to bring together another major collection of schoolgirl needlework and to preserve that collection in this book, because all of these themes resonate deeply with us, as I believe they do with you, as well. We celebrate again the lives of a talented but too easily forgotten generation.

Leslie L. Rounds

Marking Samplers

When Infant Genius First Appears

Basic marking samplers represented the introductory level of stitchery in the eighteenth and early nineteenth centuries. Typically, grade school-aged girls created these first stitchery projects to gain mastery of basic needle and thread techniques. Some of these early efforts were never framed and remain well preserved today. The styles of alphabets and numbers learned with these simple works were used to mark household linens and often-washed clothing—shirts and underwear primarily—to make for easier sorting and the proper rotation of expensive textiles.

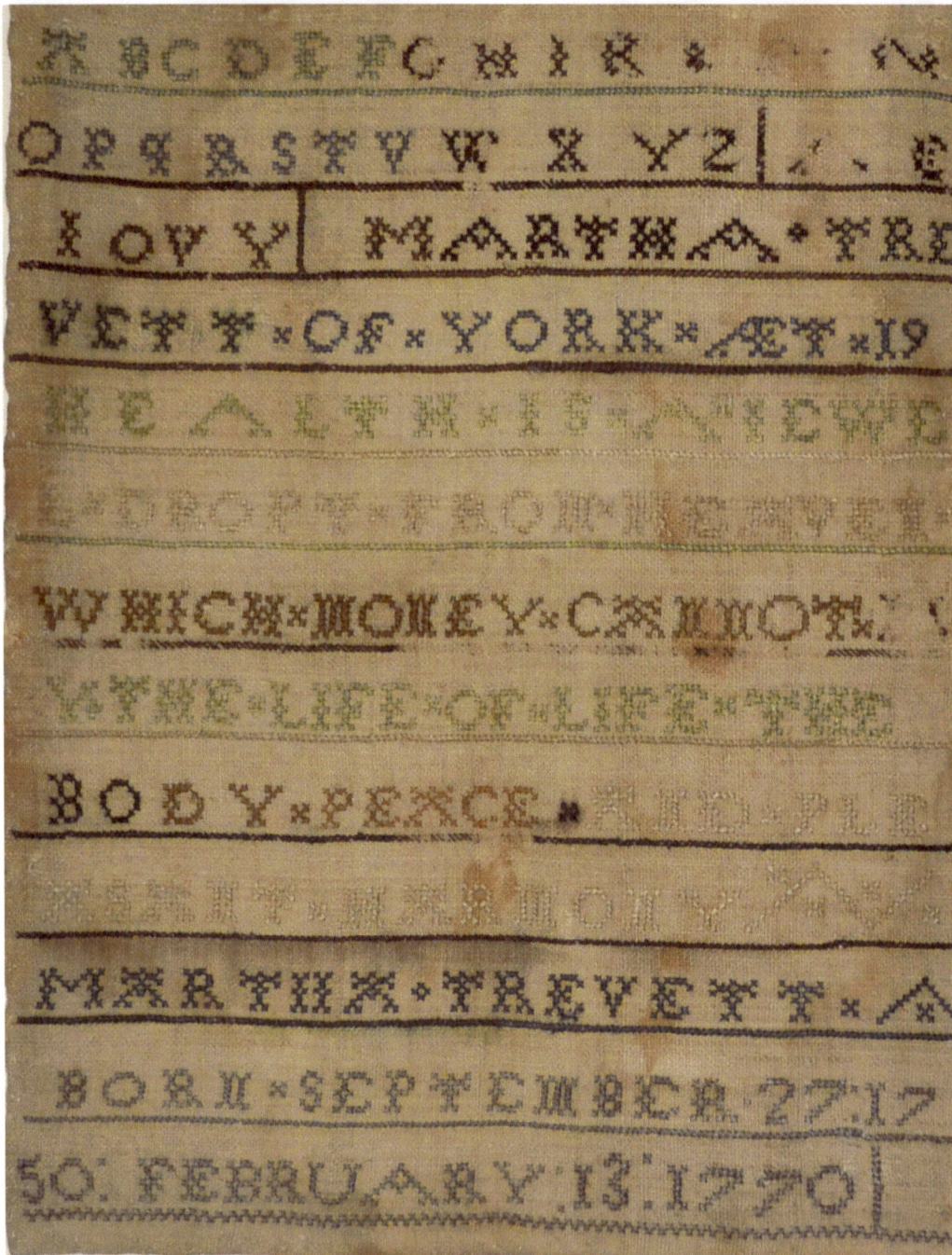

Martha Trevett (1750-1837), York, Maine, 1770. Silk thread on linen, 9 x 7 1/4". Stitches: cross. Strawbery Banke Museum.

Martha worked her marking sampler at the relatively advanced age of nineteen. She was born September 27, 1750, in York, Maine, the daughter of Hannah Sewall and her second husband, Richard Trevett. Richard was an ardent supporter of the American Revolution, serving on the local Committee of Correspondence and commanding a privateer during the conflict. After the war, he was appointed the first United States Collector of Customs in York, Maine. Martha married John Pike in 1770. The couple lived in Somersworth, (now Rollinsford), New Hampshire, where John served as a Justice of the Peace for thirty-five years. Martha and John had seven children. Sampler maker Betsy Wallingford (page 86) married Martha's son Nathaniel Green Pike in 1815. John Pike died in 1833 and Martha passed away four years later at the age of eighty-seven. They are both buried in the John H. Roberts Burying Ground in Rollinsford.

Jane Clark Haslett (1788-?), Portsmouth, New Hampshire, 1801. Silk thread on linen, 16 x 8". Stitches: hem, cross, satin. Strawbery Banke Museum.

Jane Clark Haslett was born June 8, 1788, in Portsmouth. Her father, Matthew, a leather worker, was originally from Boston. In 1766, Mathew and his older brother James came to Portsmouth and established their leather business at the "sign of the Buck and Glove." The partnership lasted until 1773, when Matthew left the business and shortly thereafter married Ann Frost. Jane was the fourth of nine children in the family. In 1813, she married Ichabod Earl of South Berwick, Maine.

Betsy Lane (?-1856), Stratham, New Hampshire, 1803. Silk thread on linsey-woolsey, 8 3/4 x 11 1/4". Stitches: cross. Collection of Glee Krueger.

Elizabeth "Betsy" Lane was one of the nine or ten children of Jabez Lane and his wife, Eunice Colcord. Jabez's father, Deacon Joshua Lane, and grandfather, Deacon Samuel Lane, were among the early settlers of Stratham. Elizabeth had three older sisters and one or two younger ones; it is quite likely that they all completed some type of embroidery as children. Betsy's simple marking sampler on linsey-woolsey might have been stitched in a district school or at home under the instruction of her mother. Her inclusion of birds, flowers, and hearts adds an additional dimension and no doubt made the work more fun for a ten-year-old. On July 25, 1815, Betsy married Charles Balker Orne, a farmer from Wolfeboro, New Hampshire, on the shore of Lake Winnipesaukee, a long distance from her former home. The births of two daughters are recorded in Wolfeboro vital records; the 1830 census hints that there might have been three little girls altogether. Like her father, Charles was a farmer, tanner, and shoemaker. According to a published Lane genealogy, Charles died at the Concord Insane Asylum, although the death date noted in that book is two months earlier than the one recorded on his grave, May 5, 1856. He is buried in Wolfeboro beside Betsy, who died January 6, 1856.

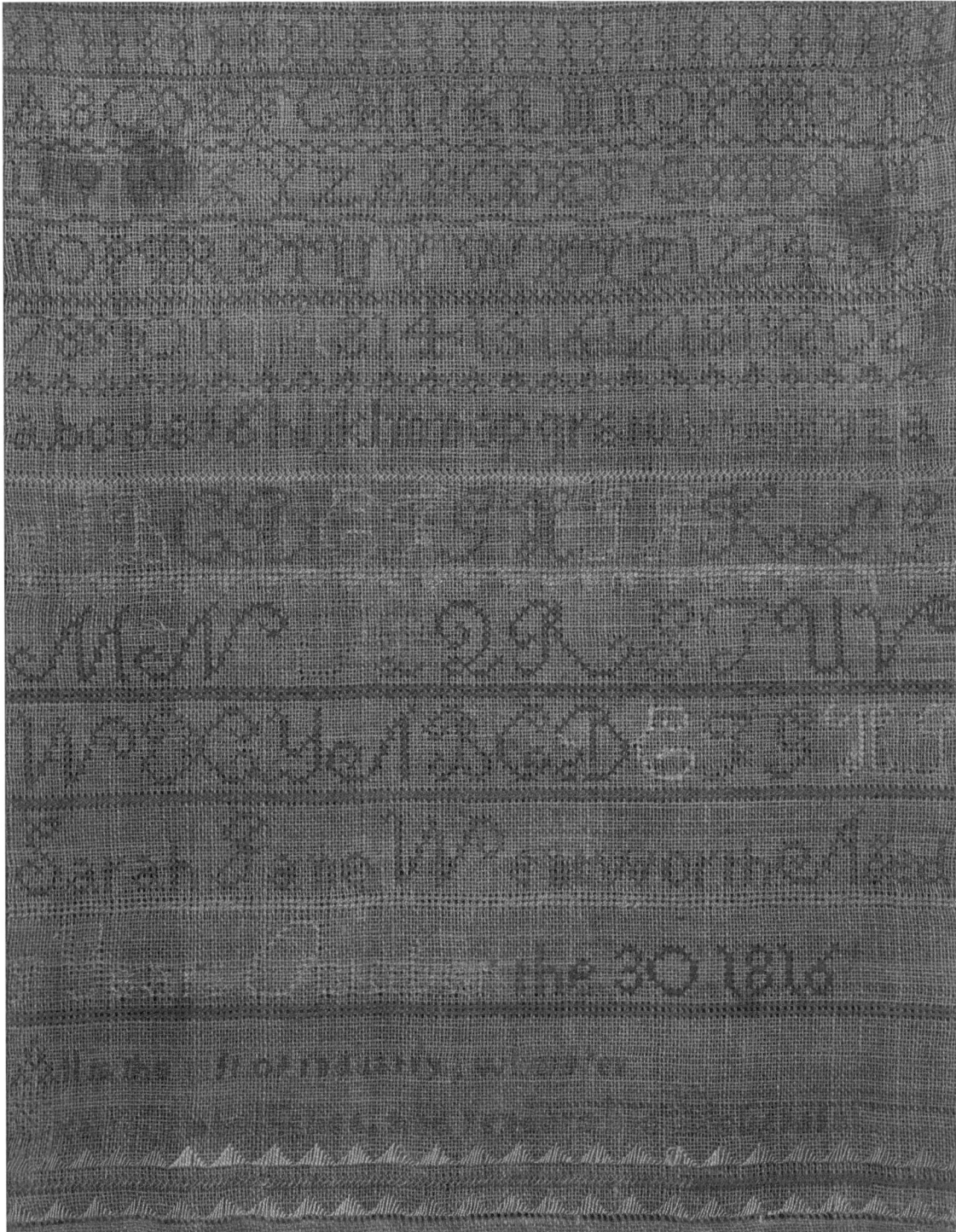

Sarah Jane Wentworth (1807-1841), Portsmouth, New Hampshire, 1816. Silk thread on linen, 15 x 12 1/4".
Stitches: cross, satin. Private collection.

Joshua Wentworth and Anne Tredick of Portsmouth married in June 1806, and their daughter Sarah Jane was born in August of the following year. Sadly, in 1816—the year Sarah worked this sampler—both her father and her younger brother, Joshua, aged seven, died. Sarah's mother, Anne, married Samuel Furnald the following year, and the couple moved to Troy, New York; it is unclear whether Sarah moved to New York as well. Anne Wentworth Furnald passed away in Troy in 1824. Sarah married Captain William Parker of Portsmouth in November 1829. The couple had three children, Ann, Robert, and Sarah. Their son, Robert, died September 15, 1841, at the age of five, and Sarah died twelve days later. She was thirty-four years old.

Laura Chapman (1799-1874), Keene, New Hampshire, 1810. Silk thread on linen, 7 x 12 1/4". Stitches: cross, satin. Collection of Leslie Rounds.

Laura Chapman's background is a bit mysterious. According to a family tree on Ancestry.com, she was the daughter of Jonah Chapman and Molly Blaisdell, who were married in Campton, New Hampshire, on February 4, 1781. Their first six children were born there between 1782-1789. The family tree states that Laura was born in Upper Canada, the early name for Ontario, on March 1, 1799, and when asked on the census in later life, Laura always stated that she had been born in Canada. Census records indicate that Jonah relocated to Newbury, Vermont, by 1790 where he lived for the remainder of his life and died on July 18, 1830. The first record for Laura appeared was when she marked her sampler in September 1810 in Keene. At that time, residing in Keene was Calvin Chapman and his wife, Sarah Nims, who were married on January 1, 1795, and were parents to at least fifteen children born between 1795-1820. The births are closely spaced and recorded on New Hampshire vital records. Could Laura be their daughter instead? On January 28, 1817, Laura Chapman of Keene married Moses Leonard, son of Noah Leonard and Bethia Wetherell. The couple lived in Danville, Vermont, for many years and all their children were born there: three sons and six daughters, several of whom died in childhood. Their eldest son, Willard, died as a Confederate prisoner of war at Andersonville Prison in 1864. By 1850, Laura and Moses had moved to Nashua, New Hampshire, with their daughter, Charlotte, where Moses worked with sheet iron. Sometime before 1870 they moved in with their son, Orin, in Illinois. Laura died August 6, 1874, in Fall River, Wisconsin, where both Moses and Laura were buried.

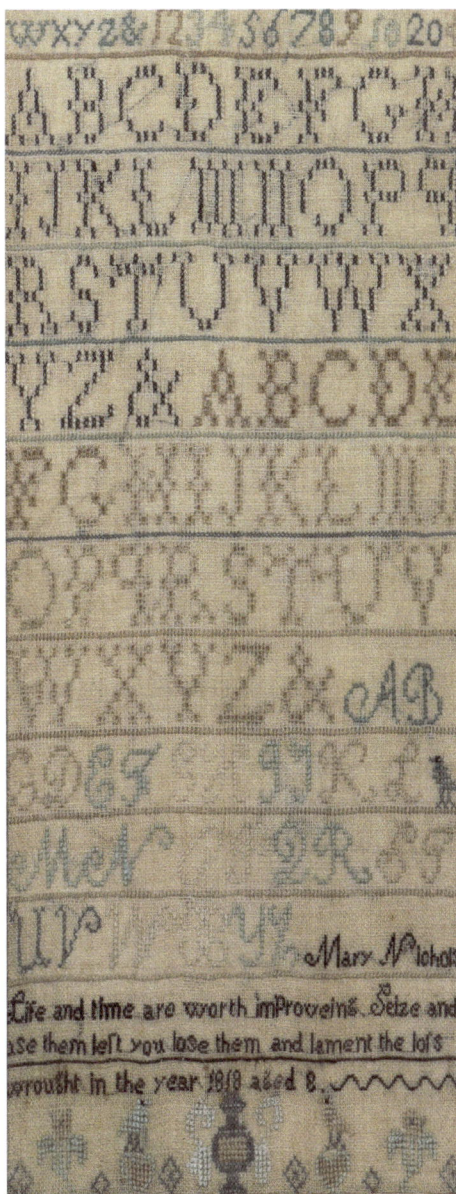

Mary Nichols (1809-1865), Antrim, New Hampshire, 1818. Silk thread on linen, 17 1/4 x 8". Stitches: cross, eyelet. Collection of Glee Kreuger.

On November 25, 1790, Ebenezer Nichols married Elizabeth "Betsey" Dix in Reading, Massachusetts. This may have been his second marriage, following closely after his first wife's death in childbirth the preceding winter. Ten children have been attributed to Ebenezer and his two wives, with the first six probably all born in Reading. By around 1803, the family relocated to Antrim in west central New Hampshire where their last four children were born, including Mary Ellen Nichols on September 23, 1809. In 1818, Miss Mary Nichols advertised in the *New Hampshire Patriot* that she "proposed to open a school near the dwelling of Mark Woodbury" and that she would teach young ladies "in all the useful branches." This Mary Nichols was not the same Mary Nichols who stitched this sampler in 1818, but her first cousin and probably her teacher. The Mary Nichols who operated an academy was the third child of Deacon Daniel Nichols and his wife, Mary Dinsmore, born September 19, 1793, and was described in *The History of Antrim, New Hampshire* as "finely educated, and became a successful teacher." She died in 1823 while on a visit to New York. Even though the travel distance from Antrim to Reading was vast, there seems to have been a considerable amount of family mobility, since, as the Nichols children grew up, most of them married people in northeastern Massachusetts. Mary Ellen married Daniel Rowe of Lynn, Massachusetts, a New Hampshire-born fisherman who was not especially successful financially. They were the parents of five boys and two girls, the youngest just fourteen when Mary Ellen died of "lung fever" in Lynn, Massachusetts, on October 12, 1865.

*Hannah McMurphy (1806-1839), Londonderry, New Hampshire, 1818. Silk thread on linen, 13 1/2 x 12".
Stitches: cross, Algerian eye. Londonderry Historical Society, Londonderry, New Hampshire.*

When Hannah and her younger sister, Mary, stitched their very similar marking samplers in 1818, the Pinkerton Academy had been providing instruction to both males and females in Londonderry for at least a year, but their works bear no resemblance to the large body of work now associated with that school. Hannah is included on the list of students who attended Adams Female Academy in 1824 and 1825, after she stitched this sampler. They were the second and third of the nine children of Alexander McMurphy and his wife, Sally Duncan, married February 2, 1797. It was not until after the sixth of their children was born, in about 1810, that Alexander moved the family from the original one-room log cabin on his ancestral family land, to a much more commodious home up on a hill. According to *Wiley's Book of Nutfield*, Hannah's younger sister Sarah (who also later attended Adams Female Academy) was "brought from the old log house by the brook in a cradle to the new house on the hill," an event that is difficult to imagine! Hannah died unmarried on January 21, 1839.

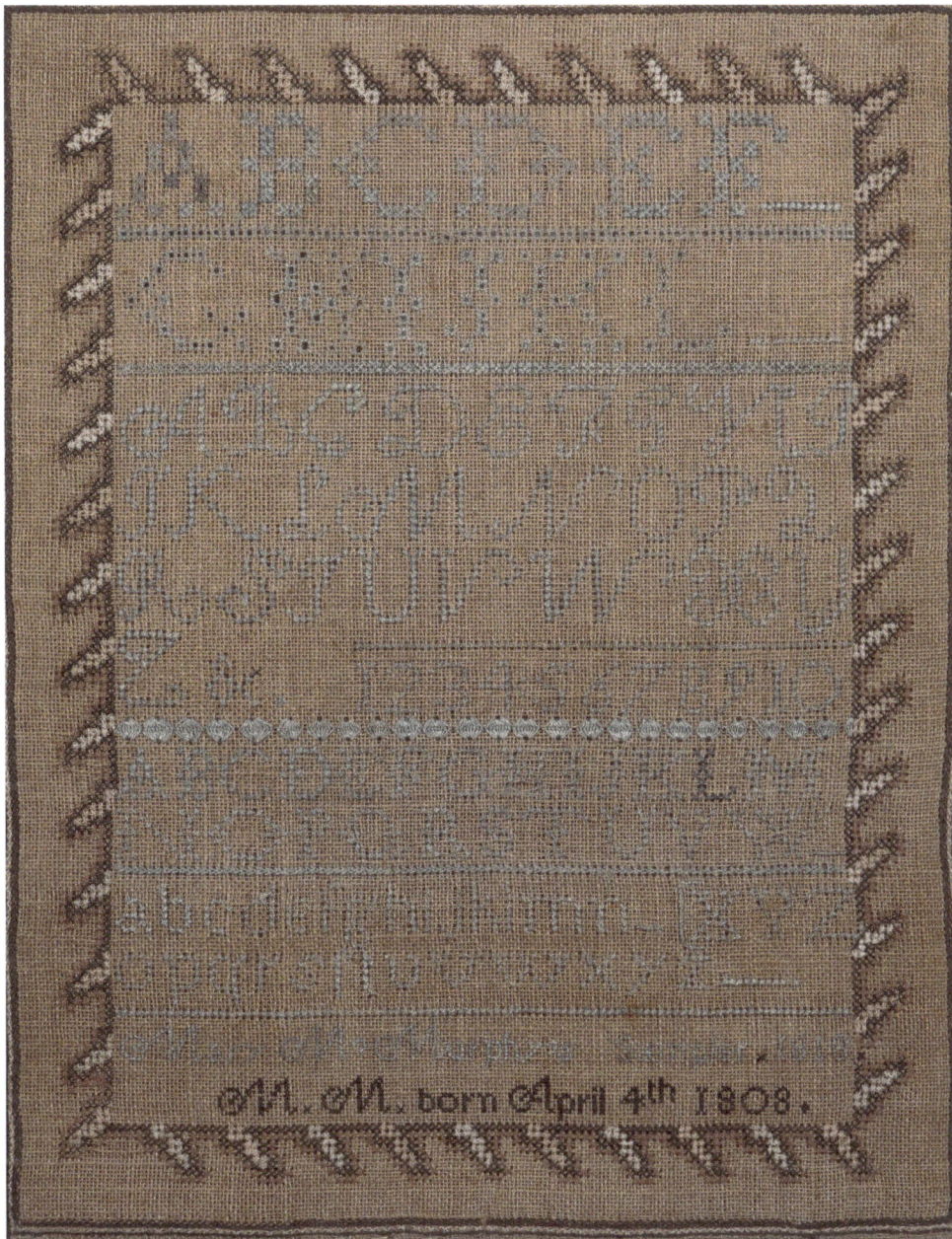

Mary McMurphy (1808-1893), Londonderry, New Hampshire, 1818. Silk thread on linen, 14 1/4 x 11 1/4". Stitches: cross, Algerian eye. Londonderry Historical Society, Londonderry, New Hampshire.

Mary is one of the few sampler makers of whom we have a photograph, taken in much later life. The second eldest daughter of Alexander McMurphy and Sally (Sarah) Duncan, she grew up in Londonderry where her father was a farmer of no more than middling means. An online family history of the McMurphys reports that she was, "one of a committee of young ladies to welcome the General Marquis de Lafayette passing thru Londonderry on his journey from Portsmouth to Concord, New Hampshire. She married Nathaniel Corning April 4, 1831. They had seven children. Mary was a graduate of Adams' Female Seminary." She is included on the list of students who attended Adams Female Academy in 1825. She and Nathaniel were the parents of five sons and a daughter. On the 1850 and 1860 censuses, they were living in Manchester, New Hampshire. In 1850, Nathaniel was listed as a laborer. In 1860, when they lived in a modest home that they owned, he was described as a "job taker," an occupational listing that might mean he hired out for the day. Shortly after the census was completed, he died of "apoplexy," a tragedy that boded ill for his surviving family. In 1870, Mary and her daughter Mary were both among the eighteen boarders in her son Alexander's large boarding house. Although Mary's occupation is illegible, her eighteen-year-old daughter was working in the hosiery mill. The final snapshot of Mary's life is provided by the 1880 census, when she had moved back to the town of her birth, Londonderry, and was living by herself but next door to her son Alexander and his family. Mary died April 1, 1893.

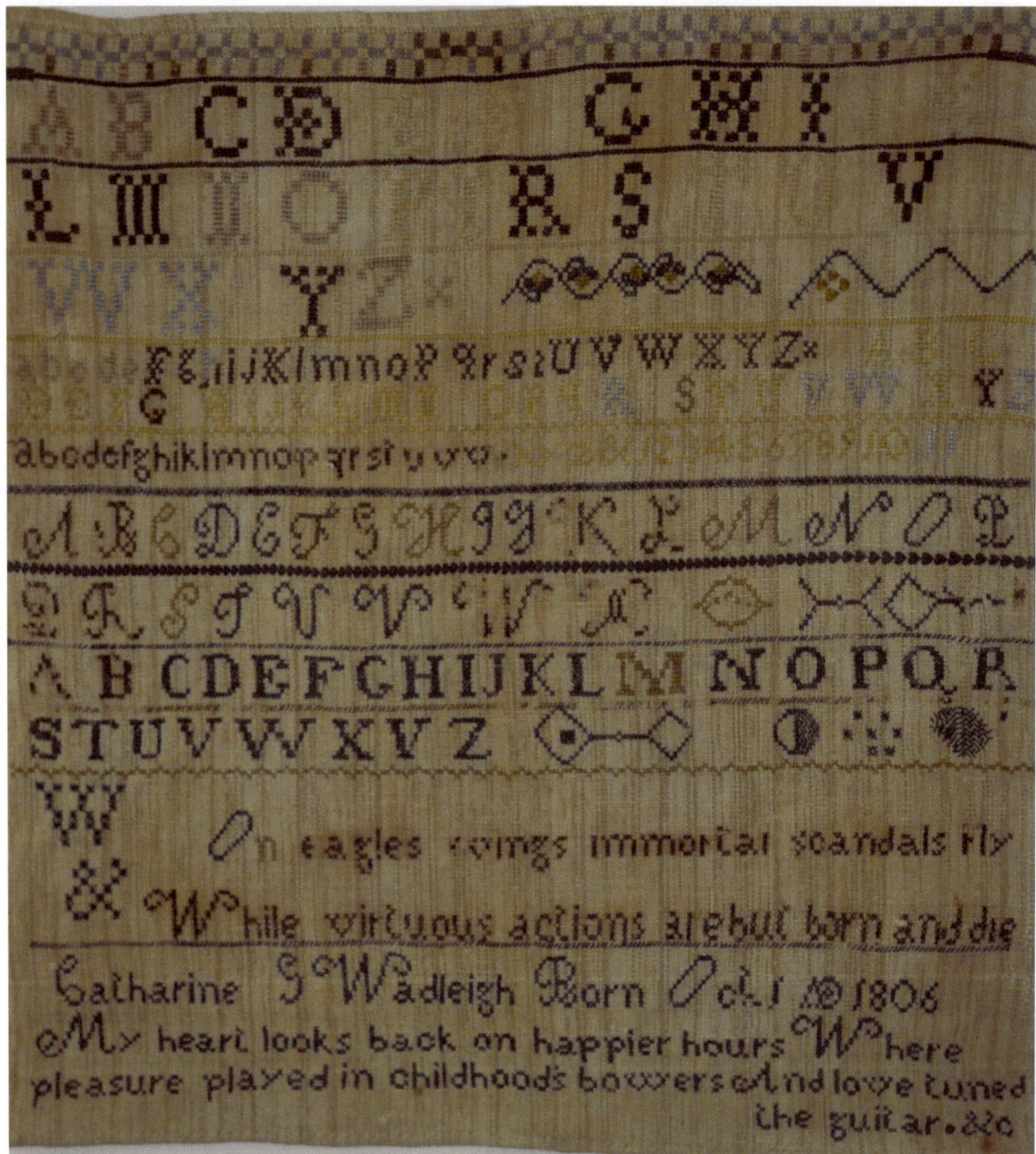

Catherine G. Wadleigh (1806-1890), Parsonfield, Maine, circa 1816. Silk thread on linen, 14 1/2 x 13 3/4".
Stitches: cross, satin, straight, French knot, Algerian eye. Courtesy of The Brick Store Museum, Kennebunk, Maine.

The youngest of Elisha Wadleigh and Sally Smith's seven children, Catherine Wadleigh was born October 1, 1806, in Parsonfield, Maine. Her parents had married in Kittery, but moved to Parsonfield by the end of the 1790s, where Elisha took up farming. In December 1834, Catherine married Stephen Wedgwood of Newport, Maine. It is unclear how many children the couple had, since no birth records were found, but the 1850 Newport census records provide some clues. In 1850, there were eight people under the age of twenty-two listed in the Wedgwood household. The three oldest, ranging in age from nineteen to twenty-two, were all too old to have been Catherine's children since their births predate her marriage. The remaining four, from ages one to five, may have been. Stephen was nine years older than Catherine and he may have been married before. The couple did have at least one daughter, named Vienna, born shortly after they married. Stephen died in 1879, at the age of eighty-two. Catherine passed away eleven years later in 1890. They are buried in the Riverside Cemetery in Newport, Maine, along with their daughter, Vienna Wedgwood Pratt, and other Wedgwood family members.

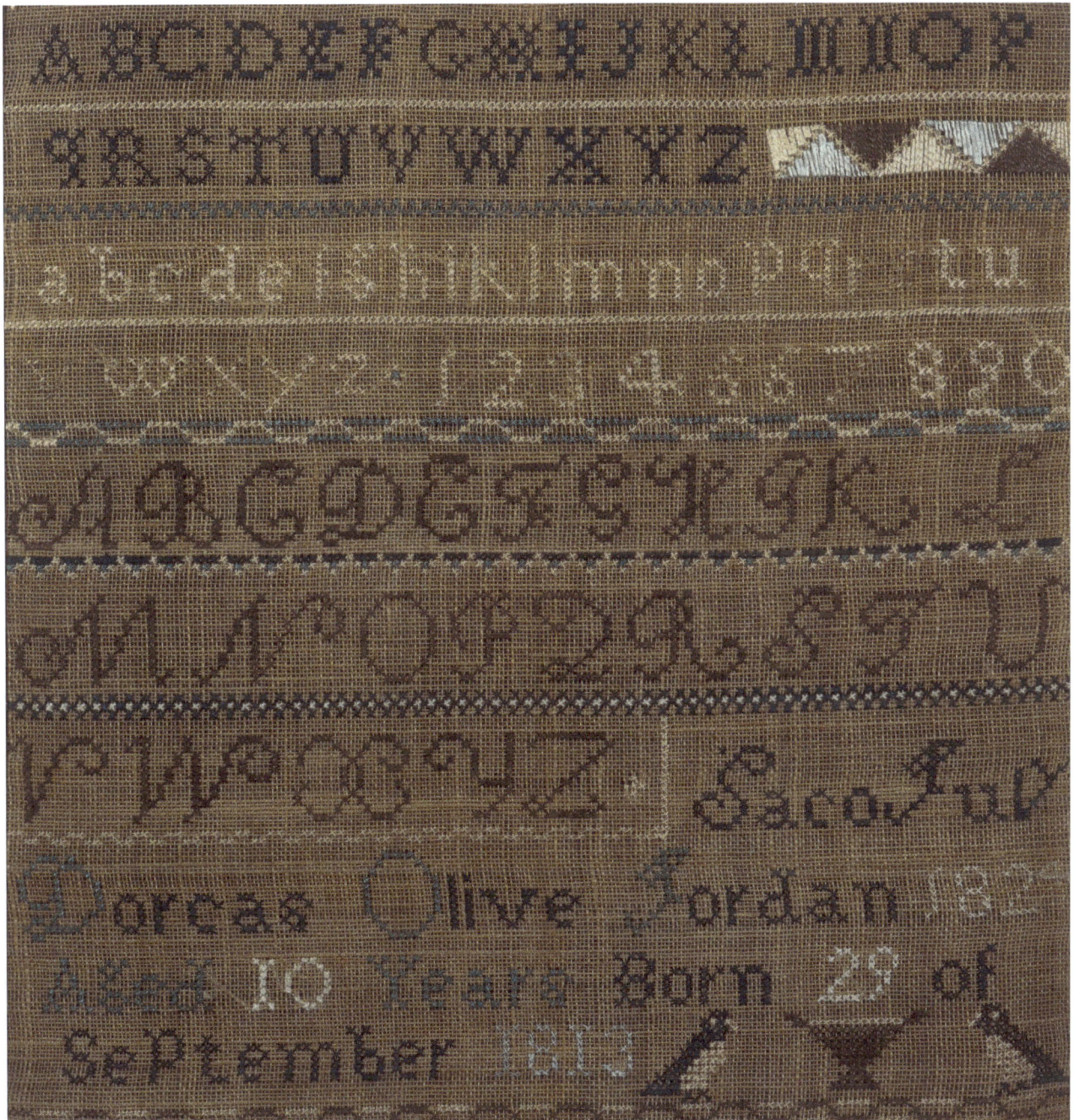

Dorcas Olive Jordan (1813-1883), Saco, Maine, 1824. Silk thread on linen, 12 1/4 x 12 1/4". Stitches: cross, satin. Private collection.

Dorcas Olive Jordan was the eldest of the eight children of Rishworth Jordan and Hannah Frost of Saco. Her parents married April 12, 1813, and Dorcas was born five months later, on September 29, 1813. Dorcas married Gilbert Sawyer on October 12, 1835. Unfortunately, they did not have a long and happy marriage. In November 1847, Gilbert was a passenger on board a schooner bound for Georgia, and was lost overboard in a serious snowstorm two days out of port. After her husband's death, Dorcas returned to her parent's home and lived with them until they both passed away, first her father in 1868 and then her mother two years later. By 1880, Dorcas was sharing her home with her younger sister, Mary H. Fogg, a widow. Dorcas died in 1883, aged sixty-nine, and is buried in Laurel Hill Cemetery, Saco, next to the marker for her husband, Gilbert.

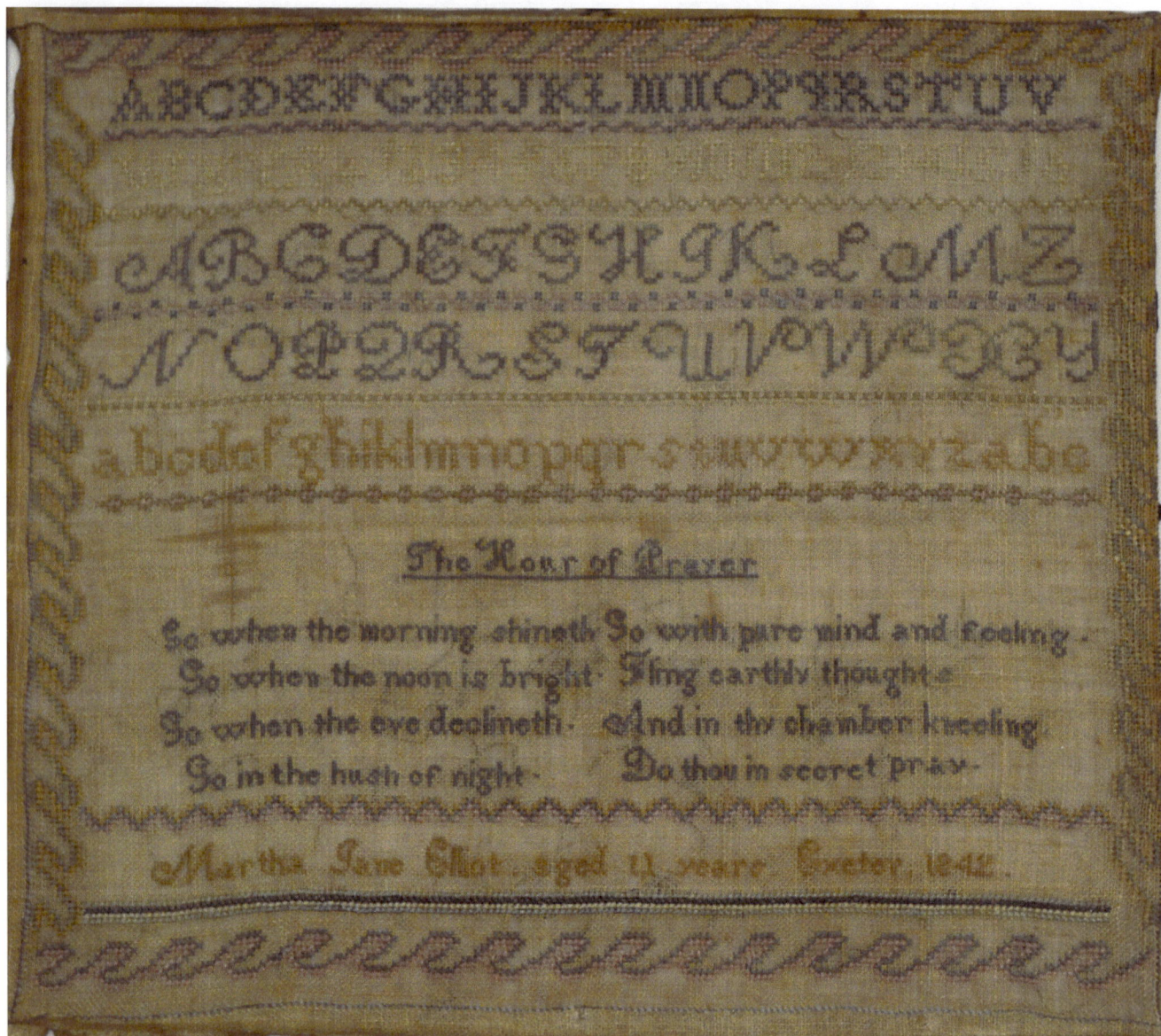

Martha Jane Elliot (1830-1902), Exeter, New Hampshire, 1842. Silk thread on linen, 11 1/4 x 12 1/2". Stitches: cross, hem. Exeter Historical Society.

Martha Jane Elliot was born on August 4, 1830, in Exeter, New Hampshire. She was the eldest child of Edmund Elliot, a prosperous Exeter merchant, and Eliza S. Gilman. Martha probably worked her sampler at the Exeter Female Academy under the instruction of Miss Emily S. Colcord of South Berwick, who taught at the academy from 1836 to 1843. In 1854, Martha married Henry R. Merrill, the son of a prominent local hat and wool dealer. Henry was also from a large family, and his younger brother, Abner Little Merrill, married sampler maker Harriet Robinson (page 17). Henry was a paint and oil dealer, and he and Martha moved to Boston. They had one child in 1855, a daughter named Sarah. Henry died in 1897 and Martha passed away five years later. They both are buried with the Merrill family in the Exeter Cemetery.

Harriet Robinson (1828-1894), Exeter, New Hampshire, 1839. Silk thread on linen, 13 x 12 1/4". Stitches: cross, satin. Exeter Historical Society.

Harriet Robinson was the second of three daughters born to Jeremiah Leavitt Robinson and Irene Fellows. She worked her sampler at the age of eleven while attending the Exeter Female Academy, just a few years after Martha Jane Elliot was a student there. In 1859, Harriet married Abner Little Merrill, a member of a well-to-do local family involved in the wool trade, and a graduate of both Phillips Exeter Academy and Harvard. The couple made their home in Boston, where he was involved in a prosperous paint business with his brother, Henry. Throughout their lives, Abner and Harriet remained involved with life in their home town of Exeter, and provided a great deal of financial support for several local institutions, including Phillips Exeter Academy.

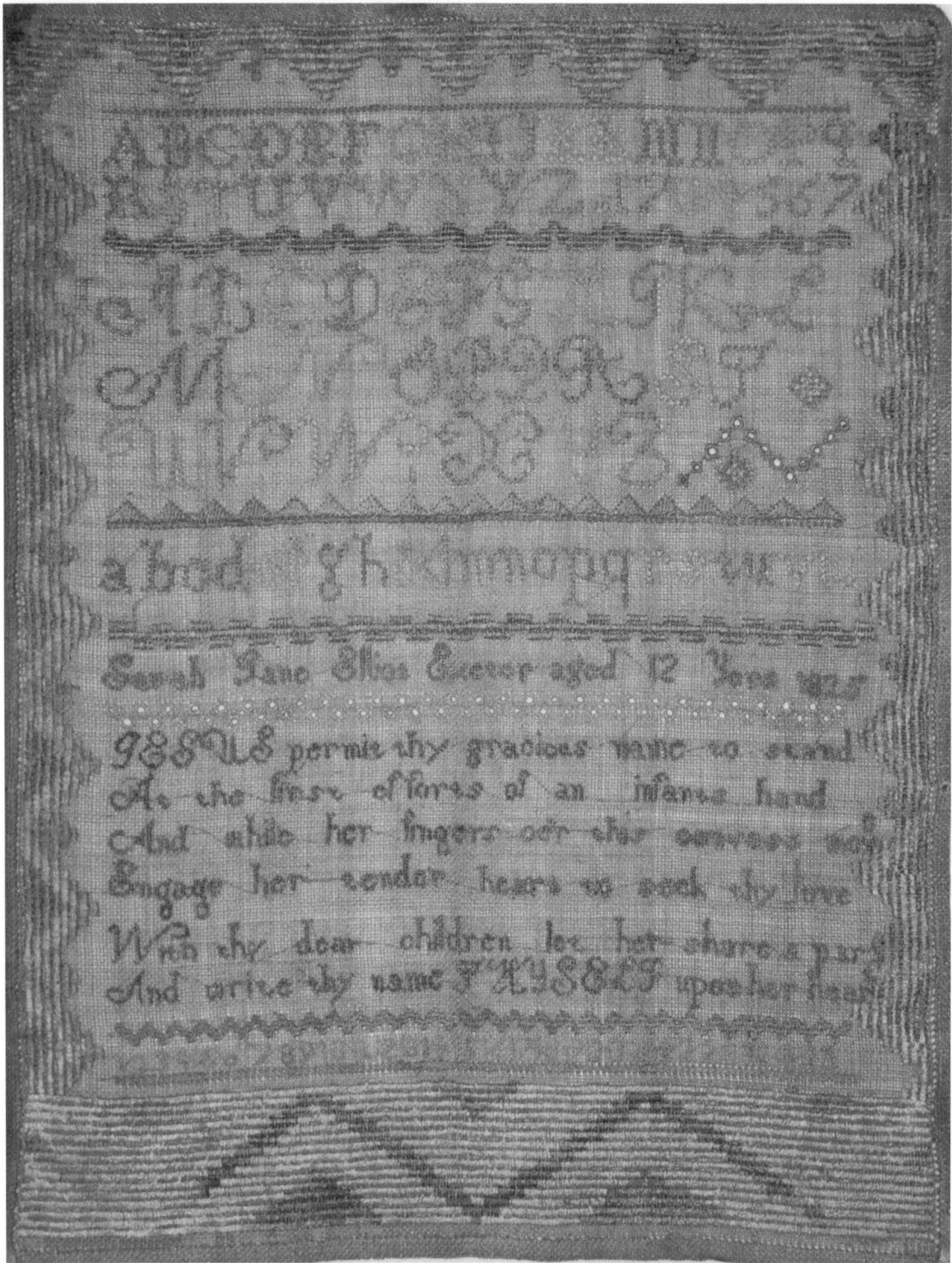

Sarah Jane Elliot (1813- ?), Exeter, New Hampshire, 1825. Silk thread on linen, 17 x 14 1/4". Stitches: cross, satin, hem. Exeter Historical Society.

Sarah Jane stitched a very unusual band across the bottom of her sampler, solidly filling the area. Although no vital records from Exeter note her birth, it is likely that she was one of the children of John Elliot, a sailor, and his wife, Nancy, or sometimes "Ann," who were the only Elliots recorded on census records in Exeter in 1810 and 1820. There is a female of the right age to be Sarah Jane in John's household in 1820. It is possible that she is the Sarah Jane Elliot who married John James in Exeter on October 13, 1835. That might be the John James who passed away there in 1842, but no further records could be found for his widow. John Elliot and his wife lived the last years of their lives at the Exeter Town Farm where they were enumerated on the 1850 census, he there because of poverty and Nancy listed as "insane."

Hannah M. Bachelder (1817-1898), Exeter, Maine, 1833. Silk thread on linen, 11 5/8 x 16". Stitches: hem, cross, satin, herringbone, eyelet. Collection of Glee Krueger.

Like many of the early settlers of rural Penobscot County in Maine, Nathaniel Bachelder was a New Hampshire native. Large areas of Penobscot County are relatively flat, fertile, easily tilled land that must have compared very favorably to the much rockier, more hilly farmland of New Hampshire. Census records indicate that Nathaniel relocated to Exeter, Maine, by at least 1820. Hannah, born August 28, 1817, was one of several children. On June 1, 1840, Hannah married George Morton of Exeter. Although they tried farming in Jackman, Maine, eventually they resettled in Garland, the town next to Exeter. Census records indicate that they were not wealthy. They were the parents of at least three sons, and perhaps a couple of daughters. Hannah died March 15, 1898, and was buried next to her husband, who had died in 1892, in Evergreen Cemetery in Garland. Her simple marking sampler gives no clues to its Maine origin and had previously been thought to have been stitched in Exeter, New Hampshire.

Judith Jane Haynes (1818-1888), Deerfield, New Hampshire, 1832. Silk thread on linen, 17 1/2 x 12 3/4". Stitches: hem, cross, eyelet. Collection of Glee Krueger.

Judith Jane Haynes stitched her marking sampler in Deerfield, New Hampshire and, unfortunately, provided us with only slender clues to her identity. When did she stitch this sampler? Judith included the letter "J" on her sampler, although not in every alphabet, and once she stitched it backward. The letter J often does not appear on eighteenth-century samplers so perhaps that is a clue that Judith did her work in the nineteenth century. Another unreliable hint is that Judith included her middle name. Middle names were less common in the eighteenth century but became very popular in the early nineteenth century. Judith Jane appears to have been the youngest child of William Haines and his wife, Elizabeth Merrill, born in Deerfield on December 27, 1818. Her father was a son of Deacon David Haines and his first wife, Mercy James. After Mercy's death, David remarried, to Jemima Pulcifer. On February 21, 1848, Judith married Samuel G. Haines, who was the son of Samuel Haines, one of the offspring of David Haines' second marriage. The couple remained in Deerfield, where Samuel was a farmer. By 1870, they seemed to have suffered a severe financial loss, no longer owning a home, and with their personal property seriously diminished in value. They were parents to a son and a daughter. Judith died in Deerfield in June of 1888.

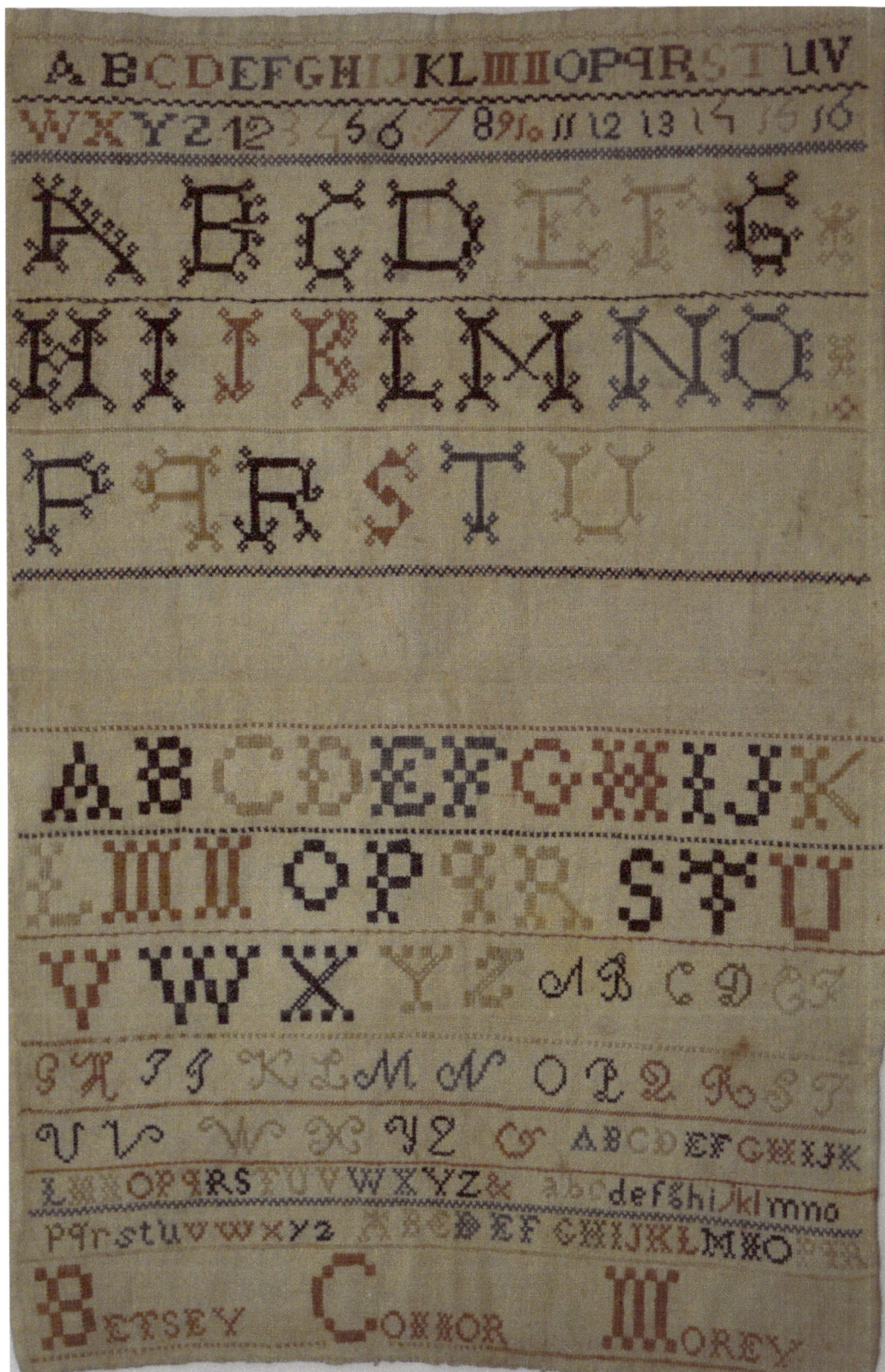

Betsy Conner Morey (1826-1898), Wilmot, New Hampshire, circa 1836. Silk thread on linen, 19 1/2 x 13 3/4". Stitches: cross. New Hampshire Historical Society.

The most notable feature of Betsy's sampler is the large, unusual alphabet near the top. Similar elaborate alphabets with curlicues are found on Scottish samplers, and they also appear on needlework produced in a number of towns close to Wilmot, including Hopkinton and Henniker. Betsy Conner Morey was the daughter of Nathan Morey and Lydia Carr of Wilmot. In 1846, Betsy married Stephen C. Howlett of Sutton; the couple had three boys. Betsy died in 1898.

Abigail H. L. Dunlap (1828-1854), Weare, New Hampshire, 1841. Silk thread on linen, 9 3/4 x 9 1/2". Stitches: cross, hem. Strawbery Banke Museum.

Abigail was the eldest of Samuel Dunlap and Lois Gove's three children. In 1852, she married Samuel Osborn of Weare. The elaborate lettering on Abigail's sampler is reminiscent of the alphabets found on Scottish samplers.

Maine Samplers

*Tis education forms the tender mind
Just as the twig is bent so the tree's inclin'd*

Portland

In the years after the Revolutionary War, Portland emerged as a center of education, culture, and refinement in Maine. By around 1800, many teachers were opening female academies in Maine's largest city, some lasting a three- or four-month term or two, but others remaining in operation for one or two decades, or longer. Among the more long-lasting were the schools of Sarah Jenkins Price, Rachel Hall Neal and her daughter, Rachel Neal, the Misses Martin, the Misses Mayo, and Mary Rea. In addition to academic subjects, these institutions offered instruction in a wide range of arts.

Mary Fernald (1789-1832), Portland, Maine, 1807. Silk thread on linen, 16 x 15 1/2". Stitches: cross over one and two, four-sided, queen, satin. Examplarery Sampler Collection.

Although Mary's sampler has suffered some stitch loss, perhaps due to the inclusion of caustic iron in dark-colored thread, it still provides key information about her family. It includes several juvenile misspellings that contribute to its charm. Mary, born on her father's birthday, was the eldest child of Joseph Fernald and Hope Cobb. As noted in the 1834 *Portland City Directory*, he was a soap maker, a career that his eldest son, Benjamin, would also take up. After she completed her needlework, Mary's parents had two more daughters, Ann and Clara, and two more sons, Samuel and James. On October 17, 1820, the marriage of Mary Fernald to Thomas Millions, both of Portland, was noted in the *Eastern Argus*, a Portland newspaper. He was a distiller. Their five-month-old daughter, Juliet, died on March 19, 1822, and was buried under a tiny slate stone in Eastern Cemetery. Mary died on March 30, 1832, and Thomas just two years later on March 14, 1834, and both are buried alongside Juliet. Mary's sampler is nearly identical to that of Mary Lewis (*I My Needle Ply with Skill*, page 34) stitched in the school of Sally Perry, also in 1807, and those of Nabby Horton and Eleanor Douglas. Sally opened her academy in 1805 and it closed upon her marriage (noted on Mary Lewis's sampler) in 1807.

Sarah Jordan (unknown), Portland, Maine, circa 1814. Silk thread on linen, 16 1/2 x 17 1/4". Stitches: cross over one and two, four-sided, queen, satin, lazy daisy, eyelet. Private collection.

Sarah Jordan's intricate Portland sampler has much in common with the group of work attributed to the academy of Rachel Hall Neal and later her daughter, Rachel Neal. While it lacks the typical pair of floral sprigs in the center section, space has been left for them. The sampler shows other evidence of being not-quite-finished: the number sequence is also incomplete. All other known samplers in this group include information—generally the maker's age and date of completion—that help provide clues to the girl's identity. Sarah has left those details out as well, perhaps a little frustrated when she realized she had not left room to include them. Since border roses in this group evolved by about 1816 into satin stitch, she might have worked on this sampler prior to that time. Jordans are numerous in Maine. Sarah may either have been the sixth of the twelve children of Morrill and Anne (Jordan) Jordan of nearby Cape Elizabeth, born May 27, 1802, or the daughter of Samuel Jordan and Rachel Humphrey of Raymond, Maine, who was born February 18, 1801, in Raymond. That Sarah married Thomas Wales, moved to Bridgton, Maine, was the mother of four, and died there in September 1858. *The Family Jordan,* a three-volume family history, reported that that Sarah's eldest brother, David, "had the privilege of attending a town school about six weeks each year" and later attended the Bridgton Academy for two months and the Hebron Academy for three months. Given his very limited educational opportunities, it seems unlikely that Sarah's parents would have been able to send her to one of Portland's premier female academies. The other Sarah's father, Morrill Jordan, was a ship's captain and presumably wealthier than Samuel Jordan. His daughter married seaman Lewis Merrill of Portland on September 27, 1828. He presumably died shortly thereafter. On March 15, 1834, she married Martin Gilpatrick of Portland who was also a mariner. By the 1860 census, Sarah was living with her daughter Sarah, a teacher who never married, in Portland. She died there January 28, 1865.

Pamela Bradford Washburn (1794-1882), Portland, Maine, 1806. Silk thread on linen, 20 1/2 x 16 1/2".
Stitches: cross over one and two, satin, queen, eyelet, couched. Private collection.

In the Federal era, young widows with children could face special challenges if they were left with limited resources, often the case when their husbands died before having time to accumulate wealth. Silvia Bradford was just eighteen, and her husband, Ichabod Washburn, was twenty-four when they were married in Kingston, Massachusetts, in 1793. Their daughter, sampler maker Pamelia (or sometimes Pamela), was born September 18, 1794, followed by twins, Charles and Ichabod, in August 1798. The twins were just two months old when their father died of "fever and black vomit," which may have been yellow fever. In 1796, Silvia's older sister married a relative of Ichabod's, Rufus Washburn, who later relocated to Portland, Maine. Silvia moved in with her married sister, which was how her Massachusetts-born daughter came to stitch an iconic Portland sampler. After Pamelia married George Warren, a very successful merchant, on November 12, 1815, Silvia joined their household and lived there for the rest of her life. Buried alongside Silvia in Portland's Western Cemetery are Charles, Edward, Elizabeth, John, and Pamela, the five who died young among the eleven children of George and Pamelia Warren. Pamelia died in 1882. Her sampler was quite likely stitched in the female academy of Rachel Hall Neal. Like all of the others in this group, her name is *not* included on the list of students who attended the equally long-lasting Portland academy of the Misses Martin, proving that school was not the source.

Martha K. Harding (1809-1874), Portland, Maine, 1819. Silk thread on linen, 19 1/2 x 16 3/4".
Stitches: cross over one and two, satin, buttonhole, four-sided, eyelet, chain. Collection of Deane Van
Dusen and David Doiron.

Martha K. Harding was just ten years old when she stitched her tour-de-force sampler, incorporating a wide variety of stitches. Hers is extremely typical of the group of samplers likely stitched at the academy run by Rachel Hall Neal for nearly the rest of her life after she was widowed only weeks after giving birth to twins, Rachel and John. Samplers from this academy always feature either a pair of urn-topped memorials or a more upbeat solidly worked scene done in cross stitch over one thread. The scene usually has a three-story house facing forward as well as a second house shown half in profile, sheep, and trees that sometimes vaguely resemble palms. Elkannah Harding's first wife, Martha Knight, died in May 1801 after giving birth to four children. The following spring, he married Hannah Elder Brown, the widow of Joseph Brown. She gave birth to an additional eight children, Martha being the fourth. All but one of the dozen lived into adulthood. Martha married Samuel Freeman, the son of Samuel and Olive, who were both raised in the celibate Shaker community, fell in love, and eloped away. By 1850, Samuel and Martha were farming in Windham. Samuel's elderly father and unmarried sister resided with them, along with three children of their own. Later in the 1860s, the family moved to Portland where Samuel became a grocer, but died of heart disease in March 1870. The census that year showed Martha living with all three of her children in Portland. Although her two sons married, none of her three offspring had any children. Martha died of consumption in Portland on March 15, 1874, and is buried in Evergreen Cemetery with her husband and children.

Lydia D. Leavitt (circa 1810-?), Portland, Maine, 1826. Silk thread on linen, 17 1/2 x 18 3/4". Stitches: cross over one and two, satin, eyelet, stem, straight, split. Collection of Deane Van Dusen and David Doiron.

In 1826, Lydia D. Leavitt stitched her rose-bordered sampler that included a village scene across the bottom worked in tiny cross stitches over just one thread. Given the similarities that it shares with the large group of samplers that have been attributed to the long-lasting school run by Rachel Hall Neal and later her daughter, Rachel Neal, it seems likely that this piece was worked under their supervision as well. By around 1816, the previous queen stitch rose border had evolved into a much more naturalistic satin stitch rendering. Rachel Neal appears to have been taking more of a leadership role by the mid-1820s and may have been doing the design work for the samplers. Although Lydia's border, unlike other known pieces, does not continue along the bottom of her work, her solidly worked scene is almost identical to others in the group. Lydia may have been the daughter of Dr. Joshua Leavitt and his wife, Sally Porter, (married July 20, 1800, in Otisfield, Maine) whose Otisfield birth was recorded on February 24, 1810. Joshua and Sally likely lived in Portland during the 1820s, since their son Joshua died and was buried there July 28, 1828, at the age of nine. No further records were found for Lydia.

Jenette Humphrey (1805-1873), Portland, Maine, circa 1820. Silk thread and watercolor on silk, 17 1/2 x 18". Stitches: satin, long and short, French knot, back, stem, outline. Examplarery Sampler Collection.

Given the many similarities between the elaborate silk embroidery of Jenette Humphrey and other works that needlework scholar Betty Ring attributed to the long-lasting academy of the Misses Martin in Portland, Maine, that was almost certainly where this piece was stitched. The central figure in Humphrey's work stands in a position exactly like that of the young woman in the work of "S.O.P." on page 253 of *Girlhood Embroidery*. The Misses Martin produced a list of their students at around the time the school closed. The only Humphrey listed was Hannah, a day scholar who may have been Jenette's first cousin, born April 5, 1798, the daughter of Ebenezer Humphrey and Polly True. Janette was born July 25, 1805, just three months after the death of her two-year-old elder sister, the daughter of John Humphrey and his first wife, Dorcas Loring. After Dorcas died in 1808, John married Mary Ann Loring and had two sons. Jenette, on January 24, 1833, married Richmond L. Storer, a North Yarmouth shoemaker. They became parents to eight children, three of whom died in childhood. Jenette died in 1873 and is buried in Old Baptist Cemetery in North Yarmouth.

Harriet Cutter (1800-1863), "The Lily and the Rose," Portland, Maine, circa 1817. Silk and watercolor on silk, 12 7/8 x 15 3/8". Stitches: satin, French knot, split, straight. Maine Historical Society.

Harriet Cutter was the third of nine children born to Levi and Lucretia Mitchell Cutter of North Yarmouth. He was a prosperous merchant. The family moved to Portland early in the nineteenth century, where he later served as mayor from 1834-1840. In 1835, when she was thirty-five, Harriet married Joseph Adams of Salem, Massachusetts. Joseph, like her father, was a merchant. The couple settled in Danvers, where Joseph was instrumental in the establishment of an Episcopal church. He was a member of the building committee, was involved with the laying of the cornerstone in 1859, and donated both the bell and a library of two hundred books for the use of the rector. Not to be left out, Harriet presented one of the silver cups as part of the church silver. The couple had no children. Harriet died in March 1863 and is buried in Walnut Grove Cemetery in Danvers, along with her husband, who passed away in 1869. Harriet stitched her iconic, lavish embroidery in the school of the Misses Martin, who had come to America from England, and who operated a large and very successful academy from about 1803 until late in the 1820s. Several other very similar pictures are known; the names of their makers almost always appear on an extant list of Martins' students.

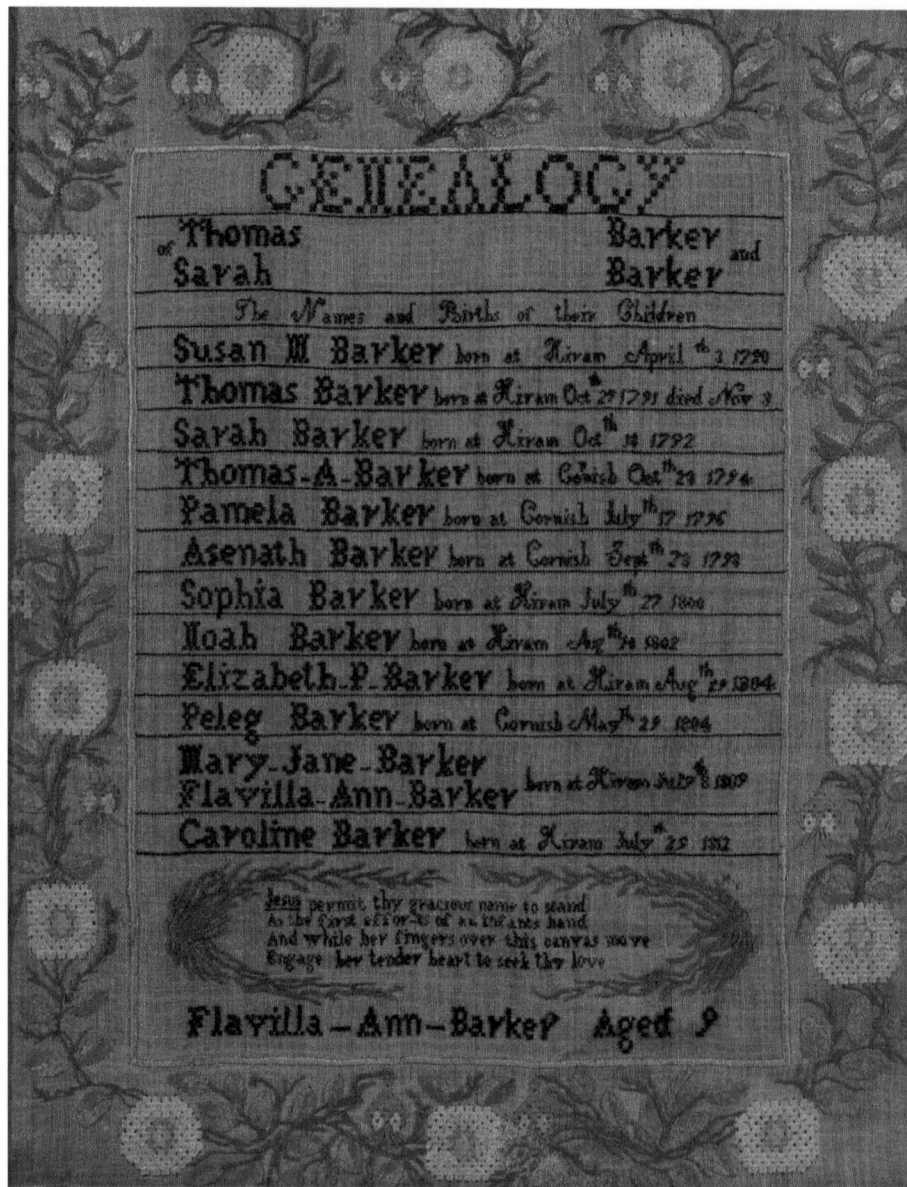

Flavilla Ann Barker (1809-1882), Portland, Maine, 1818. Silk thread on linen, 20 1/2 x 16 1/2". Stitches: cross, queen, satin, chain. Androscoggin Historical Society.

Flavilla Ann and her twin sister, Mary Jane Barker, stitched their identical samplers, probably under the instruction of Abigail Fellows. Thomas Barker sold land in Hiram in 1815; perhaps he had already moved the family to Portland where he opened a "public"—or tavern—on Congress Street. Although he died in 1819, his sons ran the tavern for many years afterward. Flavilla married James Mason Williams of Taunton, Massachusetts. She was the mother of two sons and two daughters, two of whom died in early childhood. On the 1850 census, she was residing with her husband and children, but by 1855, the family had split apart. In 1865, Flavilla was living in a Worcester, Massachusetts, boarding house, but resided in an institution for the insane in Northampton, Massachusetts, by 1870 and appears to have remained there for the rest of her life. Flavilla died on January 15, 1882, and is buried alongside her husband and three of her children in Taunton. Abigail Fellows operated a school in Portland from about 1806 until 1820, when she probably died during a visit to Havana, Cuba. She was most likely the second wife of Nathaniel Fellows of Boston, who married her sometime after the death of his first wife in 1782. Nathaniel died in Havana in May 1806. Two nineteenth-century sources identify her as running a Portland school; she is reported to have been the first teacher of Henry Wadsworth Longfellow, when he was about three or four years old. Longfellow likely attended her school around 1807. The Barker twins' samplers are attributed to her school because a Barker descendant recalled that they had been made at the school that the girls attended with Longfellow as young children (*American Samplers,* p. 125.)

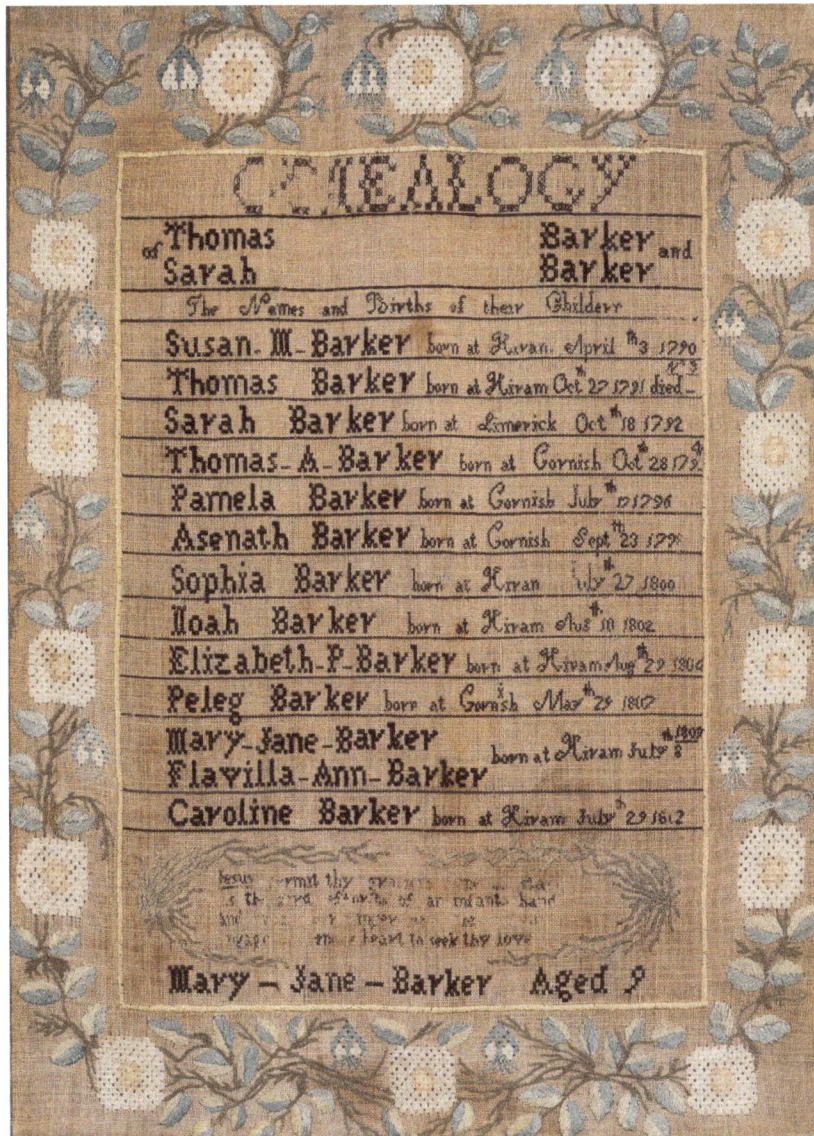

Mary Jane Barker (1809-1853), Portland, Maine, 1818. Silk thread on linen, 20 1/2 x 16 1/4". Stitches: cross over one and two, satin, straight, queen, chain. Collection of Alan and Pamela Kirby.

Mary Jane and her twin sister, Flavilla, stitched nearly identical samplers, probably at the school of Abigail Fellows. Almost the only detail that is different between the two samplers is the birth year of Peleg Barker that Flavilla incorrectly stitched as 1804, a mistake that can readily be excused considering she was just nine years old when she demonstrated her mastery of embroidery. At the time of the "I My Needle Ply with Skill" exhibition in 2013, the location of Mary Jane's sampler was unknown. It had been described by an aged descendant in *American Samplers* in 1921. It continued to pass down through the family, but was eventually sold at auction in 2000 by Butterfields in San Francisco. Since that time, it returned to New England and was kindly loaned for this exhibition, so that the twins' work could be reunited. Mary Jane was just sixteen years old when, on October 18, 1825, she married Timothy Eastman. He had been born in East Kingston, New Hampshire, studied at Dartmouth College, and was apprenticed to a Portland, Maine, physician at the time of their wedding. Not long afterward, they moved to Canaan, Maine, a small village near Skowhegan. There Mary Jane gave birth to five children between 1826 and 1832, almost one each year. In 1835, the family traveled across New England to New York, all the way up the Erie Canal, by sailing ship to Detroit, then by stagecoach, and finally birch bark canoe to their new home, a log cabin in the Michigan wilderness in a town first called Polktown and later Eastmanville. At the time, their oldest child was nine. Although no more children were born for ten years, the former frequency implies that perhaps there were failed pregnancies. In the winter of 1841, their cabin burned to the ground; Timothy rebuilt. Four more children were born (including their eighth, creatively named Octavia). Perhaps Mary Jane was just worn out when she died April 7, 1853. Six years later, Timothy married Mary Jane's elder sister Sophia, who was twice widowed by that time.

Sarah Ann Minott (1814-1881), Portland, Maine, 1824. Silk thread on linen, 16 1/2 x 12 1/2".
Stitches: four-sided, hem, cross over one and two. Maine Historical Society.

The most notable feature of Sarah's sampler is her choice of verse, honoring the Marquis de Lafayette, who toured America in 1824 and 1825. The verse was apparently quite popular during his tour and was published in both *A Sketch of the Tour of General Lafayette* (Portland, 1824) and the *Memoirs of General Lafayette* (Boston, 1824). Sarah's family background is unclear, as no birth records were found for her. There were a number of Minott families living in the Portland area in the early nineteenth century and she may have been the daughter of John W. Minott of Westbrook and Portland. She was probably the Sarah Minott who married Gideon Stickney on December 3, 1835, in Eastport, Maine. Originally from Newburyport, Gideon was a cabinetmaker and furniture dealer. The couple had four daughters between 1836 and 1849. Unfortunately, two of the daughters died before reaching adulthood, Sarah at the age of nine and Caroline at fifteen. Their oldest daughter, Maria, married apothecary Luther Gilson in 1864. That couple moved to Portland, and Maria's sister, Elizabeth, went with them. Sarah and Gideon remained in Eastport until they passed away, Gideon in 1874 and Sarah in 1881. They are both buried in the Hillside Cemetery in Eastport, along with their daughters, Sarah and Caroline.

Other Maine Female Academies

A Portland education was not an option for many Maine girls whose parents, nonetheless, valued education and middle-class refinements for their daughters. Augusta became a second recognized source for female instruction in the decade before it became the state capital in 1820. The Cony Female Academy and other smaller, short-lived schools are associated with attractive designs and substantial bodies of work. However, even very small towns across the state had one or more teachers who offered local girls a taste of urban sophistication.

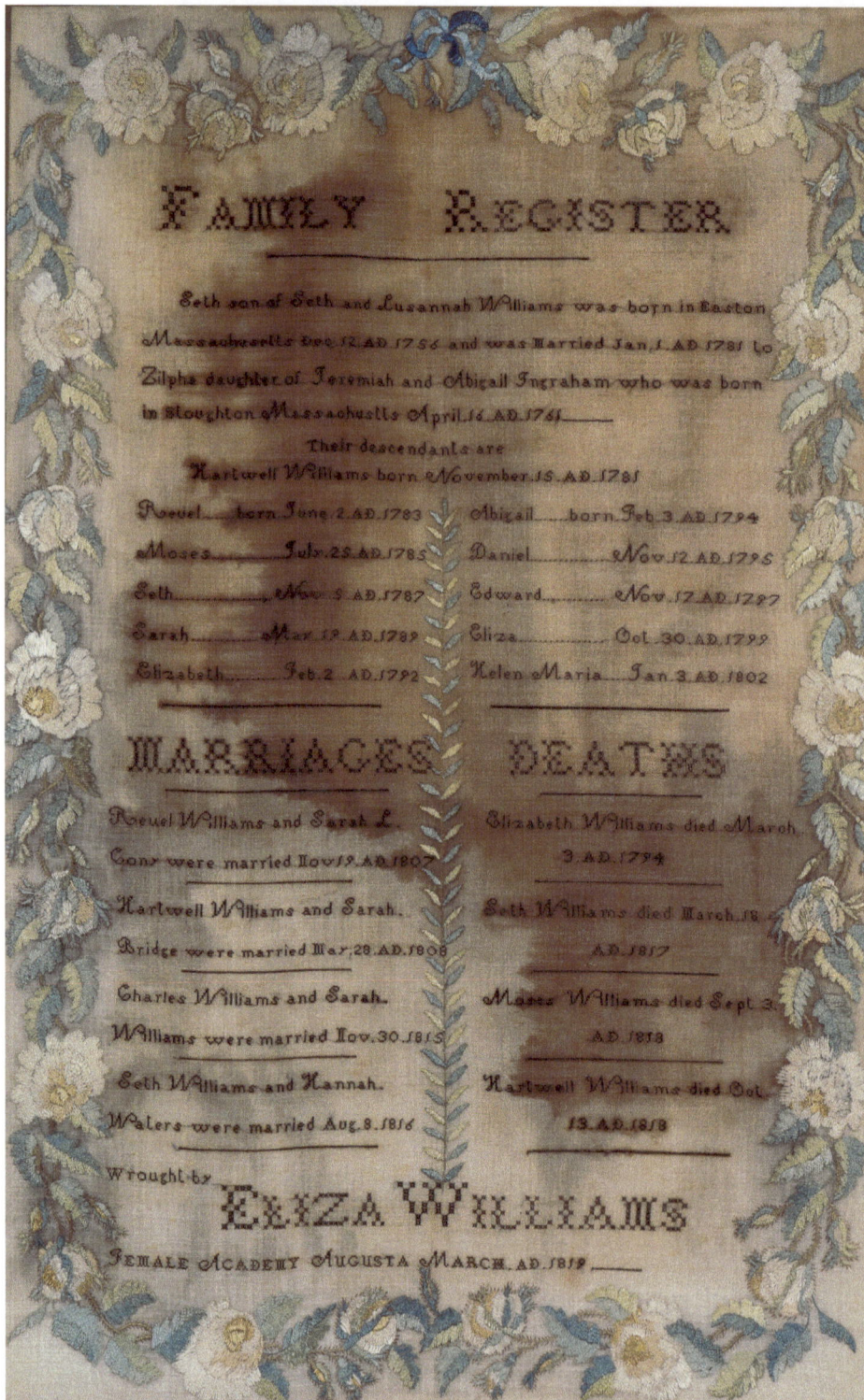

Eliza Williams (1799-1883), Augusta, Maine, 1819. Silk thread on linen, 26 x 18 1/2".
Stitches: satin, cross, eyelet, straight. Maine State Museum.

Eliza's grand and very informative sampler is typical of the best of the work that was done at the Cony Female Academy. Perhaps that is not surprising since Eliza's brother, Reuel, married Sarah L. Cony, one of the five daughters of Judge Daniel Cony, who founded the academy a bit late for his daughters to attend, but mindful of the lack of education opportunities for them in Augusta as they were growing up. Eliza included all of the details of her family, information that could be of great interest to genealogists. Eliza married Eben Fuller, a druggist, on Christmas Eve, 1824. They appear to have been parents to nine children, but at least three of them died very young. Eliza ran her own household after Eben passed away, although their unmarried daughters, Hannah and Helen, lived with her until her death on July 28, 1883.

Anna Y. Savage (1803-1846), Augusta, Maine, 1818. Silk thread on linen, 16 1/4 x 13". Stitches: cross, satin, eyelet. Maine State Museum.

Anna Young Savage was the daughter of Daniel Savage and Mary Fletcher, born in 1803. She named "Female Academy" on her sampler, a name that typically was used to refer to the Cony Female Academy that the Honorable Daniel Cony opened in Augusta in 1815. Miss Hannah B. Aldrich, who had previously advertised a female academy of her own in 1809 in Mendon, Massachusetts, was the teacher at Cony from 1815 until her marriage to Pitt Dillingham in 1820, and intermittently afterward. Although Anna's sampler is not a family register like nearly all other Cony pieces that have been identified, the leafy sprig and intricate satin stitch border are very similar to other Cony pieces. She married William Little of Kingfield on March 18, 1824. Of their four sons and a daughter, Charles, Rufus, and an unnamed infant all died very young. William was said to be originally from Bath, Maine, and on the 1850 census, his occupation was listed as "painter," although in later years he was always listed as being a farmer. His home, almost next door to Anna's brother Robert, must have been modest, valued at just $600. Anna died in Augusta at the age of forty-three in July 1846.

Mary A. Little (1825-1903), Augusta, Maine, 1838. Silk thread on linen, 16 1/4 x 13". Stitches: cross, eyelet. Maine State Museum.

Mary Ann's sampler has much in common with one stitched eleven years earlier by Mary Chase in Augusta, (see *I My Needle Ply with Skill*, page 119,) especially the unusual and intricate floral border worked in cross stitch and the format of her name and place information. It is also nearly identical to the sampler worked by Anna L. Savage and completed a month earlier than Little's. Mary Ann's mother, Anna Young Savage Little (page 37), certainly had needlework experience and could have been the teacher for her daughter and Anna L. Savage, but she was already married by the time Mary Chase stitched her work, making it less likely (but not, of course, impossible) that she was the instructor for all three works. Although these three pieces are far more like each other than to known Cony Female Academy works, it is possible that they reflect evolving changes at the academy as less emphasis may have been placed on needlework in later years. However, the family register work of Mary E. Swan (collection of the Maine Historical Society, pictured in *I My Needle Ply with Skill*, page 118) was done a year after Mary Chase's but is very similar to all the other known Cony pieces so if Mary Chase's work reflects a newer style, it was not consistently chosen by students. Mary Ann, born June 1, 1825, was the only surviving daughter of William Little and Anna Savage. She grew up in Augusta in a less-than-affluent family. She never married. After her mother died in 1846, she kept house for her father until his death. By 1880 she owned her own home, and was living just four houses away from her married brother, Daniel. On the 1900 census, she and Daniel, whose wife had died, shared a home (still standing) at 27 Chestnut Street in Augusta. She died of apoplexy—an earlier name for a stroke—on March 12, 1903.

Anna L. Savage (circa 1823-?), Augusta, Maine, 1838. Silk thread on linen, 16 1/4 x 13 1/8". Stitches: cross, eyelet. Maine State Museum.

Anna must have sat with Mary Little (page 32) as she completed her sampler since she finished hers just a month before. Augusta vital records are not as comprehensive as some, and no birth, marriage, or death records for Anna, who was born between July 4, 1823, and July 3, 1824, appear there. Some genealogists have indicated that she might have been the eldest child of Anna Young Savage's older brother, Robert, and his wife, Mary Leavett, whose farm was located almost adjacent to the Little land. If that were the case, then Anna would have been conceived prior to their marriage on March 21, 1824. On the 1830 and 1840 censuses, a female child of the right age to be Anna was enumerated in their household. By 1850, that female was no longer living with Robert and his wife. Her fate is unknown.

Lydia Rollins (1816-1918), Augusta, Maine, 1831. Silk thread on linen, 17 1/4 x 17 1/2". Stitches: cross over one and two, satin. Maine State Museum.

Although Lydia stitched her sampler in Augusta during the years that Cony Female Academy was a rich source for needlework, she neither named the school, nor does her sampler resemble those known to have been created there. When Lydia died at the age of 101, a newspaper obituary offered a good summary of her long life: *"Mrs. Lydia Wixson, the oldest woman in Augusta and with one exception the last real daughter of the American Revolution in Maine, passed away Saturday at the home of Miss Gertrude A. Choate at 167 Northern Avenue, aged 101 years and eight months. The immediate surviving relatives are a son, George F. Wixson of Sidney and a daughter, Mrs. Albert H. Mackle of Brockton, Mass. Mrs. Wixson was born in Wiscasset and was the daughter of John Rollins, who served on Gen. George Washington's personal body guard. Her parents moved to Augusta when she was but a few months old. She lived for a few years in Massachusetts and also for some years in Sidney. She often related the stories and incidents her father had told her of Gen. Washington. At the age of 18 years she was married to James Wixson, a North Augusta farmer. In 1890 they moved to East Bridgewater, Mass., and there Mr. Wixson died during the same year. Mrs. Wixson then returned to Augusta and had remained here since. She was an honored member of Koussinoc Chapter D.A.R., of the city and had figured in many of its receptions."* Lydia and James were parents to two daughters and five sons. Her grave is marked with a plaque that identifies her status as a "real daughter." The last surviving of those, Annie Knight Gregory, notably, did not pass away until 1943.

Sophia Dyer (1804-?), Cape Elizabeth, Maine, 1817. Silk thread on linen, 16 3/8 x 10 1/4". Stitches: queen, cross, four-sided. Maine Historical Society.

Sophia's sampler is one of two that is signed and dated and names Cape Elizabeth and which may have been worked in the same academy, although the teacher is not known. The Cape Elizabeth teacher was probably familiar with the embroideries worked by students at Rachel Hall Neal's Portland academy, with their queen-stitched borders and scenes with buildings. However, the Cape Elizabeth samplers do not exhibit the same level of sophistication as Portland needlework. The queen-stitched flowers are much smaller and simpler, and the buildings are not as well executed. Other than the date of her birth, which she noted on her sampler, nothing is known of the Sophia Dyer who completed this embroidery. There were a number of Dyer families living in Cape Elizabeth in the early nineteenth century, but no birth, marriage, or death records were found that match the girl who stitched this sampler.

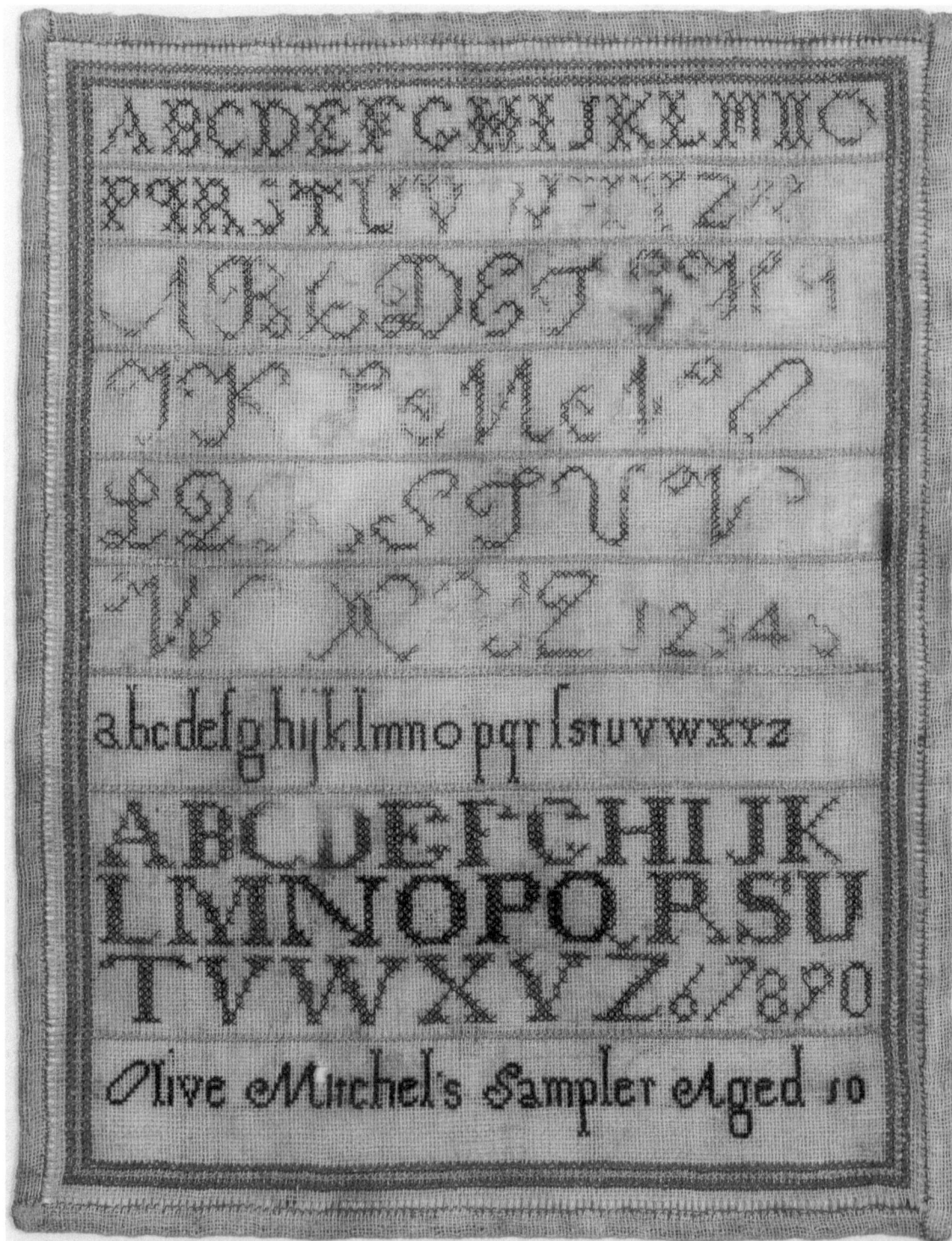

Olive Mitchell (1819-1895), Wells, Maine, 1829. Silk thread on linen, 12 5/8 x 10 1/4". Stitches: cross over one and two, hem. Maine State Museum.

Although the design of Olive's sampler is less complex than those of other Wells sampler makers, it shares enough details to make it very likely that she had the same teacher as the Littlefield girls, Jerusia Hill, and Olive Gooch. Olive Mitchell was the daughter of Olive Day of Wells and James Mitchell, who had been born in Kennebunk. They were married in Wells on September 16, 1815. James was a farmer. Olive, born February 5, 1819, was probably the eldest of at least five children. On October 29, 1839, she married William Lord Thompson, who was the grandson and son of important Kennebunk shipbuilders and who had a large residence, still standing, beside the Kennebunk River. He, too, was a well-to-do shipbuilder. They were parents to at least two sons and two daughters. William died in 1883; Olive lived on until July 25, 1895, when she died of a cerebral hemorrhage. She was buried in Hope Cemetery in the center of Kennebunk.

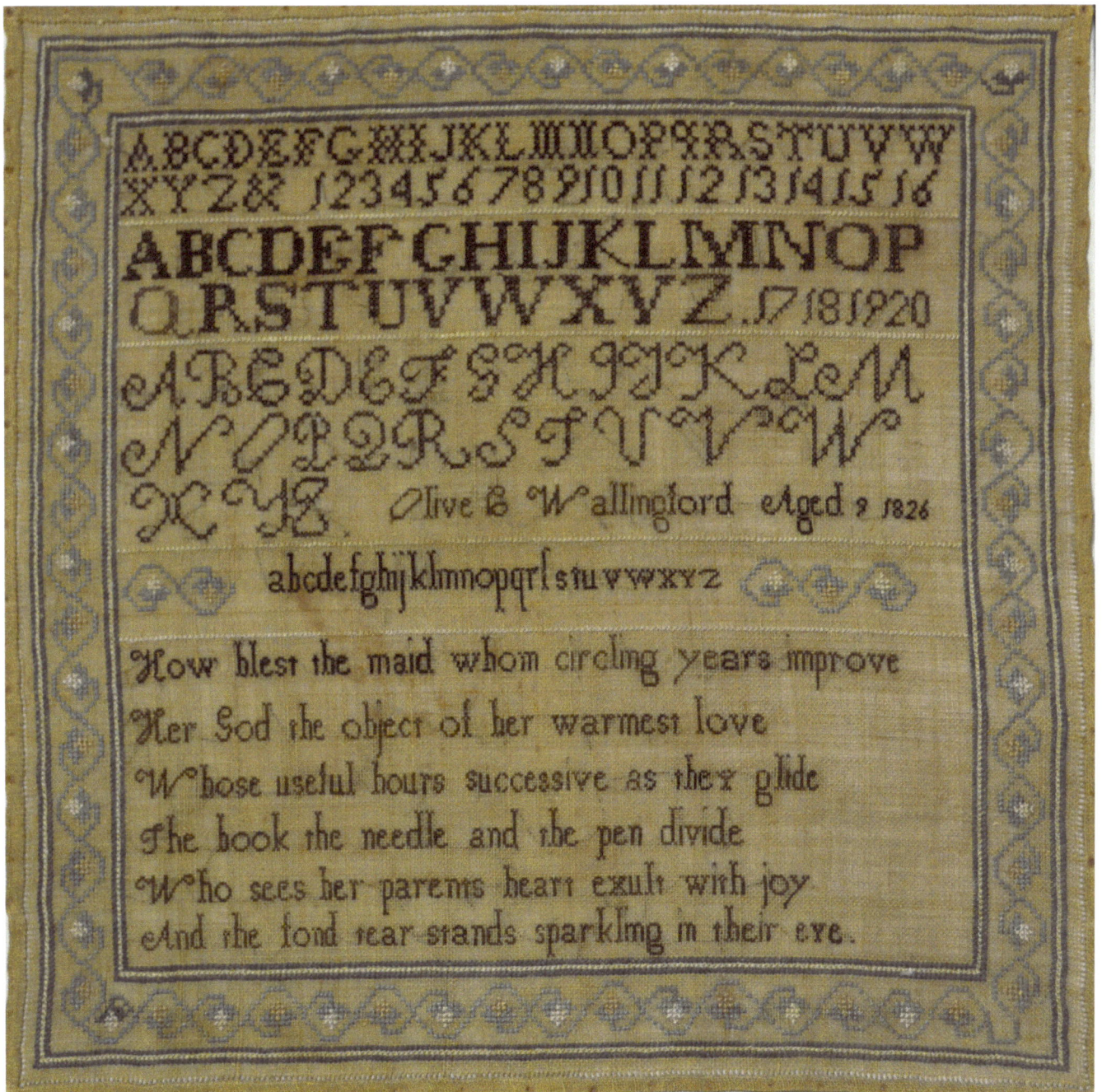

Olive Wallingford (1817-1887), Wells, Maine, 1826. Silk thread on linen, 17 1/4 x 17 3/4". Stitches: cross over one and two, hem. Courtesy of The Brick Store Museum, Kennebunk, Maine.

Olive Cushing Wallingford was the third of the five children of George W. Wallingford, an attorney, and his second wife, Mary Fisher. Two children, daughter Lucretia and son Frederick, died in early childhood. Olive's father was born in Dover, New Hampshire, graduated from Harvard College, and studied law in South Berwick, Maine, before relocating to Kennebunk, still a section of Wells, Maine, until 1820. Based on the information on her gravestone, Olive was born May 30, 1817. George died quite young, in 1824. His wife never remarried. According to a letter to Maine author Sarah Orne Jewett written years later by her younger sister, Sophia, she and Olive attended the Berwick Academy, and boarded in Berwick at the home of "great-aunt Madame Cushing." Their names are included on a list of students from 1833, seven years after this sampler is dated, so that was not the source for this group of work. Olive never married. For many years, she resided in Kennebunk in her brother's home. By 1880, she had her own home and Sophia, now widowed, lived with her. Olive died March 21, 1887, and is buried in the Unitarian Churchyard Cemetery in Kennebunk.

ABCDEFGHIJKLM
NOPQRSTUVWXY

ABCDEFGHIJKLMN
OPQRSTUVWXYZ

ABCDEFGHIJKLMNOPQRSTU
abcdefghijklmnopqrstuvwxyz & VWXYZ

Jesus permit thy gracious name to stand
As the first effort of an infant s hand
And while her fingers o er this canvas move
Engage her tender heart to seek thy love
With thy dear people let her share a part
And write thy name thyself upon her heart

Virginia 1607   Pennsylvania 1682
New York 1614   Georgia 1733
Massachusetts 1620   Vermont 1749
N Hampshire 1623   Kentucky 1775
N Jersey 1624   Tennessee 1765
Delaware 1627   Ohio 1788
Mary land 1634   Louisiana 1699
R Island 1636   Indiana 1730
Connecticut 1633   Mississippi 1716
N Carolina 1650   Illinois 1749
S Carolina 1650   Maine 1630   Alabama 1783
Missouri 1663

Wrought by Mary A Littlefield Aged 9 Wells Sept 1830

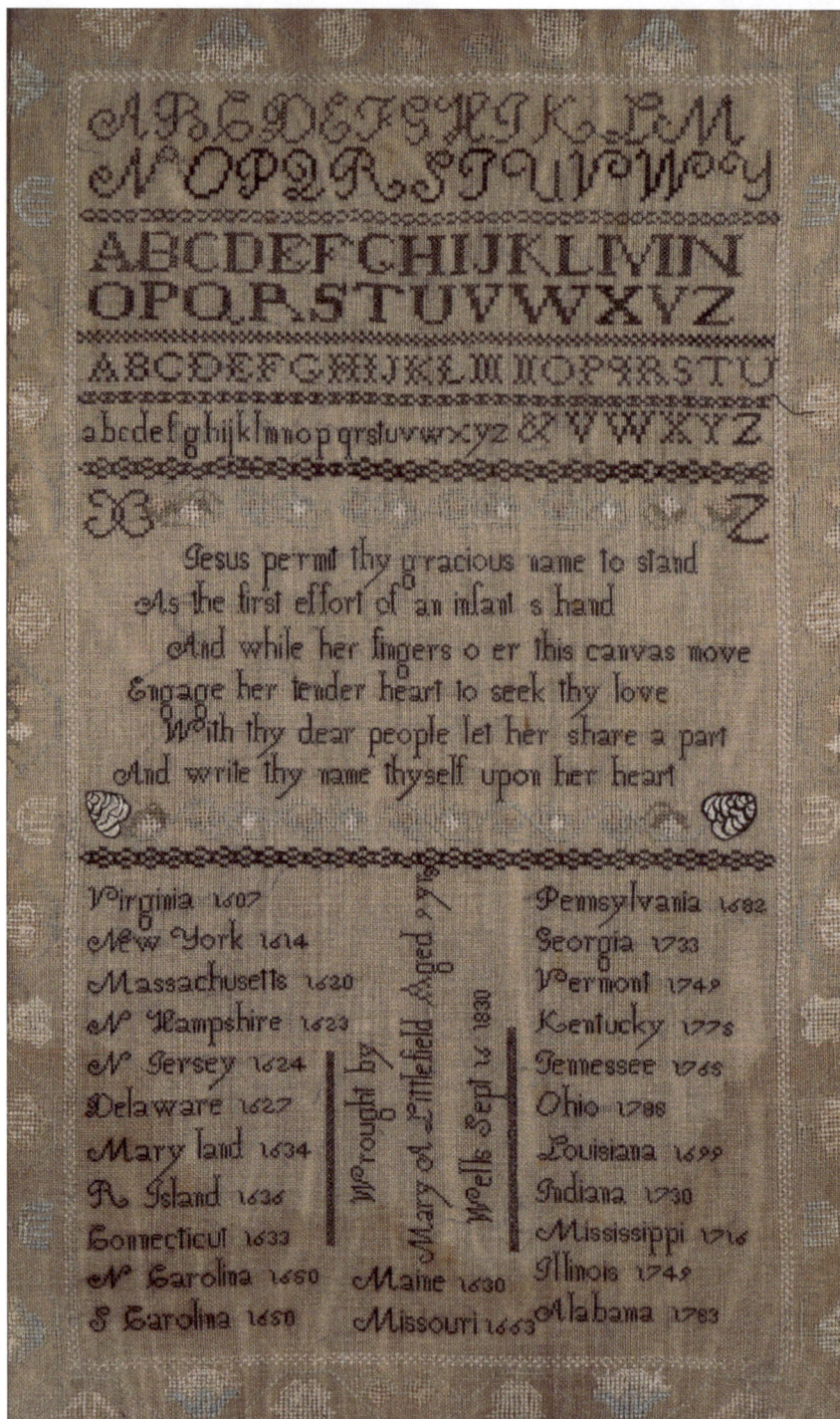

Mary A. Littlefield (1821-1882), Wells, Maine, 1830. Silk thread on linen, 24 3/8 x 15 7/8". Stitches: cross over one and two, stem, chain. Androscoggin Historical Society.

Mary Abby Littlefield was the daughter of Walter Littlefield (son of Joseph Littlefield and Anna Eaton) and Isabella Littlefield (daughter of James Littlefield and Mary Wheelwright.) Walter and Isabella were married September 27, 1817, in Wells. Their children were Albert, Walter, Mary Abby, born June 22, 1821 (in Portsmouth, New Hampshire), Ann Isabella, Joshua, and Emily Amanda. Mary Abby first married Andrew J. Webster of Portsmouth, New Hampshire, in 1840 and gave birth to daughter, Mary J., in 1842. By 1855, she was a widow. In 1863, she married a widower, Ralph W. Holman, an insurance agent who lived in Newton, Massachusetts. Widowed again in 1871, she died of a kidney ailment in Newton on November 14, 1882. She stitched a most unusual sampler, providing information about the dates of settlement of various states. In order to accommodate all the information, she squeezed her own name in vertically, a format that Abigail Bragdon would repeat two years later, implying that the arrangement was more by plan than accident. (See *I My Needle Ply with Skill*, page 67.)

Olive Jane Gooch (1822-1902), Wells, Maine, 1832. Silk thread on linen, 21 1/8 x 16 3/4". Stitches: cross over one and two. Androscoggin Historical Society.

Sampler maker Olive Jane Gooch was the daughter of John Gooch and Olive Winn who were married June 19, 1802. Wells vital records noted the births of five of their children between 1803, when Sarah was born, and August 19, 1822, when Olive arrived. Between 1812 and Olive's birth is a ten year gap that may represent births of children that went unrecorded. Although Olive's sampler includes the same arches as Hannah Hill's and the same border as Mary Abby Littlefield's, it is unique in being a memorial work, noting the dates of death of her elder brothers, Samuel and John. It seems possible that she—or her teacher—specially composed the verse she included. Although Olive later picked out the date she completed her sampler since it would reveal her age, her birth date proves that she finished it on October 1, 1832. On November 7, 1848, Olive Jane Gooch married Walter Littlefield, Mary Abby's older brother. They moved to Melrose, Massachusetts, and were the parents of two daughters. In 1900, Olive was living with one of her daughters in Melrose. She died there September 28, 1902.

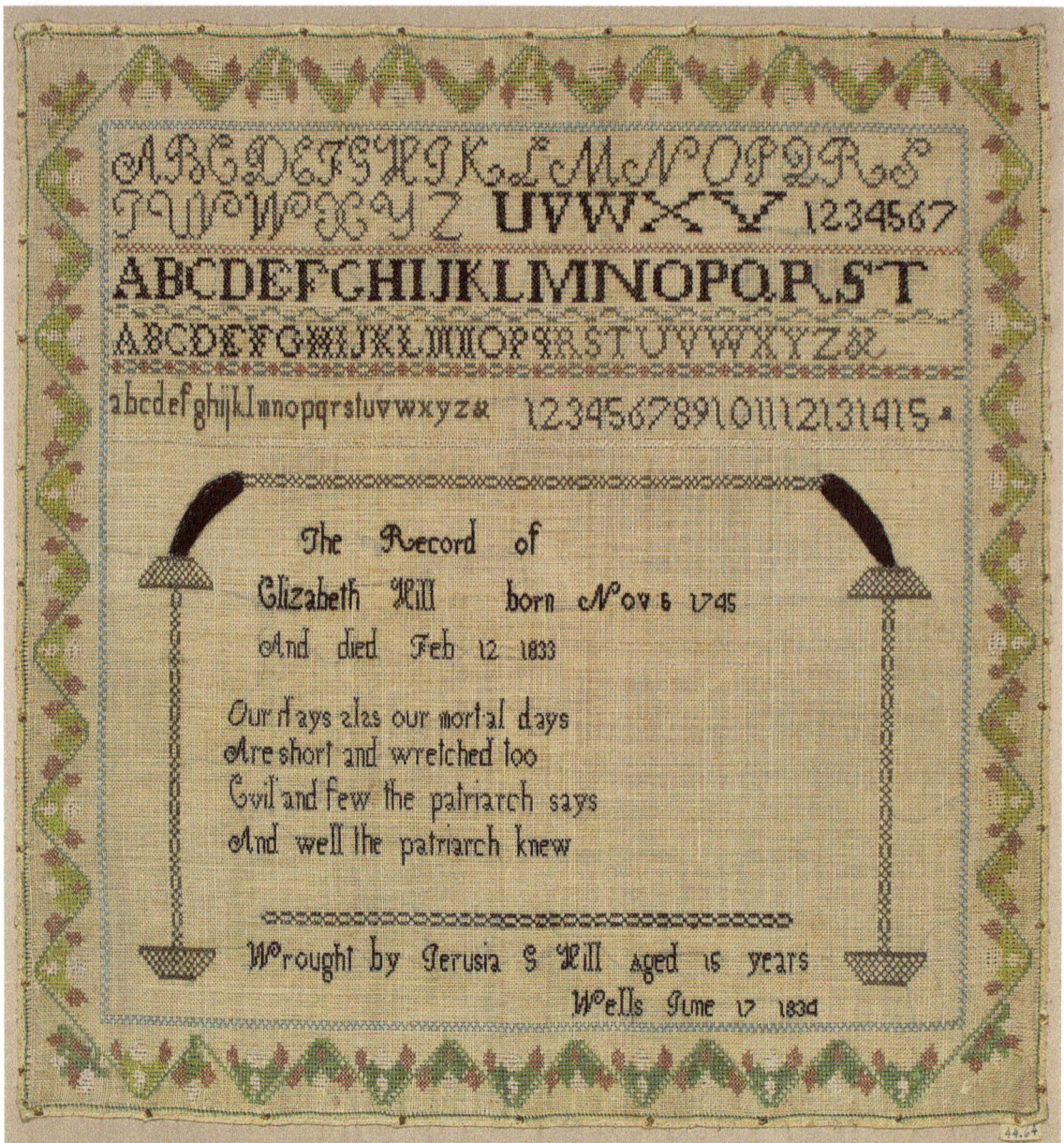

Jerusia G. Hill (circa 1819-1889), Wells, Maine, 1834. Silk thread on linen, 17 1/2 x 17 1/2". Stitches: cross over one and two, stem. Museum of Fine Arts, Boston. Bequest of Charles Hitchcock Tyler. Photograph © 2015 Museum of Fine Arts, Boston.

Jerusia G. Hill was the daughter of John Hill and his wife, Jerusha Jones (of Alfred), whose intentions of marriage were posted April 9, 1803, in Wells. They were the parents of four sons and six daughters born between 1805 and 1824 in Wells; Jerusia G. was fourth from the youngest. Her mother died in 1824, shortly after the birth of her last child. Her father, John, and Hannah Hill's father, Matthew, were brothers, probably the two youngest children among the (at least) eight offspring of Benjamin Hill and Elizabeth Gillpatrick. When Benjamin and Elizabeth married in Biddeford, Maine, on October 9, 1760, they were described as both being "of Biddeford" and baptisms of Benjamin and Elizabeth's first six children all occurred there. It is unknown where John and Matthew were born, but by 1790 the family was in Wells. Jerusia G. chose to memorialize her paternal grandmother on her very typical Wells sampler. When Elizabeth died in 1833, she was buried with her husband, two infant children of Jerusha and John Hill, and Jerusha Jones Hill in a small family plot. Jerusia married a man with the surname Bonnafoux (spelling varied) before 1855. On the 1855 Massachusetts State Census, she was residing with her married elder sister, Priscilla Whitten, and her family in Boston. On February 1, 1866, Jerusia became the third wife of David A. Hunt of Malden, a successful carpenter. By 1880, they were living in Woburn, Massachusetts, where the census noted that David had been disabled and unable to work for the past eleven months. In addition, they were now caring for his seven-year-old twin nephews. On October 10, 1889, Jerusia died of anthrax at Danvers Hospital.

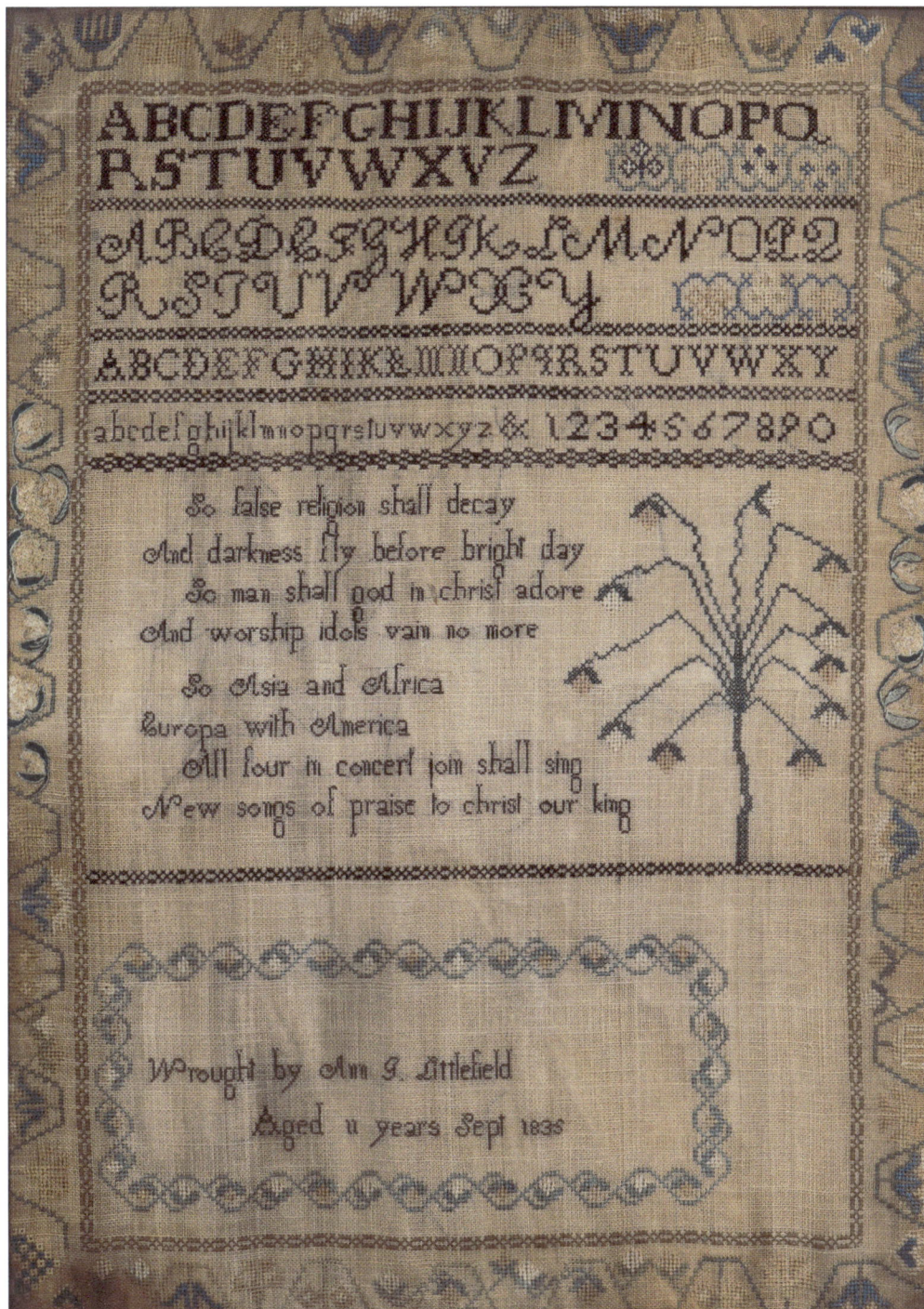

Ann Isabella Littlefield (1824-1906), Wells, Maine, 1835. Silk thread on linen, 19 3/4 X 16 1/4".
Stitches: satin, stem, cross over one and two. Androscoggin Historical Society.

Ann Isabella Littlefield completed her sampler five years after her elder sister, Mary Abby, made one. While Ann's is very obviously related to the other samplers in the group, it is also simpler and consequently somewhat less attractive. Ann married Nahum Morrill, an attorney, and relocated with him to Auburn, Maine. There they became parents to three sons, the eldest named for Ann's father, Walter. Unfortunately, their firstborn son died at the age of six months. Both of their surviving sons became attorneys. The younger, Donald, moved to Chicago where he named his firstborn son for Nahum. By 1900, Ann and Nahum were living with their son John. John's youngest child, Olive Morrill, never married. She may have been the person who collected the Wells samplers of her mother, her aunt Mary Abby, and her aunt Olive Gooch Littlefield. A period photo shows some of these hanging in her home and she was the donor, many years later, of the collection. Ann died in Auburn on September 8, 1906. Nahum lived on there and passed away at the age of ninety-eight in 1917. They are buried together with their infant son in Oak Hill Cemetery in Auburn.

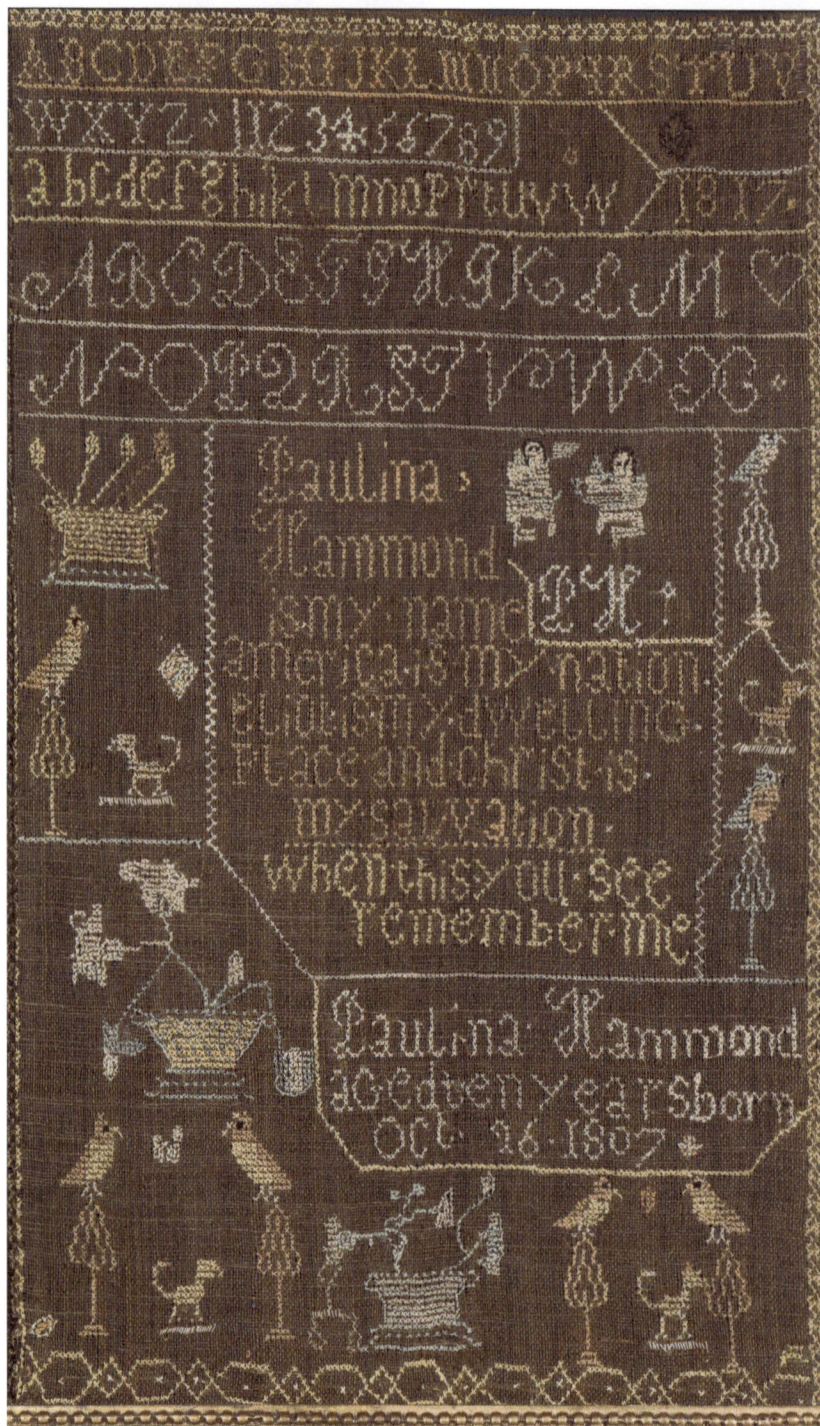

Paulina Hammond (1807-1824), Eliot, Maine, 1817. Silk thread on linsey-woolsey, 17 1/8 x 12 1/8". Stitches: cross, satin, straight. Examplarery Sampler Collection.

Paulina was fourth of the six children of Nathaniel Hammond and Elizabeth Fogg of Eliot. She was just ten when she stitched her sampler, but her life was already more than half over. Her sampler shares some motifs with the one stitched in 1819 by her first cousin, Betsey Fogg, daughter of Elizabeth's brother John, which appears in *I My Needle Ply with Skill* (page 56). Elizabeth's brother William would later marry Betsey Hill, who Betsey Fogg named as her teacher on her sampler. John would also name his second youngest daughter Paulina Hammond Fogg in 1826, two years after his niece had died. Like Mary Augusta Shapleigh, Paulina stitched her work on linsey-woolsey rather than linen. The contrast between the fabric and the thread is dramatic and attractive, but stitching on a darker ground is more challenging than on lighter-colored linen. If Betsey Hill was also Paulina's teacher, her sense of style and design was clearly just beginning to evolve in 1817, and would be somewhat more sophisticated by two years later. Paulina died on April 5, 1824, and was the first to be buried in a small family plot where her parents would also later be laid to rest.

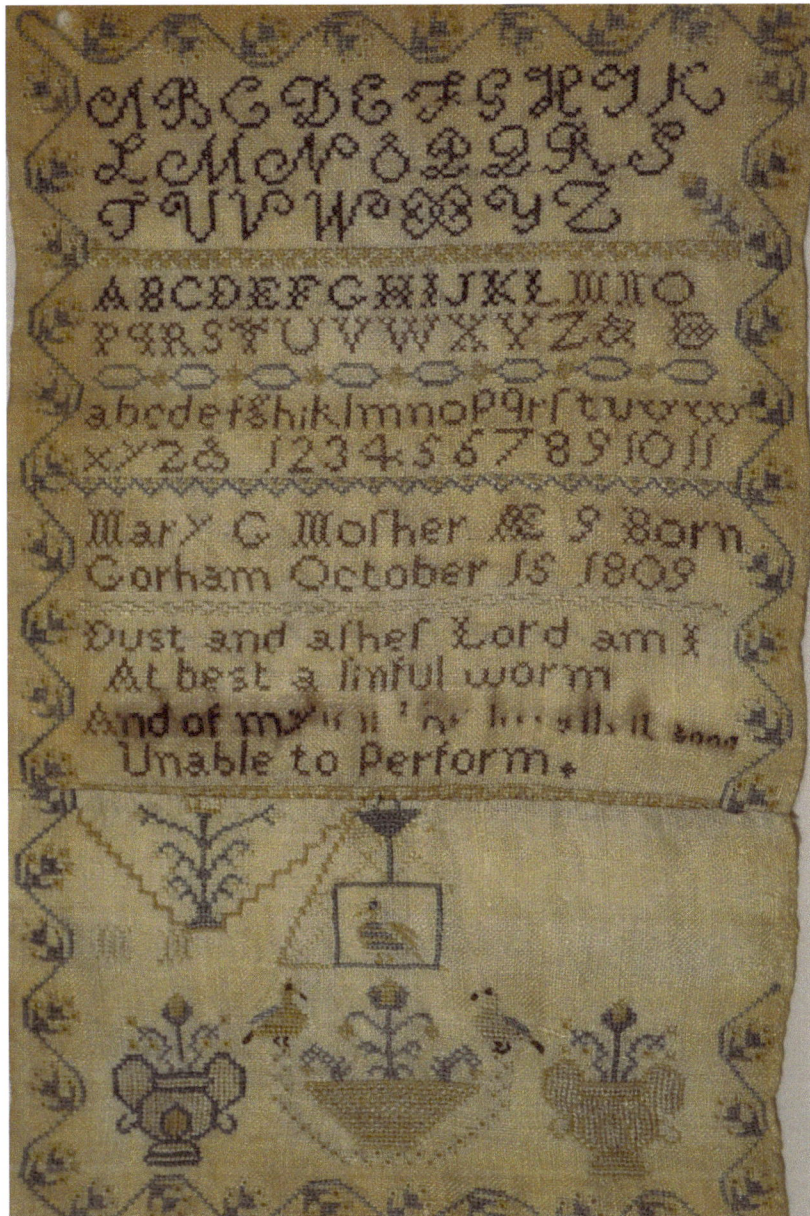

Mary Mosher (1809-1900), Gorham, Maine, 1818. Silk thread on linen, 15 1/2 x 10 1/4". Stitches: cross, eyelet, French knot, straight. Collection of Sue Merrill.

Mary's sampler was likely worked under the instruction of widow Rhoda McClellan of Gorham. Her sampler shares a number of the characteristics of others worked in Rhoda's school, including that of Eliza Stevens (page 51). Mary did not complete her sampler and it may have been damaged sometime after she stopped working on it since it has been cut apart and sewn back together below the verse. Mary Mosher was born October 16, 1809, to Nathaniel and Eunice Elder Mosher, one of nine children. On May 25, 1845, Mary became the second wife of Joseph Alexander of Brunswick. Joseph's first wife had passed away the year before, leaving him with five children under the age of fourteen. Mary and Joseph had another four children, although two of them died young. Their first child, Mary Ellen, born the year after they married, lived not quite a year. The second Mary Ellen, born later that same year, lived to adulthood. Their last child, Josephine, was born in 1851 and died just short of her third birthday. Although Joseph Alexander's father was a farmer, he was apparently interested in a life at sea and left the family farm as soon as he could. He commanded a number of vessels in his younger years and was very popular among other captains and vessel owners. A health problem with his throat forced him into early retirement and he returned to Brunswick to take up farming, although he continued occasionally to travel to Richmond and Bath where he worked as a ships' carpenter. Mary and Joseph spent their last years in the suburbs of Boston, living with their married children. Joseph died in 1890 at the age of eighty-six and Mary passed away ten years later. They are both buried in the Growstown Cemetery in Brunswick, along with their daughters, Mary Ellen and Josephine.

Amelia Dyer (1804-bef. 1850), Gorham, Maine, 1818. Silk thread on linen, 15 1/4 x 15 1/8". Stitches: cross. Private collection.

Amelia Dyer was probably the seventh of the twelve children of William Dyer, a farmer, and his wife, Rebecca Horton Huston, who was the widow of Captain William Huston who had been lost at sea in 1787. Amelia was born April 1, 1804, which would place the date of her sampler at about 1818. Amelia married Isaac Dyer, a wealthy farmer from Baldwin, Maine, on October 30, 1825. She gave birth to at least four children, the last one in 1836, but by 1850, she had passed away. On her sampler she named her teacher, Rhoda McClellan. Rhoda was the daughter of Charles and Rhoda Morris of Gorham, born February 17, 1881. She married Hugh McLellan, a sea captain, and gave birth to one child, Charles H. P., born June 6, 1803, just two months before his father died at sea in August 1803. Rhoda never remarried. Since Charles was married in Gorham in 1823, it seems likely that they remained there through at least the time of his marriage, but by June 1, 1830, she was living in his household in Portland, where he was a doctor. She moved with her son to Poughkeepsie, New York. On the 1850 census she, her son, and his wife were operating the Female Collegiate Institution there, with twenty-one live-in, teen-aged female students. She died in Poughkeepsie in 1853.

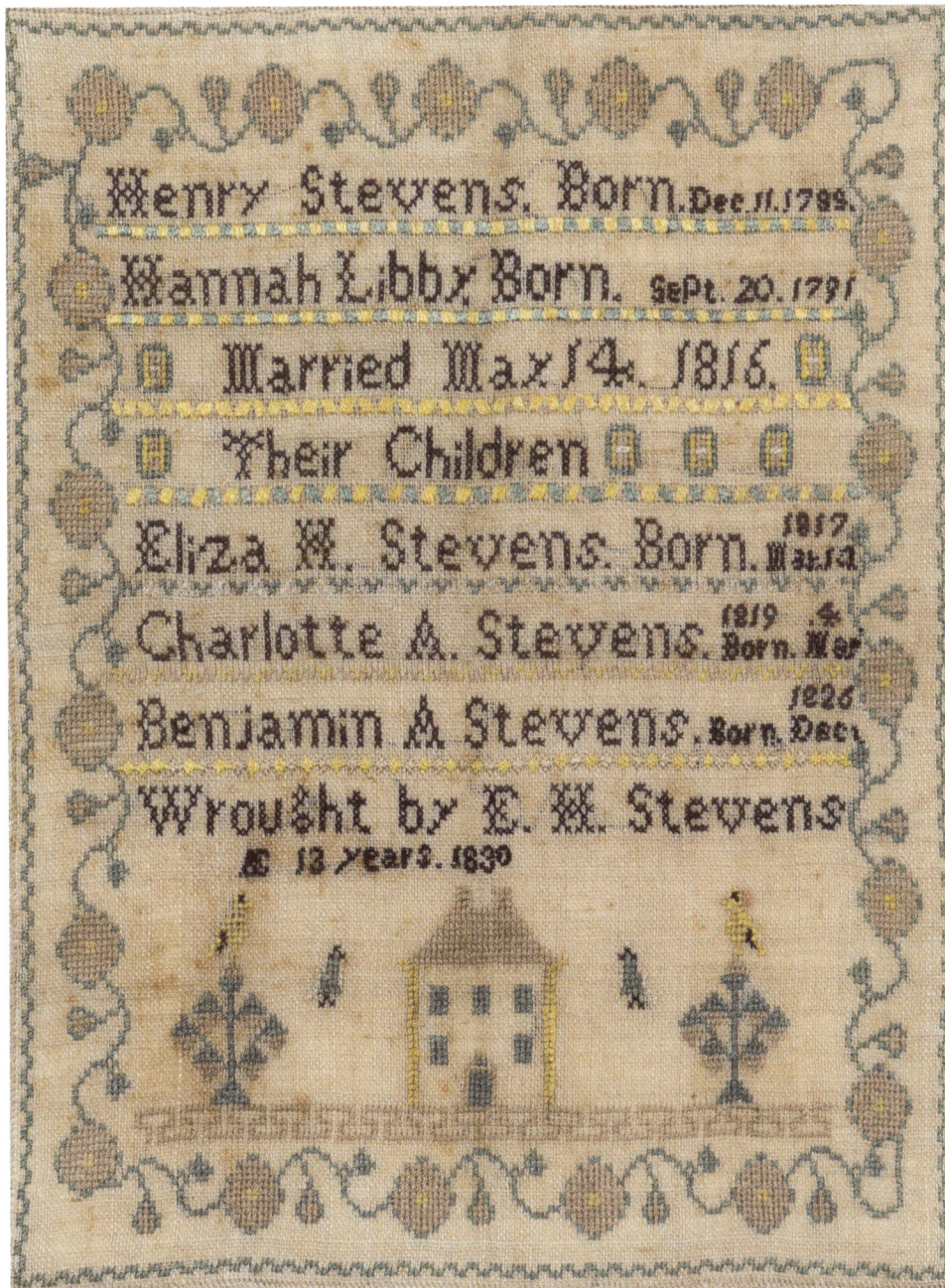

Eliza H. Stevens (1817-1893), Gorham, Maine, 1830. Silk thread on linen, 12 1/2 x 10".
Stitches: cross, hem, satin. Henry T. Callan Antiques.

Eliza H. Stevens was the eldest of the three children of Henry (sometimes called Harry) Stevens and his wife, Hannah Libby, all born in Gorham between 1817 and 1826. Henry was a carriage maker and did not marry until the age of thirty. He died only five years after Eliza stitched her sampler, and was buried in Portland, Maine. On December 22, 1839, Eliza married John Cloudman, a Gorham farmer who would later do very well as a merchant. After her marriage, her widowed mother moved in with Eliza and John, who, for the first several years of their marriage, lived with John's parents. In 1862, when Eliza was forty-five years old, she and John became parents to their only child, Alice M. Interestingly, on the 1870 census, the first one taken after her mother's death, Eliza is listed as owning $10,500 of real estate, just about twice what her husband owned. Eliza died on January 21, 1893, and John died the following June. They were both buried in Wood-lawn Cemetery in Westbrook, Maine. No further records could be found for their daughter. Eliza's sampler shares two characteristics, heavily fruited trees and poor planning of spacing, with three others that were stitched in Gorham under the instruction of widow Rhoda McClellan. She had moved to Portland by 1830, when she was recorded in a city directory. She may also have been Eliza's teacher, although it is at least as likely that some other Gorham teacher was familiar with McClellan's fruited tree motif and incorporated it into Eliza's design.

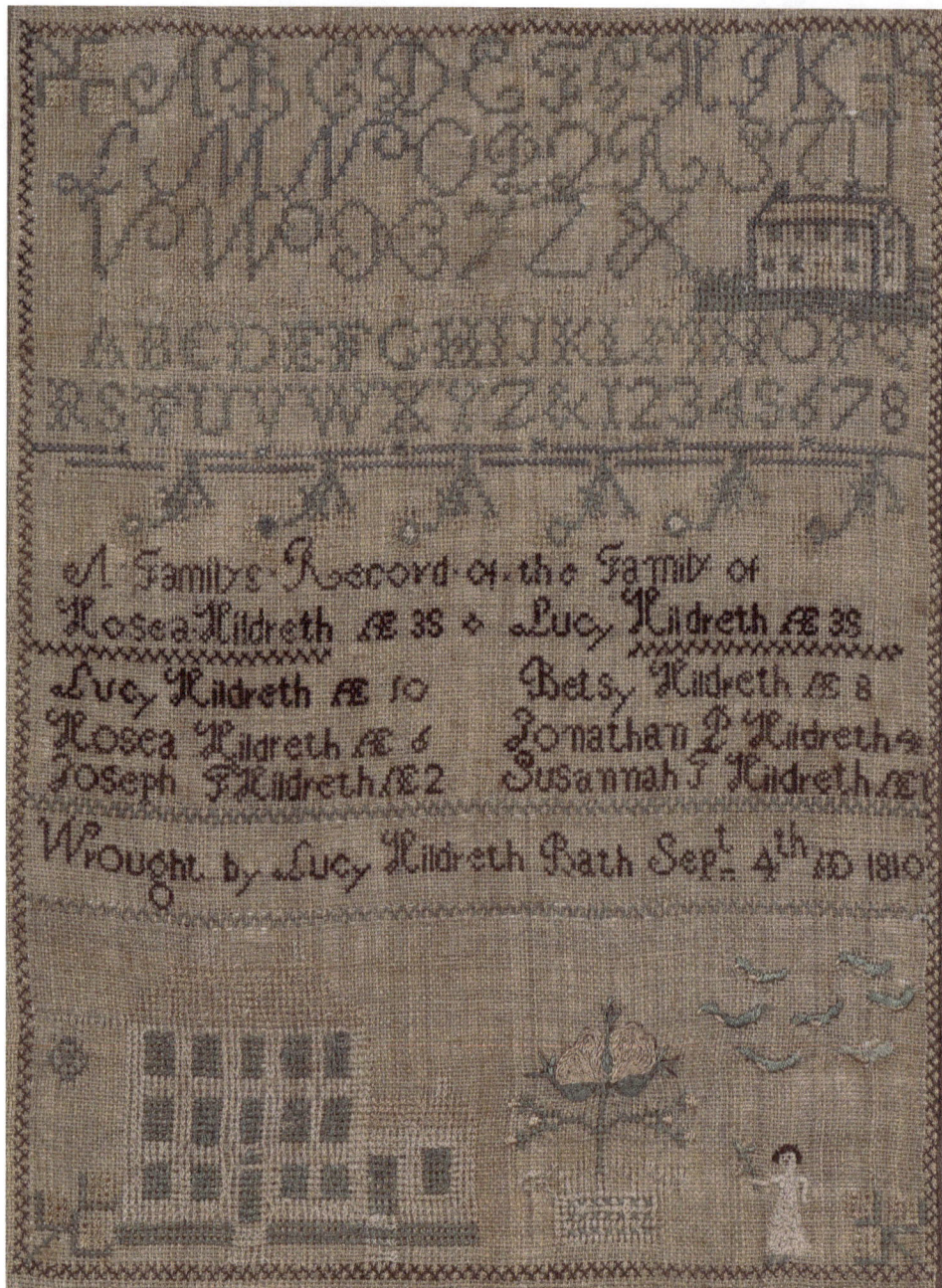

Lucy Fletcher Hildreth (1799-1869), Bath, Maine, 1810. Silk thread on linen, 15 1/2 x 12".
Stitches: cross, eyelet, bullion, satin, chain. Henry T. Callan Antiques.

Lucy titled her unusual genealogical sampler "A Family's Record of the Family" and rather than list the birthdates of family members, instead provided their ages at the time she stitched the work. Lucy was the eldest child of Hosea Hildreth and Lucy Fletcher, his second wife. She was born in Brookline, Massachusetts on February 12, 1800. Her next two siblings, Eliza—"Betsy"—and Hosea, were also born in Massachusetts, but by the time of Jonathan's birth in 1804, the family had made its way to Brunswick, Maine. The remaining five of her younger siblings (including William Jenks, 1812, and twins Samuel and Rhoda, 1814) were all born there. Lucy married James Lennan, a farmer, on October 15, 1823, in Topsham. They moved only a short distance, to Richmond, where she gave birth to seven children, with six surviving to adulthood. Her daughter Susannah, who attended Mount Holyoke Seminary, married Joseph "Jode" Hathorn and spent the first year of her marriage on board his family's three-masted schooner, recording her experiences. Her diary was published in 1997 as *A Bride's Passage: Susan Hathorn's Year Under Sail*. Susannah makes it clear how closely knit her family was. Lucy died on April 24, 1869, and is buried in Oak Grove Cemetery in Gardiner, Maine. Lucy's sister Betsy also stitched a sampler that includes a house and an over-sized person. Hers names Brunswick. Perhaps one girl named her hometown and the other the location where she completed the work?

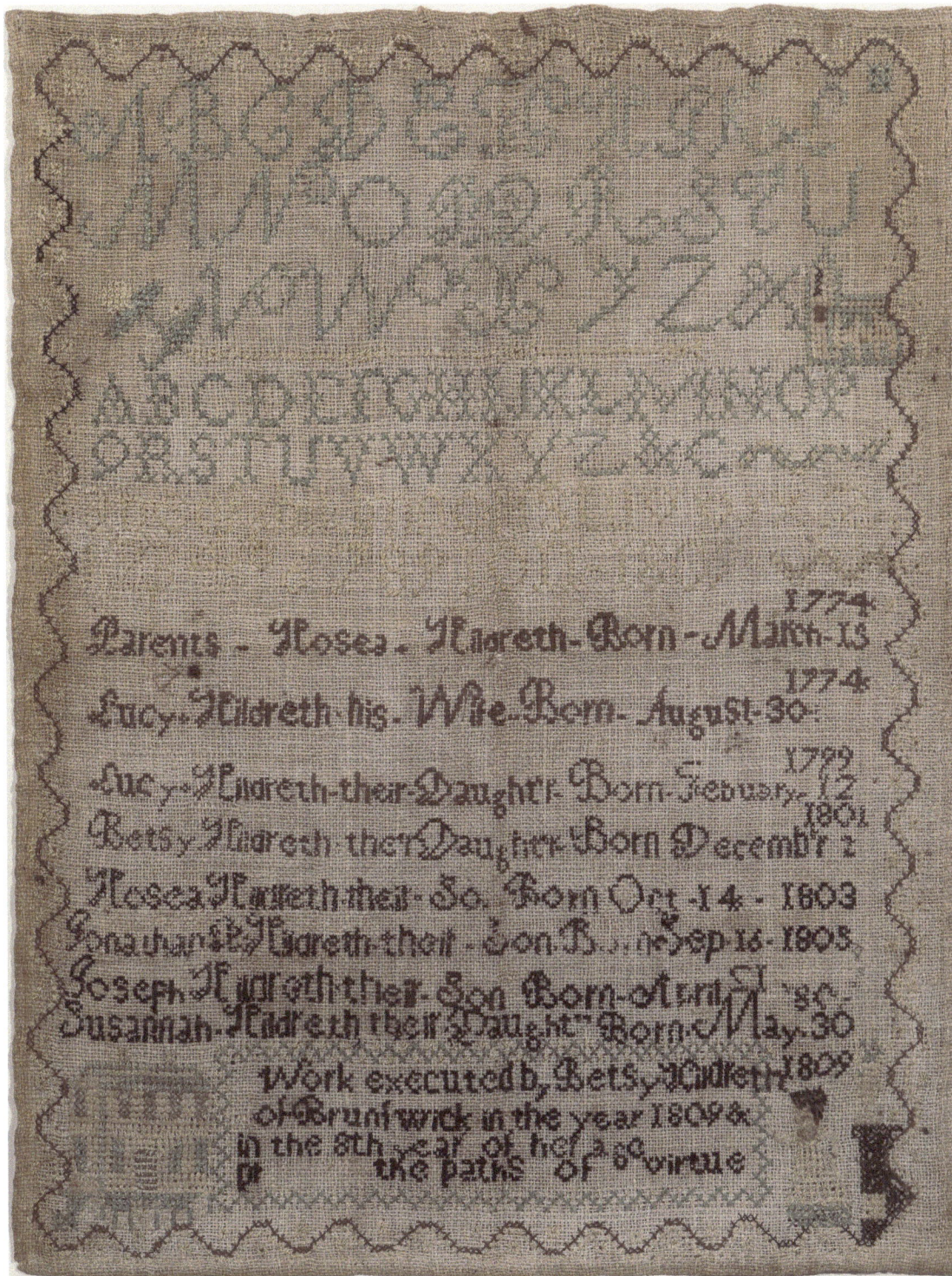

Betsy Hildreth (1801-1866), Brunswick or Bath, Maine, 1808. Silk thread on linen, 15 1/2 x 12". Stitches: cross over one and two. Maine State Museum.

Betsy Hildreth was about two years younger than her sister Lucy, and yet stitched her sampler almost a year before her elder sister is known to have worked one. On it, she carefully provided the birthdates for her entire family, although, being just "in her 8th year," (or only seven years old) she made a small mistake on her brother Joseph, stitching a mirror image of 12 and also for the year he was born: '80. Betsy noted that she was "of Brunswick," but is that also where she worked her sampler? On June 23, 1845, Betsy became the second wife of Freeman P. Patten of Gardiner, Maine, a "millman" and later a lumberman. She gave birth to a son, in addition to becoming the mother to the three surviving children of his first wife, Mary Stone. Freeman, who died in 1882, is buried with Mary Stone in Gardiner. Betsy died December 11, 1866, and is buried with the Hildreths and some Pattens in First Parish Cemetery in Topsham.

Anna M. Frost (1826-1904), Norway, Maine, 1836. Silk thread on linen, 20 1/4 x 16 1/2". Stitches: cross over one and two, four-sided, Italian hem, stem. Maine State Museum.

Anna Frost was born June 1, 1826, to Edmund Frost and Anna Pottle Lovejoy of Norway, Maine. Her parents married June 2, 1823, and had six children together. Anna was the second child and first daughter. On November 19, 1848, Anna married Osgood Perry of Norway. According to census records, the couple first lived with Osgood's father, John, but by 1860 they had established their own household on a farm. Between 1851 and 1869, Anna and Osgood had four children of their own: William, Horace, Amy Amelia, and Leland. Osgood Perry's farm appears on the 1880 Federal Agricultural Census. At that time, he had twenty-two improved acres, seventeen acres of pasture and orchards, and seventy-five acres of woodland. The farm was valued at a respectable $2500, with $50 in tools and $160 in livestock. Osgood was apparently doing all of the farm work himself, as he reported no hired hands or wages paid in the previous year. Anna and Osgood remained on the farm in Norway until the end of their lives. In 1904, Anna died at the age of seventy-seven of intestinal cancer. Osgood passed away five years later at the age of eighty-four. They are both buried in Norway Center Cemetery.

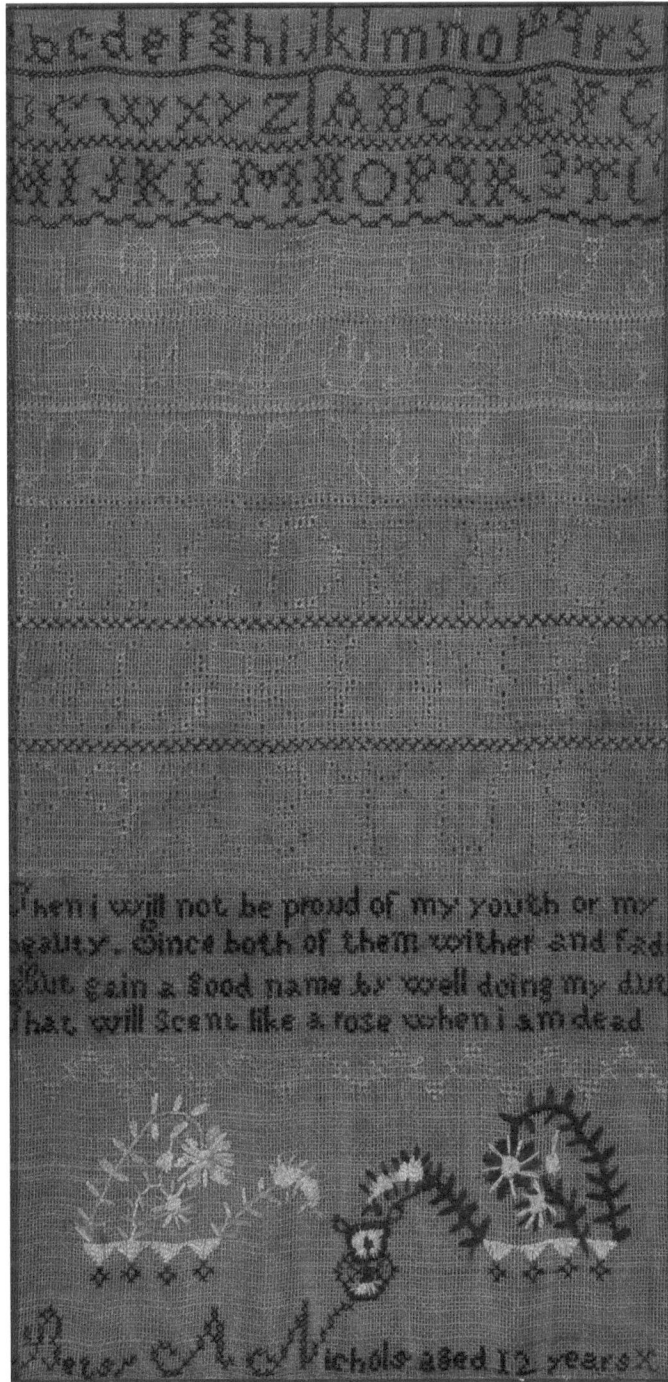

Betsey A. Nichols (1818-after 1880), Searsport, Maine, 1830. Silk thread on linen, 8 x 17 1/4". Stitches: cross over one and two, satin, eyelet, straight. Examplarery Sampler Collection.

Betsey Nichol's sampler has an elongated shape that reflects a style more common in the eighteenth century than in 1830. In addition, it features an unusual floral motif at the bottom that may be the product of an unskilled designer. No others like it have been identified. Betsey was the youngest child of the ten offspring of James Nichols, who had been born in Londonderry, New Hampshire, and his wife, Nancy Fowler. They were married in Prospect, Maine, but their children were all born in Searsport, Betsey on March 2, 1818. James was listed as the builder of the schooner *Ceres* on an 1845 Searsport property assessment. On October 7, 1838, Betsey married Howard Grant. Two sons were born in 1840 and 1843. However, on October 5, 1845, Betsey married again, to Stephen D. George, a successful farmer. They would have a daughter, Emma, and a son, Parker. By the 1870 census, Emma had married a mariner and was the mother of a one-year-old daughter, but remained in her parent's home. In 1880, the George family had moved to Winterport where Stephen was working as a grocer. That was the last record located for either Stephen or Betsey.

Susan Crosby (1810-?), Norridgewock, Maine, 1822. Silk thread on linen, 17 x 11 5/8".
Stitches: cross, eyelet, satin, back. Maine State Museum.

Susan Crosby may have been a daughter of Lucy and Jonas Crosby. Widow Lucy Tarbell Shed Crosby was the only Crosby enumerated on the 1820 census in Norridgewock. She married Jonas, her second husband, in about 1800. No records naming Susan could be found, however. Although nothing is known of the young woman who worked this sampler, she almost certainly completed it under the instruction of Catharine Swan Lyman of Northbridge, Massachusetts, who opened a school in Norridgewock around 1820. While the samplers worked in Norridgewock vary somewhat in format, they all share enough common characteristics to make a group attribution. The deeply arcaded border found on Susan's sampler appears on a number of these embroideries, including those of Elizabeth Freeman and Hadassah Thompson, which appeared in *I My Needle Ply with Skill* (pages 132-133). Catherine was the daughter of Caleb Lyman and Catharine Swan of Northbridge, Massachusetts, born on March 19, 1797. She may have moved to Norridgewock because her uncle, William Lyman, had relocated there. On August 16, 1829, she married Reverend Thomas Adams. They first lived in Vassalboro where she continued to teach for several more years, and later moved quite often, finally returning to Maine by about 1860. For the last several years of her life, Catharine was confined to the Augusta Lunatic Asylum, suffering from a mental illness that she was said to have inherited from her grandfather. She died in the asylum November 28, 1870.

Sarah Robbins (1792-1864), North Yarmouth, Maine, 1803. Silk thread on linen, 16 x 17 1/8". Stitches: cross over one and two, chain, satin, straight. Private collection.

It is easy to believe that Sarah's exuberant floral sampler is nearly as vivid as it was on the day she completed it. The profusion of attractively rendered flowers scattered across nearly all of the linen is unusual. Sarah, at some later point, picked out the last two digits of the year of her birth, but the Sarah Robbins who was the daughter of sea captain Thaddeus Robbins and his second wife, Rhoda Gray, of North Yarmouth, Maine, was born September 22, 1792, making her a very likely candidate. Her parents were married on March 27, 1787, and by the time of her birth had already lost two very young children, Ebenezer and Eunice, children of Thaddeus and his first wife, Phebe, and a second Ebenezer, who was Rhoda's infant son, making Sarah their eldest surviving child. A daughter conceived very shortly after Sarah's birth would also die as an infant. Two more sons, one of whom was lost at sea, and another daughter followed. On October 14, 1810, Sarah married Samuel Bucknum Cutter, also of North Yarmouth. Sarah had three children, Samuel, Sarah, and George. Samuel went to sea, fell from the rigging and drowned at the age of twenty-two. Sarah's husband died suddenly while out of town in 1844. She later moved to Gorham, Maine, and spent the last few years of her life living with her married daughter. After her death, on February 22, 1864, she was described, *"In circumstances more than ordinarily difficult and depressing, she was called in early life to have individual responsibility in directing and sustaining her family. Her wisdom, fidelity and success in meeting her responsibilities were such as are not common and as a consequence of what she was to her children when young and what she continued to be to them and their children through her whole life, she was loved by them with an affection almost passionate. She was remarkable for her energy, self-control, cheerfulness in trial, friendship and benevolence and for her native dignity and attractiveness of person and manner, which years did not impair."* Sarah's aunt, Olive Gray (1779-1860) attended the Hingham Academy in Hingham, Massachusetts, under the instruction of Mrs. Elizabeth Dawes who later operated a female academy in Portland, Maine. By 1816, but perhaps many years earlier, Olive was running an academy in North Yarmouth that lasted at least until about 1843. She may have been Sarah's instructor.

Elethea Soule (1800-1887), Waterville, Maine, 1811. Silk thread on linen, 18 x 12 1/2".
Stitches: cross, satin, chain. Private collection.

Elethea Soule celebrated her eleventh birthday by finishing her sampler. She was the youngest of the nine children of Revolutionary War veteran Jonathan Soule, a Duxbury, Massachusetts, farmer, and his first cousin and wife, Honor South-worth. Married in 1776, the Soules initially lived with his father in Duxbury where their first two children—both named Pelatiah—were born. In 1780, they moved to Winslow, Maine. All but one of Elethea's remaining siblings survived to adulthood, married, and started families. Elethea remained single. In 1850, she was living in the home of her ninety-three-year-old widowed mother, and they had a boarder. This home was quite close by those of the widow of her eldest brother, Pelatiah, and that of one of her nephews. She seems to have remained in the same quite modest house in 1870 (valued at just $300 that year) and 1880. When Elethea died in 1887, she was buried in Pine Grove Cemetery in Waterville, along with her parents, siblings, and numerous other relatives.

Martha Ann Nutter (1825-?), Ripley, Maine, 1835. Silk thread on linen, 17 1/4 x 13 3/4". Stitches: cross. Henry T. Callan Antiques.

Ripley, Maine, is a tiny farming community located in central Somerset County. Martha Ann Nutter was born there on March 18, 1825. Her parents were Richard Nutter, born May 28, 1785, in Wakefield, New Hampshire, and Betsey Weston, the daughter of William Weston and Betsey Clark of nearby Norridgewock, Maine. By the time Martha was born, her mother had given birth to five children, two of whom had already died. Of their five daughters, only Martha would live into adulthood. She had three surviving brothers. Sometime after 1830 but before 1840, Mehitable Hanson, born about 1765, most likely in New Hampshire, moved in with the family. She may have been a relative of Richard's. She may also have been Martha's teacher, since her sampler includes three motifs that are more characteristic of southern Maine and New Hampshire than central Maine samplers: a meandering trefoil cross border, fruit-filled baskets, and a tree with over-sized fruits. No reliable records could be found for Martha after her appearance on the 1850 census, although she may have survived to move away from Ripley; if she is buried with her family, her grave, unlike the rest, is unmarked.

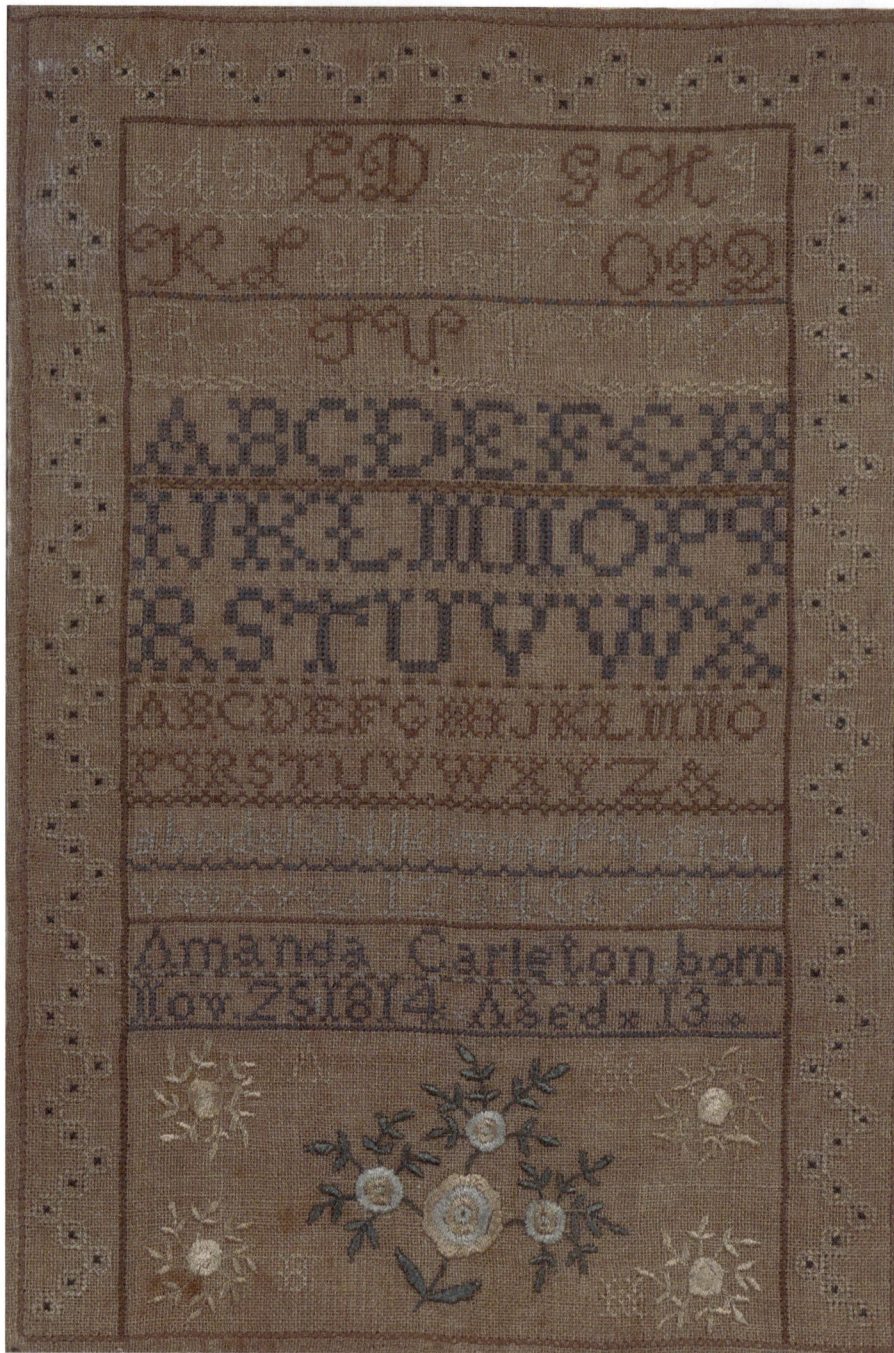

Amanda Carlton (1814-circa 1852), Blue Hill, Maine, 1827. Silk thread on linen, 12 1/2 x 17 1/2". Stitches: cross, satin, chain, hem. Henry T. Callan Antiques.

Amanda Carlton, born November 25, 1814, lived in the coastal village of Blue Hill, Maine. She was the fourth daughter of William Wallace Carlton and his wife, Pamelia Osgood. Her three elder sisters were each only a little more than a year apart in age. Her father was never more than a small-time farmer, the value of his real estate generally less than $500, with a house of only three rooms and a daylight cellar. On the 1850 census, William, who was aged sixty-four, had living in his household his wife, his son William who was aged thirty-one and had "no occupation" (although on later census records he would marry and run a very small farm of his own) and Amanda who was aged thirty-six and listed as "insane." Amanda's eldest sister, Harriet, probably left the impoverished family in order to bring in some much-needed cash. She died in Lowell, Massachusetts, likely as a mill operative, in 1835 at the age of just twenty-five. Her sister Clarissa initially taught school and then became the second wife of Captain Stephen Norton and mother to his ten children. She would go on to have eleven more! Her sister Matilda married a successful local carpenter. Amanda is believed to have died in Blue Hill on April 26, 1852. The Carleton farm still stands, a small cape-style house (that was enlarged in the late twentieth century) that William built on his father-in-law's land, and is now owned by the Blue Hill Heritage Trust.

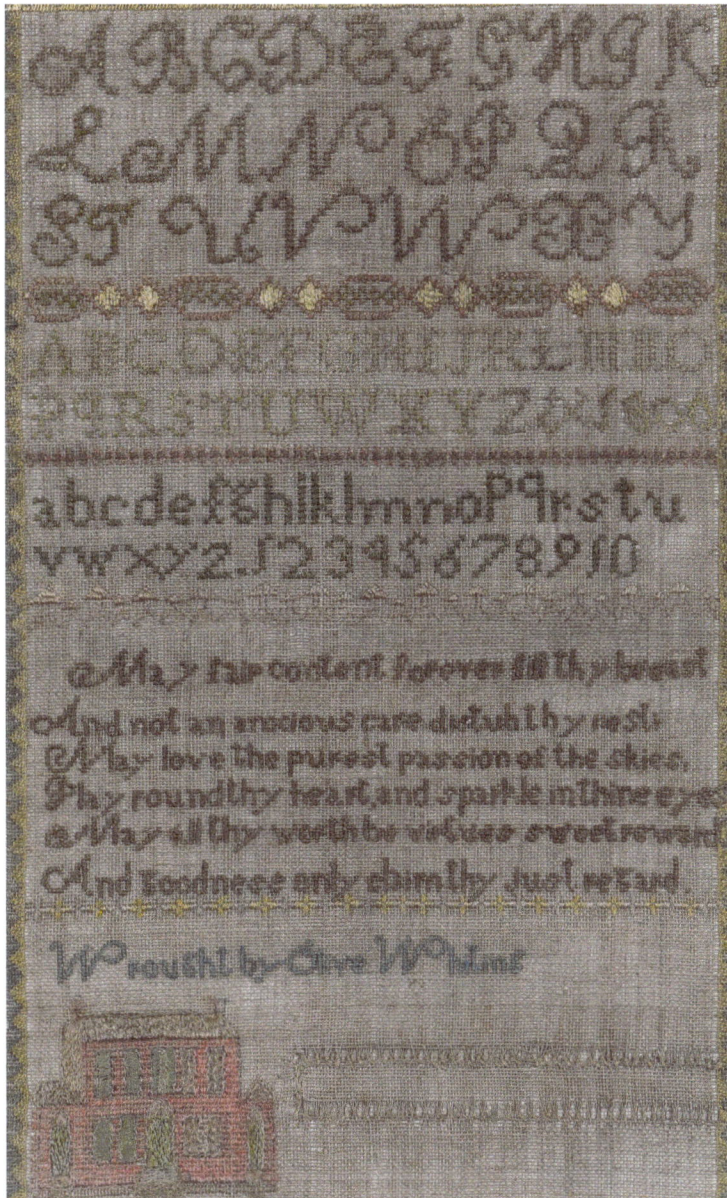

Olive Whiting (circa 1789-1819), possibly stitched in Hope, Maine, 1800.
Silk thread on linen, 12 x 8 1/2". Stitches: cross, satin, chain, sheaf-filling.
Examplarery Sampler Collection.

Olive's sampler demonstrates many of the challenges that textiles from more than two hundred years ago may offer. Olive provided few clues to her identity or the location where she stitched her work. Genealogical records can aid in filling in some of the blanks, but not all. She appears to have been the daughter and fourth child of John Lake Whiting and his wife, Olive Ross Wyman, who were married in Shrewsbury, Massachusetts, in 1782. Their first two children, Relief and Lucy, were both born in Shrewsbury. Olive Wyman Whiting died there, "insane," in 1842 at the age of eighty. Although siblings Seth, Olive, Sarah, Henry, and Mary may have been born in Massachusetts, the adult lives of Lucy, Sarah, and Henry argue strongly for a family connection to Hope, Maine. Lucy never married. On the 1850 census, she was residing in the Hope, Maine, home of her sister, Sarah and Sarah's husband, Dr. Moses Dakin, who was born in Hope. Dr. Dakin was "insane." By 1860, Sarah had died and Lucy was living as a boarder in Hope and described as "pauper." She died later that year. Henry Whiting married a woman from Hope, but later settled in Massachusetts. Phillipston, Massachusetts, vital records report that Olive married Calvin Maynard of Sterling on October 26, 1818. She died there less than a year later on July 11, 1819, of "inflammation of the brain." In 1823, Calvin remarried; the eight day old son of Calvin and his new wife, Cornelia, died later that year, and Calvin passed away in 1827. Olive's sampler includes several interesting details. Could the house be her family home? The band of elongated hexagons and diamonds has been found on several other samplers that were from southern New Hampshire and the Haverhill, Massachusetts, area but the border could have migrated to Hope with the family or some other person.

Lydia Ann Cartland (1822-1906), Vassalboro, Maine, 1833. Silk thread on linen, 12 1/2 x 11 1/2". Stitches: cross, queen. Collection of Glee Krueger.

Lydia Ann Cartland's name, along with those of her parents and siblings, appears in Friends' records at Vassalboro, Maine. Vassalboro was a vibrant Quaker community in the early nineteenth century. Lydia's father, John, had come there from Lee, New Hampshire, and her mother, Tabitha Pope, from another area where Friends were common, Windham, Maine. They were parents to six children born between 1805 and Lydia's birth on June 5, 1822. By 1850, her parents had moved to Windham where her father continued to farm. On July 31, 1867, at age forty-five, she married her first cousin, once removed, Silas Cartland, of Parsonfield, Maine, a farmer and sometime minister who was about ten years younger than Lydia. It seems likely that she and Silas had no children. Although a young woman named Harriet Cartland was living with them in 1880 and listed as "daughter" she may have been their niece since on the 1900 census Lydia and Silas were listed as having never had children. Silas died in March of 1906 and Lydia just three months later on June 27, 1906.

New Hampshire

Adorn thyself with grace and truth
And learning prize now in thy youth

Portsmouth

From an early date, the inhabitants of Portsmouth took female education seriously. By the 1760s, needlework teachers were placing advertisements in local newspapers. After the American Revolution, even greater emphasis was placed on female education and numerous schools, both public and private, were founded. Notable early nineteenth-century academies included those of the Reverend Timothy Alden and George Dame. Instructors in Portsmouth demonstrated to a remarkable degree the sharing of designs, so that very similar samplers were completed under the instruction of a variety of different teachers, rather than being attributable to a single school, as is common in other locales. Between 1800 and 1840, more than forty female teachers offered private instruction in the "ornamental branches." The only proof of existence for some of these schools is the inscription on a student's sampler.

Mary Stoodly (1753-1784), Portsmouth, New Hampshire, 1764. Silk thread on linen, 21 3/4 x 16 3/4". Stitches: cross, eyelet, satin, stem, knotted chain, couched. Strawbery Banke Museum.

Mary Stoodly's (also spelled Stoodley) sampler is unusual in a number of respects. While most girls worked their numerals from 1 to 9 with a 0 tacked on at the end, Mary included the numbers from 1 to 49. She also had her own idiosyncratic way of working several of those numbers, which makes it a challenge to interpret the dates in her inscription. While Mary completed the first repetition of her numbers correctly, when she reached the number 15, she inverted the form of her 5, creating a uniquely shaped digit. When she stitched 26, the 6 was completely backwards. From that point on, Mary consistently used her own form of these two numbers. In the late twentieth century, this led to some confusion as to the actual dates of both Mary's birth and the completion of the sampler, which were interpreted as born in 1773 and worked in 1784, instead of her actual dates of born in 1753 and worked in 1764. Mary must have truly enjoyed her needlework, because she also completed another almost-identical sampler at the age of eleven, which had a floral motif in the bottom instead of the strawberry design seen here (*American Samplers*, p.77). Mary was born in Portsmouth June 17, 1753, the daughter of tavern keeper James S. Stoodley and Elizabeth Doe. Her father was a staunch supporter of the American Revolution and his tavern was the meeting place for many of those rebelling against the king. Mary married Nathaniel Folsom of Exeter in November 1771. The couple lived in Portsmouth, where Nathaniel was a merchant. Nathaniel was also in favor of American independence. He signed the Association Test in 1776, participated in the expedition to Rhode Island in 1778 under Colonel Langdon, and was part-owner and bonder of several privateers. Mary and Nathaniel had five children between 1772 and 1779. Their only son, Nathaniel, born in 1779, died at the age of five in September 1783. Mary passed away eight months later at the age of thirty-one. She is buried in the North Cemetery, Portsmouth.

Mary Sheafe (1754-1826), Portsmouth, New Hampshire, 1768. Silk thread on linen, 20 1/4 x 10 1/2". Stitches: cross, satin, eyelet, lazy daisy, back. Examplarery Sampler Collection.

Mary stitched an elongated marking sampler that was very typical of the type of work being done at about that time. As the eighteenth century drew to a close, most sampler shapes began to shorten and became closer to square shaped. Mary separated her rows of alphabets and numbers with attractive, intricate narrow bands that add appeal and interest to her work. She was the somewhat older sister of Hetty Sheafe whose (location unknown) 1773 sampler was described in 1921 in *American Samplers* as "four alphabets, eyelet, stem, satin, and cross-stitch. Hemstitched border 16 border designs." Mary's has four alphabets and seventeen different border designs so, although stitched about five years earlier, is probably very similar. Mary was the seventh of the eleven children of Jacob Sheafe and Hannah Seavey. She married Reverend Joseph Willard who had been born December 29, 1738, in Biddeford, Maine, and who served as president of Harvard College from 1781 until his death in 1804. They had thirteen children, six of whom died young. Mary died March 6, 1826.

Mehitable Burleigh (1763-1847), New Castle, New Hampshire, 1773.
Silk thread on linen, 18 x 11 1/4". Stitches: cross over one and two,
eyelet, satin, chain, Italian hem. Examplarery Sampler Collection.

Mehitable Burleigh was the second eldest child of John Burleigh's third wife. John, who was born in Ipswich, Massachusetts, in 1717, relocated to New Castle, New Hampshire, where he ran a riverside store, served three terms in the state legislature, and was active in town politics. His first marriage in February 1739/40 was to Sarah Hall. She gave birth to five children over the next ten years and died in 1757 after a six-year long interval with no children whose births were recorded. Six months after her death, John married Elizabeth Chelsey. She gave birth to two children less than thirteen months apart who died as infants, and she died shortly thereafter. John then married Mehitable Sheafe on October 16, 1760. Mehitable began to have children as closely spaced as John's deceased wives had, giving birth to seven in the first twelve years of her marriage. Two of these were named for siblings who had already died. Mehitable was the second eldest of these, born on "April 24, 1763 Sunday" says an old handwritten listing of family information that was found in a book published in 1869. A family genealogy of 1880 said, "She had an excellent education," evidenced by her attractive sampler. With its extended length and rows of bands, it nicely demonstrates the gradual transition that was occurring when she stitched it, from the long narrow band samplers of the seventeenth and eighteenth centuries to the shortened rectangles of the nineteenth century. After John died in 1778, his wife ran the family home. Their daughter Mehitable never married, but by 1820 she had her own home where she resided for the last twenty or more years of her life with a somewhat younger woman. Mehitable died on March 23, 1847, in Newmarket.

Eliza Jane Salter (1792-1878), Portsmouth, New Hampshire, 1803. Silk thread on linsey-woolsey, 19 3/4 x 14 1/8". Stitches: cross over one and two, stem, satin, long arm cross. Portsmouth Historical Society; gift of the Sawtelle Family.

Eliza was born in 1792, the youngest daughter of Captain John Salter and Abigail Ayers. John Salter followed in his father's footsteps and went to sea at an early age. An active participant in the Revolutionary War, in 1776 John served as an officer in Commodore Hopkins's squadron, which sailed to the Bahamas to capture the island of New Providence. The following year he captured the ship *Sisters,* and in 1778, he was appointed second lieutenant of the ship *General Sullivan.* That same year John and Abigail Ayers married. Their first child, Edward, died young; he was followed by two more boys and four daughters, Sarah Anne, Lucy Maria, Abigail, and finally Eliza. Sadly, the Salter children lost their parents at a fairly young age. Captain Salter died in 1794, two years after Eliza was born, and Abigail died in 1806, when Eliza was only fourteen. Perhaps because of their parents' early deaths and the need to supplement the family income, all of the Salter daughters worked as schoolteachers at one time or another. Of the four daughters, Sarah was the only one to marry. In September 1814 she married joiner Benjamin Holmes, but he died sometime before the late 1830s. In 1839, Abigail Salter was running a private female academy with sisters Eliza and probably Lucy teaching with her. Abigail passed away in 1846 and Eliza took charge of the family teaching enterprise. Lucy and Eliza joined Sarah's household once she was a widow, and the three lived together until each passed away. Late in life, Lucy was described on a federal census as being insane; she died in 1860. Sarah passed away in 1868, and Eliza remained in the home on Pleasant Street until she died in 1878 at the age of eighty-six.

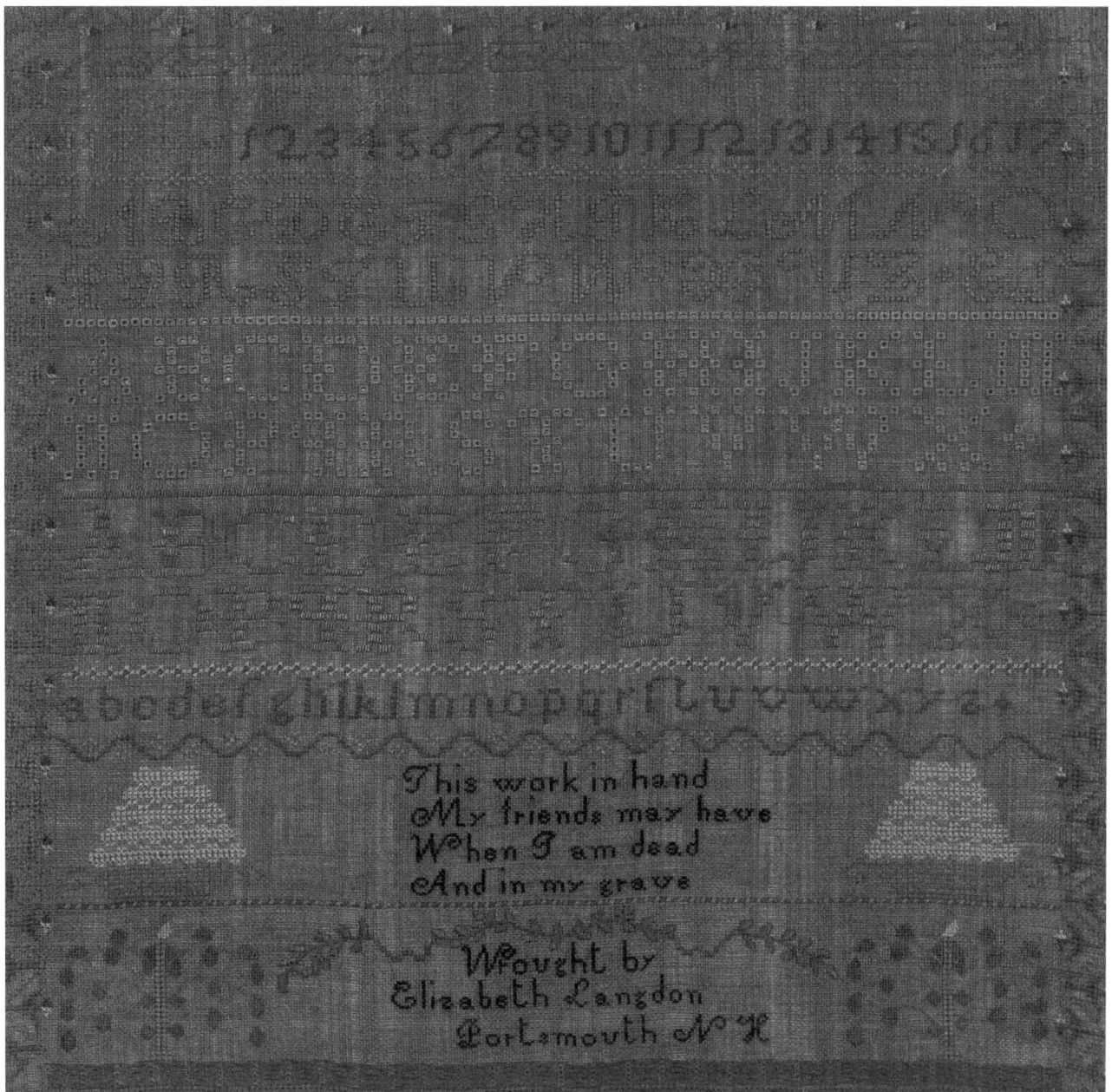

Elizabeth Langdon (1795-1875), Portsmouth, New Hampshire, 1805. Silk thread on linen, 16 3/4 x 17 1/2". Stitches: cross over one and two, satin, outline, eyelet, basketweave. Newington Historical Society.

Elizabeth was the daughter of Reverend Joseph Langdon of Portsmouth and Patience Pickering of Newington, New Hampshire. Joseph and Patience married in December of 1790; Elizabeth was born in 1795, the second of four daughters. Joseph was a graduate of Dartmouth and a minister in Newington, New Hampshire, where he began preaching in 1788. Joseph arrived in Newington at a transitional time for public church support, when many residents were discontented with paying taxes to support the Congregational church. Many "polled off" and pledged their support to other denominations, greatly reducing both the size of the church congregation and its ability to support a minister and his family. The Langdon family stayed in Newington until 1810, when Joseph was dismissed by his congregation, and then moved to a farm Portsmouth. In March 1827, Elizabeth married Samuel Whidden III. Samuel was a prosperous farmer and the couple lived on Lafayette Road in Portsmouth. They had five children, four boys, one of whom died as an infant, and one girl. The family did well, and according to U.S. census records, the household usually included at least one or two farm laborers as well as an Irish maid. Of their children, only their son Langdon married. The other three—William, Elizabeth, and Samuel—remained at home for the rest of their lives, helping their parents run the farm. Samuel Whidden III died in January 1875, and Elizabeth's death followed in December of that year. She is buried in the Whidden Family Cemetery in Elwyn Park, Portsmouth, along with her husband, son William, parents, sisters Elizabeth and Temperance, and other Whidden family members.

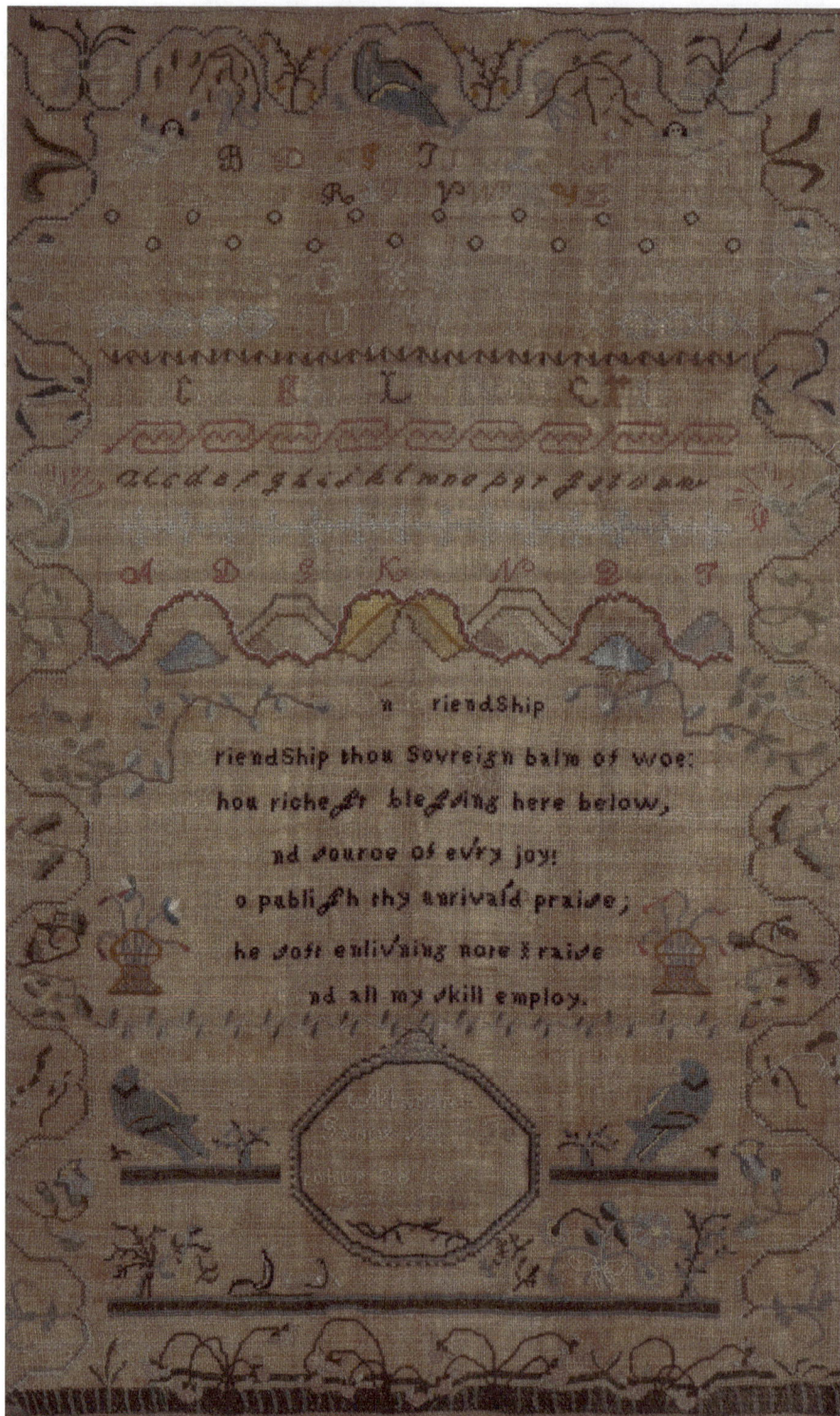

Martha Gaines (1794-1858), Portsmouth, New Hampshire, 1804. Silk thread on linen, 25 1/2 x 15 3/4". Stitches: hem, chain, cross over one and two, bullion, couched. Newington Historical Society.

Martha's sampler shares several characteristics with those of Sarah Catherine Odiorne and Mary Gerrish. All three samplers have unusual oval-shaped cartouches, and the blue birds on Martha's and Sarah's samplers are clearly related. While Sarah's and Mary's samplers are both memorials to family members, Martha chose to include a verse on friendship. Martha was the daughter of George Gaines and Sarah Pickering of Newington, New Hampshire. George was a cabinetmaker and house carpenter, the only son of John Gaines III of Portsmouth, a prominent cabinetmaker himself. Martha's parents married in July 1782 and had at least three children. George Gaines passed away when Martha was only fifteen. Martha never married and died in 1858 at the age of sixty-four of a "bilous fever."

Sarah Catherine Moffatt Odiorne (1794-1868), Portsmouth, New Hampshire, 1806. Silk thread on linen, 16 3/4 x 24 1/4". Stitches: hem, cross over one and two, bullion, couched. Moffatt-Ladd House and Garden.

Sarah Odiorne worked her sampler in memory of her grandmother, Sarah Catherine Moffatt (1742-1802), wife of Samuel Moffatt, who lived in the Moffatt-Ladd House in Portsmouth, New Hampshire. Sarah was born March 10, 1794, the fourth of the eleven children of William Odiorne and Lucy Moffat of Kittery. On November 11, 1814, Sarah married Andrew Leighton. The couple made their home in Eliot, Maine, where they had nine children between 1815 and 1839. Andrew was a farmer who was active in politics, and he served as both a state representative and senator from Eliot. Sarah died in 1868 and is buried in the Mount Pleasant Cemetery in Eliot along with her husband, who passed away in 1882. On her sampler, Sarah named her teacher, Miss Ward. It is difficult to be certain about just who Miss Ward was. She did not advertise her school in any local newspapers or list herself as a teacher in the Portsmouth city directories. So far, all of the known Portsmouth samplers worked in this style were completed by girls whose families were members of the North Church. Nahum and Margery Greenleaf Ward were also members of that church. They had four daughters: Dorcas, Margery, Elizabeth, and Mary Ann. According to sampler scholar Rita Conant, daughter Elizabeth was Sarah's teacher. However, it seems unlikely that Elizabeth was the instructor for all of the girls who worked samplers in this style since she would have only been fourteen when the first one was completed by Mary Langdon in 1800. It is possible that more than one of the Ward sisters taught needlework and made use of similar motifs.

Mary Gerrish (1801-1876), Portsmouth, New Hampshire, 1811. Silk thread on linen, 20 x 16 1/4".
Stitches: hem, cross over one and two, long, chain, bullion, satin, outline, basketweave, eyelet, couched.
Newington Historical Society.

Mary Gerrish was born in Portsmouth in 1801, the daughter of Timothy and Dorothy Patterson Gerrish, and the youngest of ten children. Timothy was a prominent silver and goldsmith in Portsmouth, where he also served as deputy sheriff and jailor from around 1800 to 1815. Mary worked her sampler in memory of her brother, Thomas Patterson Gerrish (1789-1811). It shares several characteristics with those of Martha Gaines and Sarah Odiorne, and probably was completed under the instruction of the same teacher. Mary's sampler also has cartouches, although hers are oriented vertically rather than horizontally as on Martha's and Sarah's. In common with Sarah's sampler, the cartouches are surrounded by leafy vines. Although the urn on Mary's sampler is different in configuration than the one on Sarah's, they are both worked very finely over one thread. Mary Gerrish never married. In 1850, the U.S. census recorded her as boarding at the Franklin House in Portsmouth, along with Mary Walden Barnabee, a former needlework teacher and sister of Elvira Walden Potter, the instructor named on Adeline Ferguson's sampler. By the 1860s, she was listed in the city directories as "Miss Mary Gerrish," first boarding at 19 Anthony Street and later living at 19 Union Street, where she remained until her death in 1876 at the age of seventy-five.

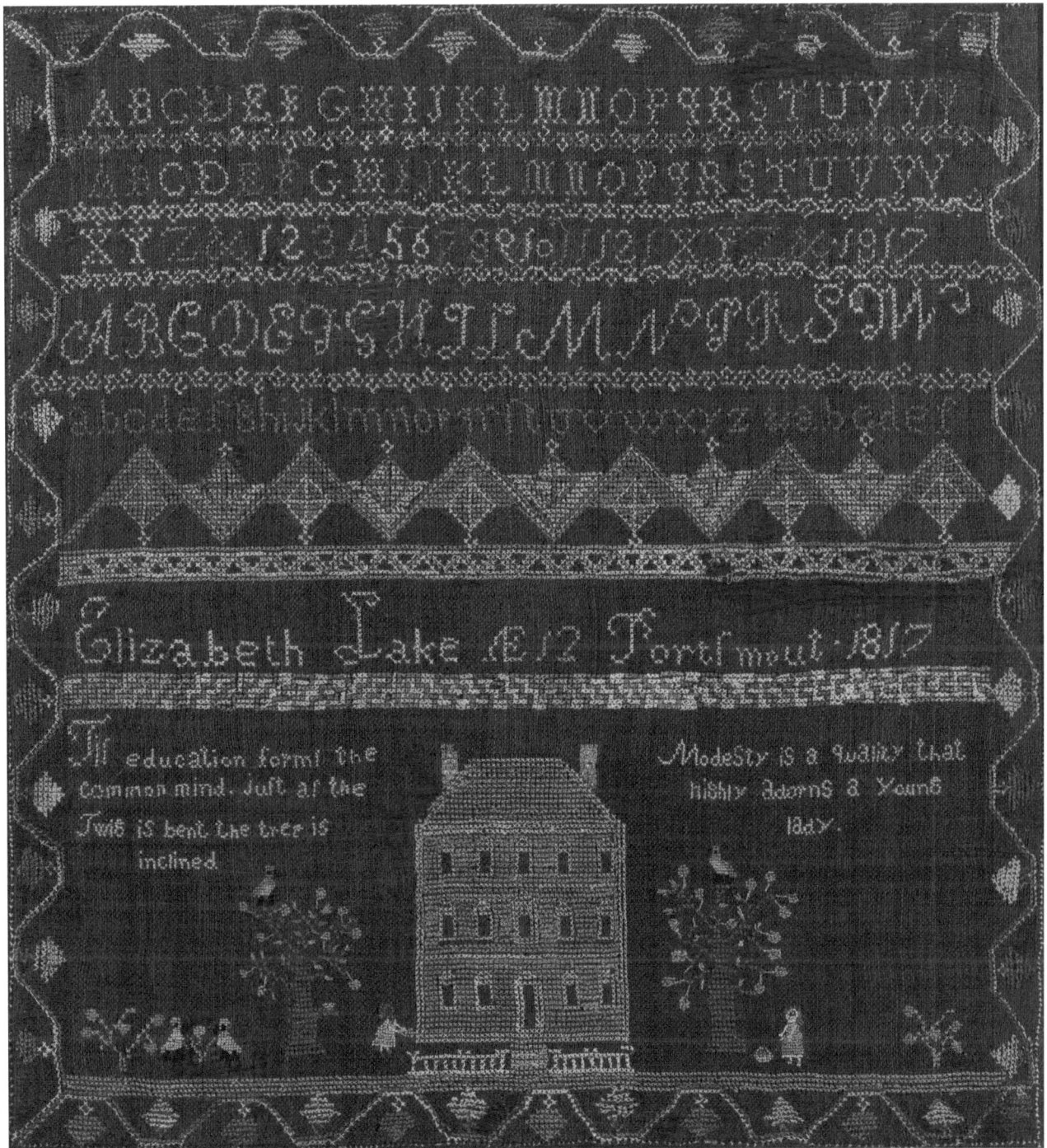

Elizabeth Lake (1805-1843), Portsmouth, New Hampshire, 1817. Silk thread on linsey-woolsey, 17 x 16 1/8". Stitches: cross over one and two, stem. Portsmouth Historical Society; Gift of Mrs. E. E. Cummings.

Although many samplers completed in Portsmouth in the 1820s and 1830s include a scene with buildings at the bottom, Elizabeth's work is somewhat atypical. She placed a single, large three-story, hipped-roof brick house at the bottom center, along with two small figures of children who appear to be gathering fruit. Elizabeth was the daughter of John Lake, a shipmaster, and Hannah Salter, who were married on June 26, 1796, in Portsmouth. In November 1826, when she was twenty-one, Elizabeth married Rufus Hubbard. Elizabeth and Rufus had one child, John Wesley Hubbard, born in 1828. Rufus was apparently a druggist, because on July 23, 1830, a Gardiner, Maine, newspaper reported the death of "Mr. Rufus Hubbard, Apothecary, of Portsmouth" who had died the previous Friday "aged about 35." Elizabeth died December 17, 1843, at the relatively young age of thirty-eight. In 1852, their son married Pamelia Wesley Philbrook. The couple had a daughter in December 1853 whom they named after John's mother, Elizabeth Lake Hubbard.

Mary L. Starbird (1815-1894), Portsmouth, New Hampshire, 1825. Silk on linen, 25 1/2 x 21 1/4". Stitches: cross over one and two, satin, eyelet, French knot, lazy daisy, Italian hem. Strawbery Banke Museum.

Mary Libbey Starbird was born in Portsmouth, New Hampshire, May 18, 1815 to Samuel Starbird of Durham and Mary Libbey of Portsmouth. In 1834, she married John Pike, a widower with four children, becoming, at the age of nineteen, the stepmother of three girls and one boy, ranging in age from nine to three. Mary and John went on to have four children of their own. After their marriage, John and Mary moved to Danvers, Massachusetts, where John was a farmer. By 1880, when John was eighty-two, the couple was living in Lexington and John was working as a farm laborer. He died at age ninety-one on July 14, 1890. Mary died four years later in November 1894, at the age of seventy-nine. They are buried together in the Walnut Grove Cemetery in Danvers. Mary worked her sampler under the instruction of E. M. Robinson, probably Emiline Robinson, the same teacher who taught Frances Whidden. Although the two samplers are different in size and shape, they share some of the same crossbands and sawtooth borders, and, at the bottom, both have scenes with buildings. Both girls also included a giraffe, or "cameleopard," as Mary calls it, finely worked over one thread. A sampler by Harriet Ann Dockum worked in 1825 (in the collection of the Portsmouth Historical Society) may have also been worked under Miss Robinson's instruction. Although Harriet did not name a teacher on her sampler, it shares the same lozenge border with its satin-stitched flowers and large fruit baskets. Emiline was the daughter of Abednego Robinson of Stratham and Mary Sawyer of Dover. The couple had twelve children between 1794 and 1817; Emiline was the sixth. The family first lived in Stratham, but by 1821 Abednego had purchased a large farm on Sherburne Road in the Plains district of Portsmouth. In April 1825, the Selectmen of Portsmouth appointed Emiline to teach at the school in the Plains, where "…the higher branches of Education, Reading, Spelling, Writing, English Grammar, Geography, Arithmetic, History and Philosophy were taught in the four months of summer by Misses, and in the winter months by the Masters." Emiline probably supplemented her income the remainder of the year by giving private needlework lessons. She does not appear to have placed any advertisements for her school in the local newspapers, so she may have recruited prospective students from among her public school pupils. In 1830, Emiline Robinson married Reverend Samuel Kelly, a Methodist minister. Over the next few decades the couple lived in several different towns in Vermont, returned to Portsmouth for a while, and then moved to Newburyport, Massachusetts, by 1860. Emiline died in 1865 and is buried in Harmony Grove Cemetery in Portsmouth.

Frances Whidden (1816-1855), Portsmouth, New Hampshire, 1828. Silk thread on linen, 16 3/4 x 16". Stitches: cross, satin, queen, bullion, running. Strawbery Banke Museum.

Frances Whidden chose to work her sampler as a memorial to her maternal grandparents, William Seavey and Anna G. Trefethen, who lived in Rye, New Hampshire. Her grandparents married in 1766 and had eleven children; Frances's mother, Abigail, was next to last. During the Revolutionary War, William Seavey served as First Lieutenant under Captain Joseph Parson at New Castle, New Hampshire. Abigail Seavey married Joseph W. Whidden Jr. of Portsmouth in 1808. Joseph's farm was located on Lafayette Road and the couple raised their family of eight children there. Their eldest daughter, Mary Ann, taught needlework in the early 1830s; Sarah Marden's sampler names her as teacher. In September 1840, Frances Whidden married Richard L. Palmer. They made their home in Dorchester, Massachusetts, where they had one daughter, Annie Seavey Palmer. Frances died May 3, 1855, at the young age of thirty-nine. She is buried in the Whidden graveyard in Portsmouth. Frances worked her sampler at the school of E. Robinson, who was probably Emiline Robinson, Mary Starbird's teacher. Frances included small depictions of her grandparents in the middle of her sampler. Enclosed within a sawtooth border is a verse on death, with her grandfather on the left reading a book and leaning on his cane and her grandmother, on the right, sporting a large bonnet and carrying a bag. At the bottom, she worked two gravestones in a cemetery. Above the cemetery fly two angels that look nothing the smaller winged cherubs that appear on a number of other Portsmouth samplers. In the bottom right corner, Frances placed a finely worked giraffe that appears to be identical to the one on Mary Starbird's sampler .

Sarah Elizabeth Marden (1823-1906), Portsmouth, New Hampshire, 1832. Silk thread on linen, 20 1/2 x 16 1/4". Stitches: cross over one and two, satin, lazy daisy, straight. Portsmouth Historical Society.

The samplers of Sarah Marden and Frances Whidden are similar in a number of respects, although they were completed under the instruction of two different teachers. For instance, they have the same borders, footed fruit bowls, and church at the bottom. The depiction of the building, St. John's Church in Portsmouth, is particularly notable because it shows the facade as it was originally constructed in 1808 with a series of flat-topped parapet walls ornamented with ball finials. In 1848 the building was altered and only a few period representations of the church's first appearance are known. Sarah worked her sampler under the tuition of Mary Ann Whidden, sampler maker Frances Whidden's sister, who obviously borrowed some of the motifs from her sister's earlier sampler. Mary Ann's teaching career was relatively short since she died at the age of twenty-four on January 12, 1839. Sarah Marden was the eldest of the eight children of James Marden and Mercy Page of Portsmouth. In 1842, she married salesman Daniel Brewster. The couple lived in Boston and had six children: three girls and three boys, including a pair of twins. The daughters all lived to adulthood, but the boys were less fortunate. James died at age two of a lung infection in 1858. Four years later, twins Charles and Franklin were born, but Charles died at the age of three months. Sarah's husband, Daniel, passed away at the end of 1864, leaving Sarah with a two-year-old boy and three daughters ranging in age from eleven to nineteen. In her old age, Sarah moved to Winthrop and lived with her married daughter Emily and her husband. She died there in December 1906 at the age of eighty-three. She is buried in the Daniel Woodlawn Cemetery in Everett, along with her husband and son Franklin.

Ann Mary Gerrish (1821-1850), Portsmouth, New Hampshire, 1832. Silk thread on linen, 17 x 15 1/2". Stitches: cross over one and two, satin. Portsmouth Historical Society.

Ann was the daughter of Samuel Gerrish Jr. and Mary Griffith Fernald of Eliot, Maine. They married in 1807, settled in Portsmouth, and had twelve children; Ann was the fifth, born in October 1821. Her childhood must have been somewhat sad, as five of her younger siblings died as young children. The family was fairly well off, since her father was a prosperous brass founder who operated his business on Bow Street and lived on High Street. Ann married Thomas H. Odion, a mast and block maker, in Portsmouth. She died at age thirty-seven in February 1850 and is buried with her parents in Union Cemetery, Portsmouth. Ann's sampler has a number of the same features as Mary Starbird's sampler, worked in 1825 at E. M. Robinson's school. The outer lozenge border is similar, although the center of Ann's is worked in cross stitch instead of satin stitch. The treatment of the large buildings at the bottom is also reminiscent of those found on the Starbird sampler. Ann did not include the name of a teacher on her sampler. Although her work certainly was influenced by that of the Robinson school, it was unlikely to have been worked under Miss Emiline's instruction, since she had married Reverend Kelly in 1830, two years before Ann completed her needlework.

Elizabeth Fabyan Willey (1821-?), Portsmouth, New Hampshire, 1834. Silk thread on linen, 19 5/8 x 17 5/8". Stitches: cross over one and two, satin, lazy daisy, French knot, Italian hem. Portsmouth Historical Society.

We know little more about Elizabeth Willey's family than the information she included on her sampler. Her father, Stephen, was born in 1797, her mother, Elizabeth Hoit, in 1800, and the couple married in November 1820. They had three children, Elizabeth, John, and Stephen, born between 1821 and 1825. On November 9, 1839, the *Portsmouth Journal* published the announcement of Elizabeth's marriage to William Innis. William was a Canadian sea captain, and he and Elizabeth apparently moved to Nova Scotia after their marriage. The couple had at least three children, two daughters and a son. The couple was recorded on the Liverpool census in 1890; no further records were found. Although Elizabeth's sampler looks quite different than that of Ann Gerrish, they do have the same large abstract trees at the bottom. Beneath those trees, Elizabeth chose to include miniature versions of the type of trees with birds that appear on Portsmouth house and barn samplers.

Lucy Maria Wiggin (1815-1889), Portsmouth, New Hampshire, 1822. Silk thread on linsey-woolsey, 14 1/2 x 17 1/2". Stitches: cross over one and two, satin. Strawbery Banke Museum.

The pattern of Lucy's sampler—known as "house and barn"—is probably the most well-known of the Portsmouth sampler designs. Between 1818 and 1840 at least fourteen samplers of this type were completed, worked on both linsey-woolsey and natural linen, with five different teachers named. All of these samplers include a house at one end, a number of trees (usually with birds) placed behind a fence line, and a small barn or carriage house at the other end. They also often include a large birdhouse that towers over the barn. Lucy Wiggin was only seven when she completed her house and barn sampler. She was the second of four children born to Joseph and Rhoda Sinclair Wiggin. Joseph was a prosperous farmer in Portsmouth who held both town office in Portsmouth as well as serving in the state legislature from 1826-1833. In 1838, Lucy married Calvin Hodgdon. Calvin was a farmer and, according to census records, the Hodgdon family lived in several towns in Rockingham County between 1850 and 1870 before finally settling in Exeter. Lucy and Calvin had three children, none of whom married. During the Civil War, their son Joseph served in Company C of the First Massachusetts Cavalry; he died at Brentwood, New Hampshire, in June 1865 at the age of twenty-four. Daughter Rhoda was felled by liver disease in 1888 at the age of forty-eight. Lucy passed away in 1889, and Calvin died the next year. Only their daughter Abbie outlived her parents, dying in 1902. Lucy, Calvin, and all three of their children are buried in the Exeter Cemetery.

Eliza Dore (1809-1864), Portsmouth, New Hampshire, 1822. Silk thread on linen, 15 x 16 3/4". Stitches: cross over one and two, satin. Collection of Dan and Marty Campanelli.

Eliza Dore was the daughter of John Dore Jr., probably a farmer, and his wife, Betsey. Very little is known about them. Both John Jr. and his father appeared on the 1810 census in Somersworth, New Hampshire. Their daughter, Eliza, was born sometime in 1809, according to the information she stitched on her sampler. However, later census records would suggest she was born as late as 1813. Eliza had a younger brother, William, who was described on the 1860 census as "idiotic," which might mean that he had a severe congenital intellectual disability. On August 29, 1829, Eliza married Ezekiel Dyer, who may have been a mariner. He died in 1832, not long after she gave birth to their son, Ezekiel. Her father died before 1840, as well, making life much harder for both Eliza and her mother. The city directory of 1834 revealed that Eliza was working as a laundress, a terribly hard job that she kept up for the next twenty or more years. In 1850, Betsey and Eliza had an eight-year-old girl, Alvira Dyer, living with them. She was born July 6, 1842. By 1860, Alvira (or sometimes Elvira) had married Thomas Entwistle, a man from England, and the couple was living with Eliza, along with Eliza's disabled brother. Thomas Entwistle would eventually become the chief of police of Portsmouth. He and Alvira would have five children; when she died in 1914, her death record stated that her parents were Eliza Dore and Ezekiel Dwyer—although she would have been conceived about a decade after his death. Betsey Dore died before the 1860 census and Eliza, at age fifty-five, on March 17, 1864. She is buried in Old North Cemetery in Portsmouth.

Adaline M. Ferguson (1809-1884), Portsmouth, New Hampshire, 1822. Silk thread on linsey-woolsey, 15 5/8 x 17 1/4". Stitches: cross over one and two, eyelet, satin, long arm cross, lazy daisy. Collection of Dr. Jeffrey and Sharon Lipton.

Adaline was the eldest of five daughters of James Ferguson, a joiner, and Rebecca Parrot Richards, who married on April 28, 1805. Adaline married carpenter Reuben L. Hobart of Boston and lived there the rest of her life. In 1884, Adaline committed suicide at the age of seventy-five, "while insane." Her husband passed away less than two months later. Adaline's sampler is worked on green linsey-woolsey and includes a brick house and barn at the bottom, flanked by two large fruit baskets. Above the house scene is a pair of cherubs holding a banner. As she noted on her sampler, Adaline completed her needlework at E. Walden's School. Her teacher was probably Elvira Walden, whose sister Mary also taught needlework. They were the daughters of William and Mary Walden of Portsmouth. Elvira's school must have been fairly short-lived, because she married Oliver Potter in 1823 (and probably stopped teaching), the year after Adaline completed her sampler. Oliver was a tavern keeper for at least a time. In the 1827 Portsmouth city directory, he was listed as the keeper of the Bell Tavern on Congress Street. However, Oliver must have fallen on hard times because by 1850 his occupation was recorded as "sailor" on the census. A decade later, Oliver was working as a porter and the couple and their five children were living near the Rockingham House on State Street; both Elvira and her daughter Frances are listed as tailoresses on the 1860 U.S. census. The family moved to the Boston area by the late 1860s. Oliver Potter died in 1870. Elvira lived another thirteen years, dying at the age of eighty-one in Hyde Park, Massachusetts.

Mary Ann Walton (unknown), Portsmouth, New Hampshire, circa 1825-1830. Silk thread on linen, 21 3/4 x 10 1/2". Stitches: cross over one and two, lazy daisy, satin, twisted chain. Collection of Mr. and Mrs. Dan Scheid.

Nothing is known about the Mary Ann Walton who worked this sampler. She did not include the date she completed her work, and she appears to have picked out her birth date at a later time. The right-hand swag at the center of the sampler has damaged threads and the wavy decorative band worked in pink does not seem to match the quality of the stitchery in the rest of the sampler; it may have been added in an attempt to cover up the damaged threads. Mary Ann's sampler is also somewhat unusual in its format. Most Portsmouth house and barn samplers are almost square while Mary Ann's is rectangular. The border she chose is also not typical of Portsmouth samplers. Although Mary Ann did not include the name of her teacher, her sampler does share several common elements with those of both Mary Ann Marden, worked at the school of M.A.F. Hall, and that of Adaline Ferguson, completed under the instruction of Elvira Walden. All three have similar flower baskets with distinctive curled handles, as well as paired flying cherubs. On the Walton and Marden samplers, the cherubs support the tasseled ends of a double swag. The houses on the latter two samplers are also similar, both of which are two-story and set at an oblique angle.

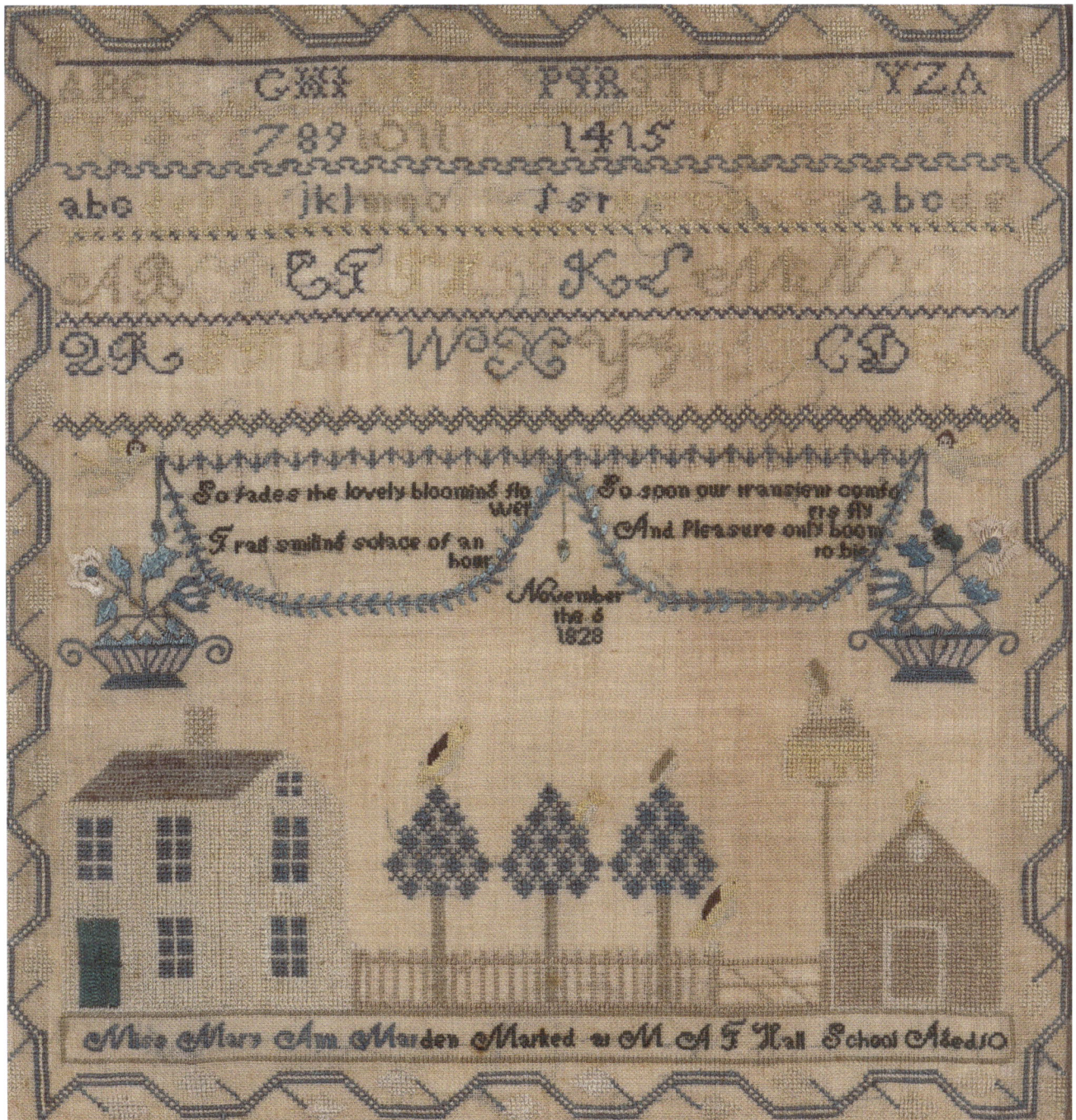

Mary Ann Marden (1818- ?), Portsmouth, New Hampshire, 1828. Silk thread on linen, 16 1/2 x 16 1/2". Stitches: cross over one and two, lazy daisy, satin, chain. Portsmouth Historical Society; gift of the Sawtelle Family.

Although Mary Ann Marden's sampler shares a number of common features with that of Mary Ann Walton, the two do differ in several respects. The border on the Marden sampler is much more like that found on a number of other similar Portsmouth samplers, including those of Mary Ann Davis, Eliza Dore, and Adaline Ferguson. In addition, the square format of Marden's is much more typical of Portsmouth house and barn samplers than the rectangular arrangement of Walton's. It is clear that Portsmouth teachers were aware of each other's work, and freely borrowed and adapted from each other the elements that they liked the best, incorporating them into their own student's final projects. Unfortunately, we know nothing about the Mary Ann Marden who completed this needlework. So far, no birth, marriage, or death records have come to light, but she may have been the daughter of Jonathan and Sarah Marden of Portsmouth. Jonathan was a joiner who lived on Ladd Street. Mary Ann named her teacher on her sampler, M.A.F. Hall, but so far her identity also remains unknown.

Mary Ann Davis (1816- ?), Portsmouth, New Hampshire, 1828. Silk thread on linen, 16 1/4 x 16 3/4". Stitches: cross over one and two, eyelet, basketweave. Newington Historical Society.

The Mary Ann Davis who worked this sampler may have been the daughter of an E. or A. Davis who operated a shop selling West Indies goods on Congress Street in Portsmouth in the 1820s. She might also have been the daughter of a John S. Davis who was a shipmaster, and who appeared in the Portsmouth city directories from 1821 through 1834. No birth, marriage, or death records have been found so far. Mary Ann included a rather unusual house on her sampler; unlike most of those found on Portsmouth samplers, it has two front doors instead of one. Although she did sign her name at the bottom, Mary Ann did not finish her sampler. The windows and doors of the house are unworked and the large fruit baskets unfilled.

Mary Ellen Cleaves (1821-1863), Portsmouth, New Hampshire, 1832. Silk thread on linen, 15 3/4 x 17 1/2". Stitches: cross, satin, eyelet. Moffatt-Ladd House and Garden.

Mary Ellen Cleaves was born in Portsmouth on November 3, 1821, a year after her parents, Samuel Cleaves and Abigail Wingate Paul, had married. Samuel was a soap and tallow chandler and a prominent man in town, serving as a director of the Portsmouth Whaling Company and deacon of the Middle Street Baptist Church. In 1839, Mary Ellen became the second wife of Horton Dudley Walker. Horton was also a tallow chandler and he became Samuel Cleaves's partner in the candle and soap manufacturing business. Mary Ellen and Horton had two children: Susan, born in 1840, and Henry Cleaves, born the following year. Mary Ellen died at the age of forty-two of a "bilious fever." Two years after Mary Ellen passed away, both of her children married, as did Horton Walker—for a third time. By 1867, Henry had joined his father in the soap business. Henry and his wife, Martha, also had two children, both of whom were named for their paternal grandparents. Sadly, Henry also died young, passing away in 1876 at the age of thirty-four, two years after his daughter was born.

This needlework of mine was taught
not to spend my time for naught

A cross the state of New Hampshire—from the seacoast to tiny isolated towns on the southern edge of the White Mountains—small female academies run by talented teachers became sources for elegant and complex needlework. Although Portsmouth and Canterbury have long been well recognized as rich sources of iconic samplers, numerous other smaller bodies of work were discovered in preparation for this exhibition. It remains unclear what exact combination of talent, perseverance, value for education, and economic climate fueled the refinement and delicacy that distinguish the needlework of rural New Hampshire.

Betsy Wallingford (1789-1879), Somersworth, New Hampshire, 1801. Silk threads on linen, 16 1/8 x 12". Stitches: cross, eyelet, stem, satin, French knot. Strawbery Banke Museum.

Betsy was born October 9, 1789, the second child of Amos and Phebe Brewster Wallingford of Somersworth, New Hampshire. Sampler maker Mary Wallingford was her older sister. In October 1815, Betsy married Nathaniel Green Pike, the son of sampler maker Martha Trevett, and grandson of the Reverend James Pike, the first pastor of Somersworth. Nathaniel and Betsy lived in his grandfather's house on Old Dover Road in Somersworth (now Rollinsford), where they raised their four children: Martha, John Gilman, Amos, and Phebe. Nathaniel Pike was a farmer who prospered enough to send at least one child to Berwick Academy; their son Amos appeared on the 1839 roster of students there. By 1850, Betsy and Nathaniel's children had all grown and started their own families except for daughter Martha, who never married. Betsy's sister Polley was also living with them by this time. Nathaniel passed away in 1858, and after that date Betsy, Martha, and Polley all moved into the home of Betsy's son Amos and his family. Betsy died in 1879 at the age of ninety.

Mary E. Wallingford (1786-1881), Somersworth, New Hampshire, circa 1800. Silk thread on linen, 15 7/8 x 10 3/4". Stitches: cross, satin, eyelet, straight. Strawbery Banke Museum.

Mary was the first child of Amos Wallingford and Phebe Brewster, born September 20, 1786. Phebe was from Berwick, Maine, but Amos was born in Somersworth, and that is where the couple settled after marrying in 1785. Mary, known as Polley for most of her life, never married and probably lived at home with her parents until they passed away. According to U.S. census records, in 1850 Polley was living with her sister Betsy and her husband, Nathaniel Pike, in Rollinsford, New Hampshire. After Nathaniel's death in 1858, Polley moved with her sister Betsy and niece Martha into the home of Betsy's son Amos. Although Amos farmed for a time, by 1880 he was working as a school teacher, as was his daughter Lillian, while his son Robert was a law student. Both Martha and Polley remained in Amos's household until their deaths. Polley lived a long life, dying in 1881 at the age of ninety-four. She is buried in Old Town Cemetery, Rollinsford, along with many members of the Pike family.

Mehitable Frost (1799-1879), probably Durham, New Hampshire, circa 1810. Silk thread on linen, 17 7/8 x 15 1/2". Stitches: cross, eyelet, satin, lazy daisy, chain, straight. Private collection.

George Frost of Durham and Margaret Burleigh of Newmarket married in April 1797. George was a merchant, farmer, and magistrate, as well as serving as a representative from Durham to the General Court in 1807. Mehitable was their eldest child, born in 1799. She had two younger siblings, a brother named George who arrived in early 1801, and her sister, Elizabeth, who was born in May 1805. Their parents obviously took female education seriously, because both daughters appear on the list of students at the Female Seminary at Saugus, Massachusetts, originally founded in Byfield in 1806 with the Reverend Joseph Emerson serving as principal. Mary Lyon, founder of Mount Holyoke, was among the early students. The seminary placed its educational emphasis on academic subjects rather than the ornamental branches. Worked ten years before she attended the academy (at the relatively advanced age of twenty,) Mehitable's sampler was probably produced under the tutelage of a needlework teacher in the Durham or greater Portsmouth area. In April 1823, Mehitable married John Prentiss Mellen. John was a merchant and the family moved several times while raising their children, living in Durham, Saco, Maine, Dover, and Durham again. Their first child, Margaret Ann, was born April 12, 1824, but died in July of the next year. Eight more children followed over the next seventeen years, six boys and two girls. Sadly, Mehitable outlived quite a number of her children. Four died before the age of eighteen: Margaret (fifteen months) in 1825, Elizabeth (twelve) in October 1847, Frank (sixteen) in October 1853, and Caroline (seventeen) in October 1859. Mehitable passed away in 1879 at the age of eighty, two years after her husband, John, had died.

Lucinda Burley (1812-1878), Ossipee, New Hampshire, 1882. Silk thread on linen, 15 1/8 x 14 7/8". Stitches: cross, straight, satin, stem. New Hampshire Farm Museum.

Lucinda Burleigh (spelled "Burley" on her sampler), was born in Ossipee, New Hampshire, on February 29, 1812. She was the first of Nathaniel and Betsy Hodsdon Burleigh's four children; she was followed by two brothers, and a sister who died at age two. Lucinda married John Young, a farmer, and they lived in Ossipee. The couple had two daughters, Eliza, born in 1827, and Mary, born in 1843. Unfortunately, neither of her children had long lives. Eliza died in 1843 at the age of six—the same year that Mary was born. The 1850 U.S. census records, in addition to John, Lucinda, and daughter Mary, list a young man by the name of Joseph Burleigh living in their household. He was probably a member of Lucinda's father's family, and may well be the same Joseph Burleigh that daughter Mary married in February 1865. Mary and Joseph had one son, Arthur, born in 1866. Mary died of a fever in October of that year, leaving behind the infant for her husband and parents to raise. By 1870, John and Lucinda were providing a home for not only Lucinda's mother, Betsy, now a widow, but also their son-in-law and grandson. John Young died in 1875, and Lucinda passed away three years later. After both of his wife's parents died, Joseph remarried and moved to Lynn, Massachusetts, with his new wife and his son, Arthur.

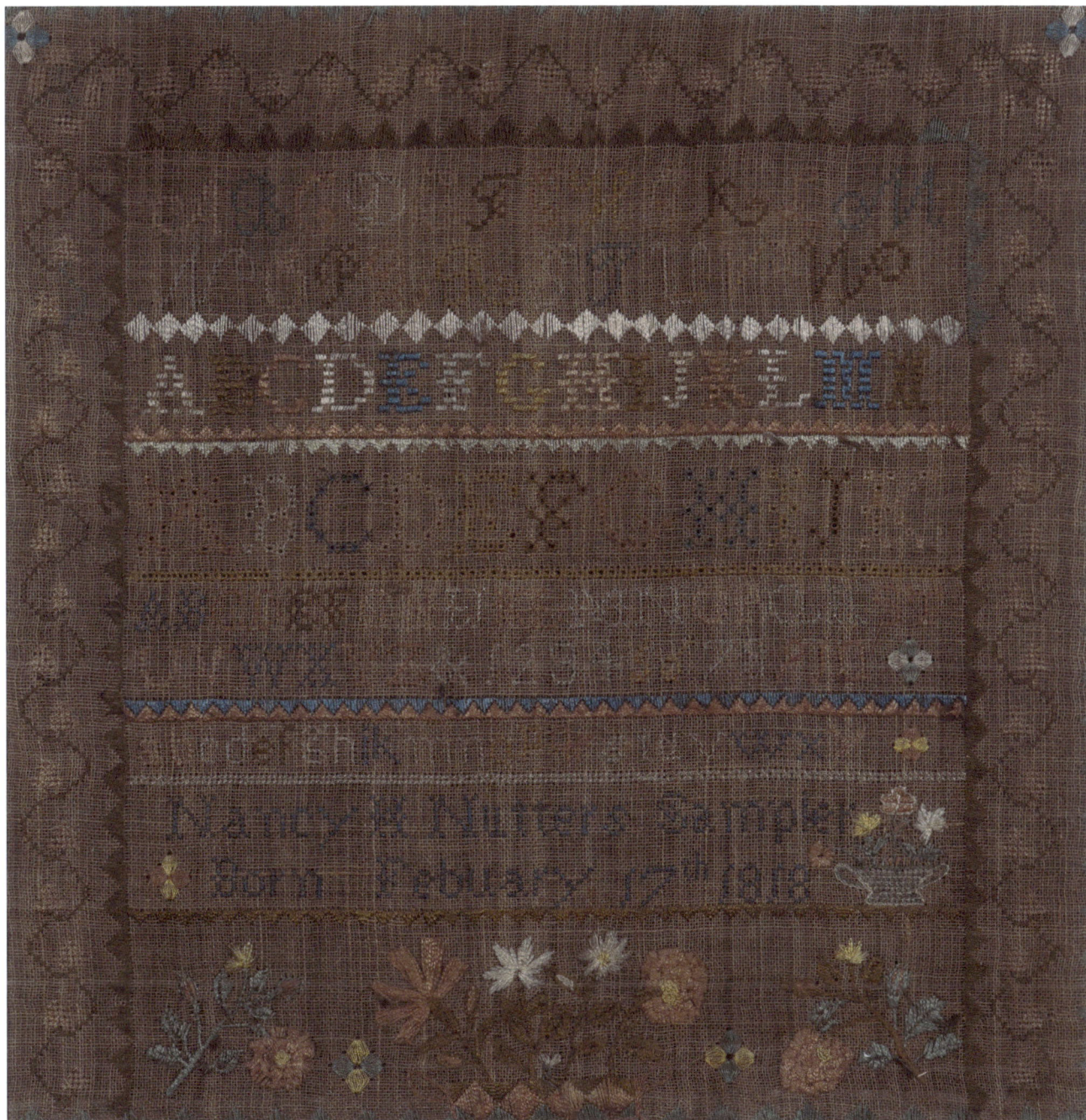

Nancy Ham Nutter (1818-1889), Milton, New Hampshire, circa 1830. Silk thread on linen, 17 x 17". Stitches: satin, cross, eyelet, overcast, bullion, chain, running, couched. Strawbery Banke Museum.

Ruth Wentworth and William Shackford Nutter of Milton, New Hampshire, had eight children. Nancy was the fourth, and sampler maker Ruth Hall Nutter was her younger sister. By 1840, the Nutter family had moved to Waterboro, Maine, with at least four of their children. Nancy probably did not go with them because she married William Augustus Kimball of Rochester, New Hampshire, on October 24, 1841. William Kimball practiced law from 1849 until 1854, when he sold his practice and took up farming, occasionally teaching school, and serving on the superintending school committee for eighteen years. Nancy and William had three children: John, Elizabeth, who died at fourteen, and Mary, who graduated from the "academical course" of Boston University in 1879. Nancy Nutter Kimball died of pneumonia in May 1889. Her husband, William, died three years later in 1892. Nancy and Ruth's samplers were passed down through the family of Nancy's daughter, Mary, who married John F. Springfield of Rochester in 1886. Their daughter, May, attended Boston University and also became a school teacher. May never married and lived in her parents' home at 82 Summer Street in Rochester; she donated the pair of samplers to Strawbery Banke Museum in 1979.

Ruth Hall Nutter (1822-1909), Milton, New Hampshire, circa 1830. Silk thread on linen, 16 1/4 x 17 1/4". Stitches: satin, cross, eyelet, satin, chain, bullion, basket fill. Strawbery Banke Museum.

Born on August 17, 1822 in Milton, New Hampshire, Ruth Hall was the sixth of eight children in the family of Ruth Wentworth and William Shackford Nutter. In the late 1830s, her parents moved to Waterboro, Maine. Unlike her sister, sampler maker Nancy Nutter, Ruth moved with her parents. In 1843, Ruth married Seth Philpot of Waterboro. Seth was a farmer and the couple had three children, William, Susan, and an infant who died in 1857, the same year that Seth passed away. By 1860, Ruth was living with her older sister Elizabeth, also a widow, and her daughter Elizabeth Jr.; Elizabeth's husband had died only three years into their marriage. Ruth remained in her sister Elizabeth's household until the late 1870s. By 1880, she moved into the Rochester, New Hampshire, home of her daughter, Susan, who had married Abraham Chadborne, a brick mason. Ruth died November 9, 1909, after living in Rochester for thirty-six years. She was buried in Waterboro along with her husband, and their infant child.

Sarah Molton, (1791-1871), Hampton Falls, New Hampshire, 1801. Silk thread on linen, 15 1/2 x 12 1/2". Stitches: hem, cross, bullion, herringbone, satin, half cross, Smyrna cross. Henry T. Callan Antiques.

The Moulton (also spelled "Molton") family of Hampton Falls, New Hampshire, lived in one of the original homesteads of the town in a farmhouse that dated to the eighteenth century. In front of their house stood an enormous elm tree that was, for many years, called "the Moulton Elm." Thomas Moulton married Ellesbeth Brown on December 16, 1789. They were the parents of Sarah, Nathan, Benjamin, Joseph, and Nancy Moulton, who probably died young. No other record was found for her besides her mention on this sampler. Benjamin drowned in the Hampton River in 1820. Ann and Sarah never married. Sarah, Nathan, and Joseph were all founding members of the town's First Christian Baptist Church in 1833. After Thomas's death in 1841, Joseph took over the family homestead, but Sarah remained at home, as was very typical for unwed women of the time. She lived with Joseph, his wife, and children until her death on April 26, 1871. She is buried in Westview Cemetery in Hampton Falls along with Joseph, his wife, and some of their children. There are a few interesting elements to this sampler. The genealogical information runs from line to line with little concern for spacing. Is Nancy's birthdate worked in black thread because she died shortly thereafter? The artfully rendered scattering of farm animals adds a substantial level of charm. Finally, does the date 1801 rather oddly placed in the lower left hand corner, signify when the sampler was completed?

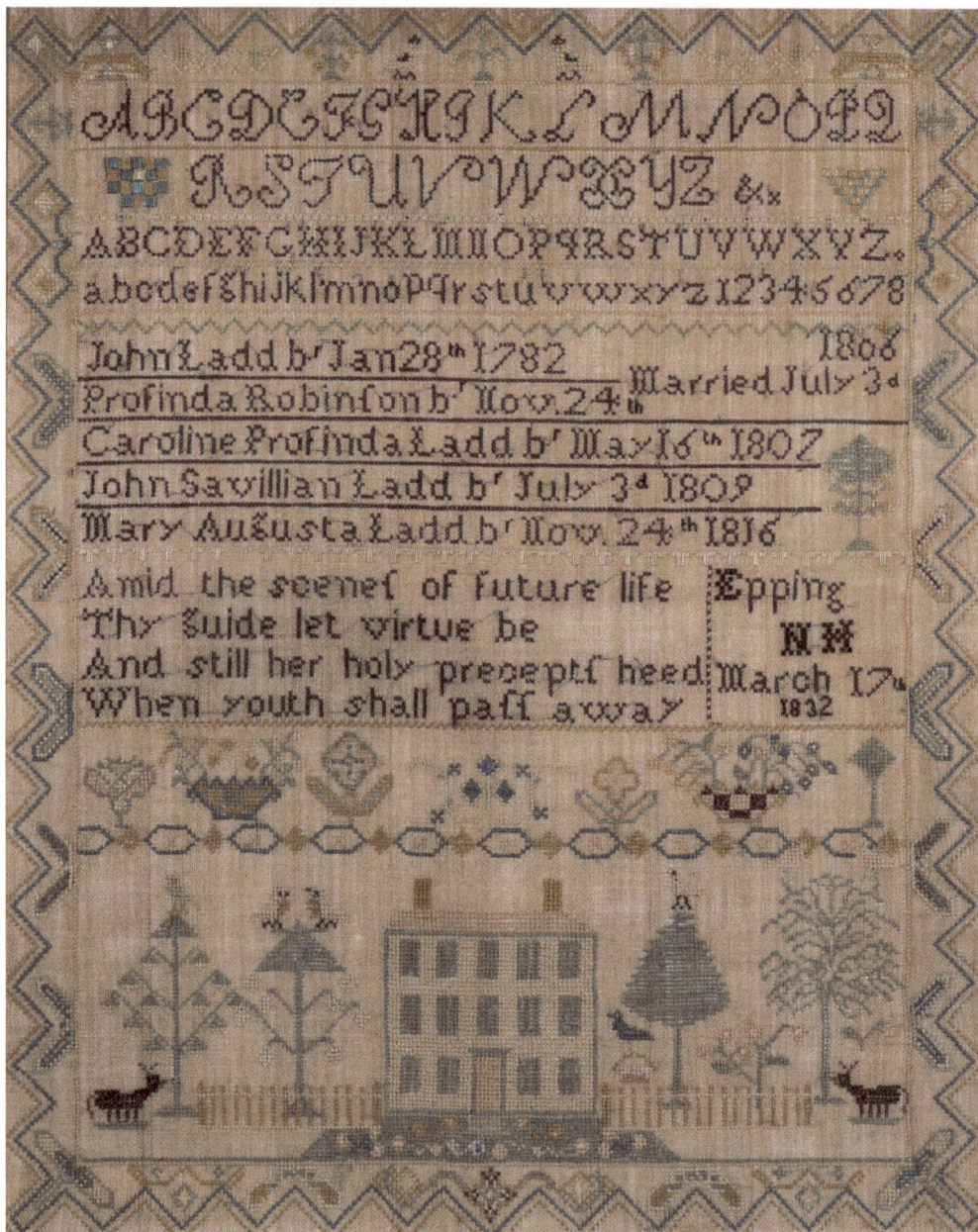

Mary Augusta Ladd (1816-1900), Epping, New Hampshire, 1832. Silk thread on linen, 20 1/4 x 17". Stitches: cross, satin, basketweave, hem, eyelet. Henry T. Callan Antiques.

Mary Augusta Ladd, who provided some details of her family's record but withheld others—such as the year of her mother's birth—stitched her charming sampler in Epping, New Hampshire, where she was born on November 24, 1816, the youngest of the three Ladd children. Her father, a doctor, served in the War of 1812. Lowell, Massachusetts, vital records reveal more of Mary's story. On May 4, 1840 in Lee, New Hampshire, she married merchant Benjamin P. Brown "of Lowell." On December 11, 1841, their ten-month-old daughter, Lucy, died in Lowell. On March 5, 1843, Benjamin died there of consumption. Their daughter, Frances Adelia, died at the age of one on August 14, 1843. Just three days later, Mary's sister, Caroline Prosinda, the wife of Benjamin Watson, died of chronic pleurisy in Lowell. A little more than a year later, Mary was wed to her widower brother-in-law, also a merchant. They named their first daughter, born in 1849, for Mary's sister. A short-lived son, Clarence, and two more daughters would be born before the family moved to Tewksbury, Massachusetts, and Benjamin took up farming. By the summer of 1900, Mary was the widowed head of a household that included her daughter, Effie, who was separated from her husband, two granddaughters, a grandson, and two boarders. Mary, eighty-four years old, listed her occupation not as the typical "keeping house" but as "farmer." The census noted that, sadly, only one of her six children still lived. On September 25, 1900, she died of a cerebral embolism in Tewksbury. Mary's work bears no resemblance to the undated Towle family register, sold by Stephen and Carol Huber, which was stitched in Epping a few years earlier

Polly Cochran Adams (1797-1836), Pembroke, New Hampshire, 1809. Silk thread on linen, 25 3/4 x 20". Stitches: cross, eyelet, satin, lazy daisy, chain, running, straight. Collection of Glee Krueger.

Polly Cochran Adams stitched her attractive sampler in memory of her father, Dr. Thomas Adams, who had died the year before, and her older brother, John, who died at the age of thirteen when she was just four years old. Her mother, Sarah Fillebron Tufts, was from Lincoln, Massachusetts, and her father from Ipswich, Massachusetts. Some of her six older siblings were probably born before the family's arrival in New Hampshire. Polly was born March 21, 1797, in Pembroke. The reason for her middle name—Cochran—is uncertain, although there were numerous Cochrans in Pembroke at the time of her birth. Polly seems very likely to be the Polly C. Adams who became the second wife of John Cleaveland Cogswell, and died childless. His parents were from Ipswich, but had relocated to Derry, New Hampshire, sometime after his birth in 1793. That Polly died June 3, 1836, and is buried with John Cogswell, his equally short-lived first and third wives, his brother, and one of his children in Boscawen, New Hampshire. The Pembroke Academy, which continues to serve as the town's high school, was not founded until 1818 so was not the source for Polly's sampler.

Polly Foster (1774-1869), Canterbury, New Hampshire, 1787. Silk thread on linen, 16 7/8 x 16 1/8". Stitches: cross over one and two, satin, hem, eyelet, stem. New Hampshire Historical Society.

Through the attention of sampler scholar Betty Ring and the 1990 exhibition at the Hood Museum in Dartmouth, New Hampshire, "Lessons Stitched in Silk," samplers stitched in Canterbury, New Hampshire, and the surrounding farming towns of Northfield, Sanbornton, and Loudon have become some of the most recognizable and admired that emerged from New Hampshire in the last quarter of the eighteenth century and well into the nineteenth century. Mary "Polly" Foster was the seventh of the nine children of Reverend Abiel Foster and his second wife, Mary Rogers, and stitched the second earliest of the known samplers in the group. In addition to his ministerial duties, Abiel served in the Continental Congress and was a United States Congressman. After he took up leadership of First Congregational Church in Canterbury, his father and four brothers also relocated to Canterbury from Andover, Massachusetts. Several of the earliest of the Canterbury samplers were stitched by their daughters. Of Abiel's female children, four including Polly completed a stint of teaching in district schools, but given the chaotic nature of many if not most of New England's early public schools, with large groups of children of all ages and just one beleaguered teacher, it is hard to imagine this level of needlework instruction going on there. Polly was born October 1, 1774. On June 7, 1796, she married Henry Gerrish Jr. of Boscawen. They were parents of two boys, four girls, and an infant that died unnamed. By 1850, Polly and Henry were living with their son Abiel in Boscawen, along with his wife and growing brood of five children. Polly died there on September 23, 1869.

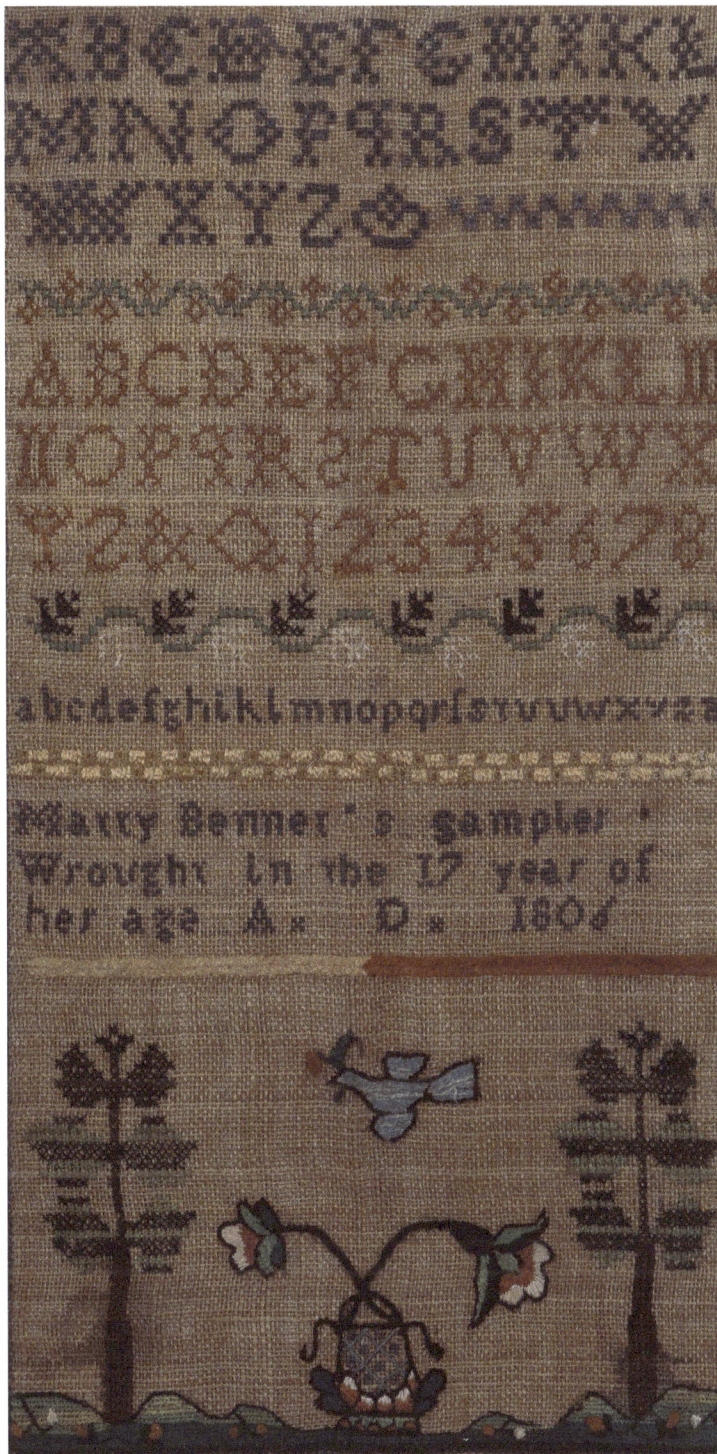

Matty (or Marry) Bennet (1789-?), possibly Canterbury, New Hampshire, 1806. Silk thread on linen, 14 x 7 7/8". Stitches: cross over one and two, satin, stem, chain. Private collection.

Because of her tight, tiny cross stitches, it is difficult to be sure of this sampler maker's name. The end letter of her last name resembles the t in her lowercase alphabet. In her first name, the double letters are also—perhaps—the letter t making her likely to be either Matilda or Martha (for Matty) Bennet. If she was a Bennet, the only likely parents for her, based on census records, would be Joseph Bennet and his wife, Elizabeth Moore. He was born in 1762, but lived first in Loudon, a town adjacent to Canterbury, and by the 1810 census, in Canterbury. The only recorded birth for this couple was that of Levi in about 1788, but vital records are quite incomplete. This sampler, although simpler than the grandest of the Canterbury works, nonetheless includes layered trees like Polly Foster's and a flying bird with a flower in its beak, like Mary Osgood stitched. No records could be found for this uncertainly named young lady.

Joanna Smith (unknown), possibly Canterbury, New Hampshire. Silk thread on linen, 9 3/4 x 7 7/8".
Stitches: cross over one and two, satin, stem, hem. Henry T. Callan Antiques.

Joanna Smith provided almost no clues to her own identity. Her sampler has much in common with those stitched in Canterbury and also in nearby Northfield from the last quarter of the eighteenth century up to the 1830s. David Smith resided in Canterbury and was enumerated on the 1800 census with a large household; perhaps she was one of his daughters. Nothing more is known about her, unfortunately.

Harriet Peverly (1813-?), Canterbury, New Hampshire, 1826. Silk thread on linen, 16 1/4 x 16 1/4". Stitches: queen, outline, satin, bullion, cross, long and short, couched. Collection of Glee Krueger.

Harriot—as she was named on her birth record—was born August 7, 1813, in Canterbury, the third daughter and youngest child of John Peverly and Betsey Sanborn. She was just thirteen when she stitched her tour-de-force Canterbury-style sampler, employing all of the vibrant motifs that are associated with this enduring group of iconic samplers. The most recognizable aspect of the Canterbury group is the use of a black outline stitch that sets up a sharp, eye-catching contrast between the decorative elements. Many of the samplers also include numerous bright birds, a strawberry cross border, oversized flowers, and a leafy basket. Some feature a pair of flame-shaped trees and others a pair of tiered pines that resemble trees from coastal New Hampshire samplers. Harriet Peverly and Mary Davis stitched virtually identical samplers. They each have a pair of objects that may be pineapples out of which are growing lovely flowers. Although Harriet was probably still living at home as a young woman—a female aged twenty to twenty-nine on the 1840 federal census may be she—that is the last known record of her existence. Her older brother, George Washington Peverly, named his first-born daughter after her.

Mary Davis (unknown), Canterbury, New Hampshire, 1826. Silk thread on linen, 16 1/2 x 15 3/4". Stitches: queen, satin, cross over one and two, bullion, outline, long and short, seed. Collection of Glee Krueger.

Mary Davis stitched her sampler in the same year as Harriet Peverly and her sampler and Harriet's are so similar, including an unusual verse that names the sampler maker, that it seems all but certain they shared the same teacher. Sampler scholars Betty Ring and Mary Jaene Edmonds concluded that the widow Hannah Wise Rodgers, who operated a female academy in Ipswich, Massachusetts, but who may have relocated to Canterbury, might have been the original designer and teacher for this group of samplers. Ruthy Foster (1779-1858), a maker of one of the group herself in 1800, may have been the primary teacher after the early years. Ruthy Foster was the ninth child of Daniel Foster and Hannah Kittredge. She never married and worked as a school teacher through most of her adult life. Although she taught more than one generation of Canterbury's children, she merited only mention of her birth in the lengthy Foster Genealogy. Ruth seems never to have had her own home; census records positively note her presence in the household of her nephew, Jonathan B. Foster, in 1850, but she is likely to be the woman recorded living with his family in 1830 and 1840, as well. If Mary Davis was from Canterbury, then it is likely that she was the child of one of three Davis heads of households noted on the 1810 census with a daughter in the correct age bracket: Stephen, Caleb, or Hezekiah. No certain records for Mary have been found.

Sophia Woodbury (1803-1877), Northfield, New Hampshire, 1818. Silk thread on linen, 16 7/8 x 16 7/8". Stitches: cross over one and two, eyelet, hem, satin, stem, chain, bullion knot, French knot, fishbone. New Hampshire Historical Society.

Sophia stitched an exuberant garden inhabited by a leopard, butterfly, birds, and enormous flowers, all in sharp, cheerful contrast to her two ominous warnings, "PrePare for Eternity," and "Time is short." Her sampler shares a series of characteristics with the unfinished Northfield sampler of Betsy C. Knowles, including the strawberry cross band, the use of alternating buttonhole stitched squares to form a zig-zag border, a pair of very similar trees at the bottom, and the use of an unusual uppercase alphabet. The strawberry cross border has sections that resemble railroad tracks, created with pairs of cross stitches separated by a space. That, as well as the same upper case alphabet, zig-zag border, and Sophia's fern-leaf cross band all also appear on the iconic Canterbury samplers of Polly Foster, 1787 (page 95), and Mary Davis, 1826 (page 99), and several others. Her sampler shows how the Canterbury motifs spread to surrounding towns, even as Canterbury-style works continued to be made in Canterbury. Sophia is said to have been born September 27, 1803, in Northfield. The identity of her parents is unknown, but it seems possible that she was the sister of two other Northfield Woodburys, Josiah and Rufus. On January 4, 1822, she became the second wife of Jonathan Clough who had been born in 1790. Jonathan inherited the Clough family farm in Northfield, described in a *History of Northfield* as "one of the most beautiful places in New Hampshire." She took over the care of his four children and gave birth to an additional five. All nine lived to adulthood, and five of them eventually settled in Illinois. The Cloughs' youngest child, Rufus George, died in the Civil War. Jonathan and Sophia spent the rest of their lives on their Northfield farm. He died in 1850 and Sophia passed away May 11, 1877.

Betsey C. Knowles (1808-1882), Northfield, New Hampshire, 1821. Silk thread on linen, 13 7/8 x 15 7/8". Stitches: cross over one and two, eyelet, satin, hem, stem. New Hampshire Historical Society.

In 1802, William Knowles traveled south to Haverhill, Massachusetts, to bring back to Northfield his intended bride, Betsey Clement. Tragically, she died on the eve of her planned wedding, within days of arriving in his New Hampshire village. In 1805, he married Zilpha Thorn, who was from Amesbury, Massachusetts. They were the parents of five children. Betsey was their second, born March 11, 1808, and named for her father's deceased bride-to-be. Betsey became the second wife of Baptist and later Methodist minister Reverend William D. Cass on August 2, 1832, two years after the death of his first wife, Laura Worthen Sanborn. She had passed away only weeks after the birth of her only child, Laura. (Laura Sanborn's simple—also unfinished—marking sampler is in the collection of the New Hampshire Historical Society as well.) Betsey became mother to her husband's surviving daughter, who passed away in 1843, but never had children of her own. After Betsey's father died in 1864, her mother, Zilpha, moved in with her and remained there for the last years of her life, outliving Reverend Cass who died in 1867. Betsey died May 3, 1882, and is buried in Tilton, New Hampshire. Although Betsey got off to a good start on her sampler, she never completed it, even though she did stitch in the year she was working on it. Typically, sampler makers would have copied from charts the alphabets and many of the other counted thread designs that were included on their samplers. However, the inked shapes that Betsey never filled in demonstrate how the more abstract elements were done, most likely drawn by the teacher and then stitched by the student.

Mary Osgood (1814-1881), Northfield or Canterbury, New Hampshire, 1830. Silk thread on linen, 20 3/4 x 16 5/8". Stitches: cross over one and two, eyelet, stem, satin, queen. Collection of Dr. Jeffrey and Sharon Lipton.

Nine years after Betsey Knowles of Northwood stitched her variation on a Canterbury-style sampler, Mary Osgood worked one that is far more Canterbury in flavor, yet she, too, was from Northfield. Mary was the only daughter and fourth among the five children of Nancy Kezar and Edward Osgood, who were both born in Northfield, but who were married in Canterbury on December 27, 1810. Edward was a stonemason. The Osgoods, according to *The History of Northfield*, were all originally from Canterbury. Perhaps that connection led Nancy and Edward to send their daughter there for additional schooling beyond what was available in district schools. Or perhaps the teacher responsible for Sophia Woodbury's and Betsey Knowles's samplers was no longer teaching in Northfield nine years later and Canterbury presented the closet educational opportunity for Mary. Mary's youngest brother achieved local renown by outliving five of his six wives, tying a record for Northfield. A year after the death of Albert Merrill's first wife, Mary married the carriage maker from Conway, New Hampshire. She became mother to his son, Laroy, and two daughters, Emmeline, who probably died young, and Augusta. Mary also had children of her own: Laticia, born in 1847, and who had died by 1860, and Otis. After Albert, who accumulated significant wealth and owned a commodious home, passed away in 1877, Mary resided with her son, Otis, and his wife. Just up the street, Laroy continued the carriage making tradition. Mary died May 11, 1881.

Lucinda Currier (1806-?), Salisbury, New Hampshire, 1819. Silk thread on linen, 16 5/8 x 17 1/8". Stitches: cross over one and two, satin, hem, stem, French knot, chain, bullion knot. Private collection.

Lucinda Currier helpfully provided not only the date of her birth, but also the name of her teacher. Lucinda was probably born in Salisbury, New Hampshire, but her parents are unknown. There were three Currier patriarchs who could have been her father, and two of those, Nathan and James, were living in Salisbury in 1820, two years after she completed her sampler, and had females of the right age in their households, but she is not named among their children on vital records. Although a Lucinda Currier had her own household in Concord in 1830 and 1840, her age makes it unlikely that this was the sampler maker. Even though Lucinda did not provide enough information to successfully identify her, she did provide the name of her teacher, "Tryphena Wheler." This may be the Tryphena Wheeler who was born March 24, 1796, in Salem, New Hampshire, the daughter of Abner Wheeler and Sarah Stickney. She married Phineas How on October 17, 1819. Since the other three Salisbury samplers are similar to each other but have less in common with Lucinda's, it is very likely that Tryphena was not the teacher for those. Tryphena gave birth to three sons and three daughters with two of those births, in 1820 and 1835, recorded on Haverhill, Massachusetts vital records. She died in Haverhill, November 15, 1854.

Abigail Pettingill (1814-1868), Salisbury, New Hampshire, 1827. Silk thread and ink on linen, 14 1/8 x 16 7/8". Stitches: cross over one and two, eyelet, satin, hem, chain, French knot. Private collection.

Abigail's attractive but unfinished needlework is one of four known samplers stitched between 1819 and 1827, probably all in Salisbury, New Hampshire. It is possible that these all were completed at the Salisbury Academy that was founded in 1795. A two-story building was completed by 1796 and the academy opened for business. By 1805, it was in financial difficulty, attributed at the time to its isolated location. The building was then moved closer to the center of town. Two extant printed programs from end-of-year performances in 1809 and 1819 list both male and female students. However, a town history names only male teachers, so it is unclear whether this academy was the source for the samplers, or, just as likely, that its female teachers were not considered as worthy of mention. Abigail was the daughter of Lieutenant Benjamin Pettingill and Hannah Greeley. They were parents to thirteen children with Abigail second from the youngest. She and three of her siblings all married members of the Smith family. Abigail became the third wife of Dr. Robert Smith who had practiced medicine in Amesbury, Massachusetts, and then relocated to New Hampshire. When Abigail married him in Franklin, New Hampshire, on February 24, 1842, he was already the father of four young children. They moved to Salisbury and Dr. Smith gave up medicine in favor of farming. Abigail gave birth to three boys and then a pair of twins, Lucy and Sarah. She died on February 22, 1868, just one day after her fifty-fourth birthday, of typhoid fever.

Rhoda Stevens (1813-1848), Salisbury, New Hampshire, 1827. Silk thread on linen, 16 1/8 x 16 1/4". Stitches: cross over one and two, satin, chain, French knot, eyelet. Private collection.

As Rhoda Stevens helpfully noted on her sampler, she completed it on July 28, 1827. Of the four known samplers in this group from Salisbury, three have connections to the Greeley family. Rhoda Stevens was the daughter of Isaac Stevens and Margaret Greeley, who were married November 19, 1789, in Salisbury. Rhoda had at least six siblings, most or all of whom were older than she. On May 21, 1835, she married farmer John Pressey who was the son of a hat maker. According to a local history, Pressey "was familiarly called" by the not especially familiar "Colonel Pressey." Rhoda gave birth to two sons, and a daughter who died at three years of age. Rhoda died on April 6, 1848. Roxanna, whom John married six months later, was even more unfortunate. She and her infant son were dead within three years of her marriage. John married for a third time and had two more children with that wife, who outlived him. Like the other two 1827 Salisbury samplers, Rhoda's features attractive cross borders, plants growing out of a satin-stitched basket, and an unusual satin-stitch variation on a "Quaker" style upper case alphabet with block letters and some elements two stitches wide, as if shaded.

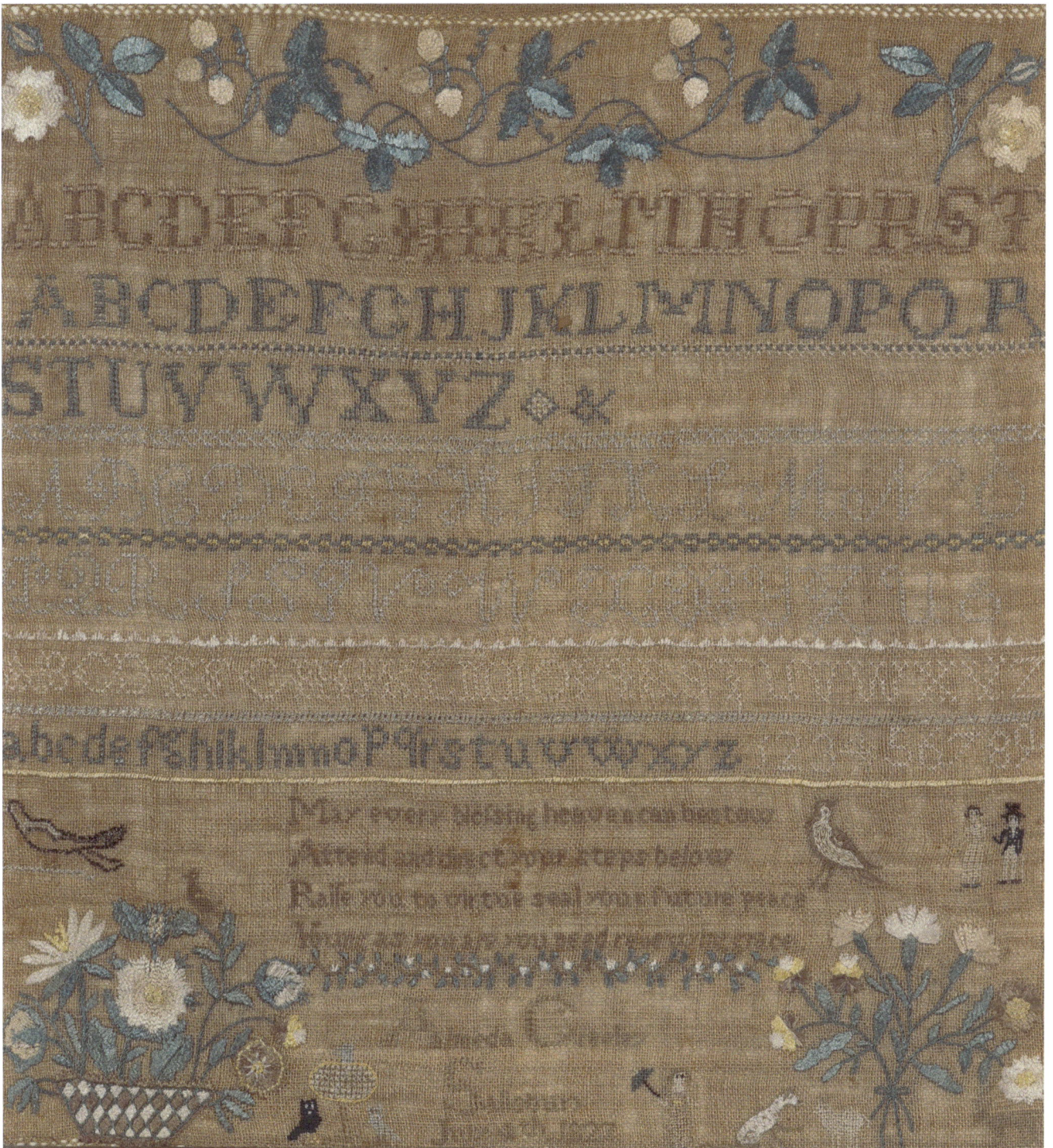

Almeda Greeley (1813-1869), Salisbury, New Hampshire, 1827. Silk thread on linen, 16 1/4 x 16 1/8". Stitches: cross over one and two, satin, chain. Private collection.

Almeda was among the eldest of the eight children of Benjamin Greeley and Rebecca Witcher. She was born March 22, 1813, the same day as fellow sampler maker Rhoda Stevens. Her family remained in Salisbury through the mid-1820s but sometime after Almeda's mother died in 1826, Benjamin relocated first to nearby Franklin, New Hampshire, but later to Illinois where he lived out the last years of his life. Perhaps Almeda did not accompany him to Illinois since on May 13, 1835, she married John Couch of New Hampshire, who in 1842, "felt himself called to preach the gospel as an Adventist." In later years, they moved to Warner and then Concord, New Hampshire. They had two daughters and a son. After Almeda died on May 9, 1869, John remarried. He and his two wives are buried under a substantial monument in Blossom Hill Cemetery in Concord, New Hampshire.

Probably Frances Mehitable Kimball (1820-1899), Salem, New Hampshire, circa 1832. Silk thread on linen, 17 1/4 x 17 1/2".
Stitches: cross, satin, stem, New England laid. Collection of Lynne Anderson.

In the early nineteenth century, samplers were often used to honor family ties and document vital statistics for posterity. Most family record samplers begin with information about the parents, followed by names and birth dates for each of their children. This family register is unusual in that no parents are listed. Eight of the thirteen children have the last name Austin and five that of Kimball. All thirteen children were born to Nancy Stevens, the daughter of Simeon and Mariah Stevens, born September 2, 1782, in Billerica, Massachusetts. The Stevens family later moved to Salem, New Hampshire. On July 27, 1800, Nancy married Abial Austin III and their first child, Cordelia, was born two months later. Recorded on the sampler, but not documented in family genealogies, is the birth of their first son, Aaron, about a year later. Aaron only lived for a day, and this sampler may be the only record of his existence. The last of six more children, Abial Austin IV, was born four months after his father's death on Christmas Day, 1815. About 1819, Nancy married Tristan Kimball, a farmer; they had five children. The most likely person to have been the sampler maker is Frances Mehitable Kimball. Although dates were later added in red thread, the sampler was probably originally completed about 1832, as the last date in brown thread is August 23, 1831, when Frances was about twelve. Frances was the only adult child living with her parents in 1850 and on the 1860 census she and her Irish-born husband, Michael Haley, a day laborer, and their five children, including a set of twins, lived in a second very modest house on the same property. After Michael's death in 1863 and Tristan's death in 1864, Nancy and her daughter shared a home in Salem with Frances's four remaining children. After her mother's death in 1873, Frances moved to Lawrence, Massachusetts, where three of her surviving children lived.

Hannah Newhall (1797-1878), Lynn, Massachusetts, 1814. Silk thread on linen, 20 3/4 x 17 1/4". Stitches: cross, back, satin, chain, hem, French knot, split. Lynn Museum and Historical Society, Lynn, Massachusetts.

During the first and second decades of the nineteenth century, girls from Lynn, Massachusetts, stitched family register samplers that share a number of characteristics, including delicate borders primarily worked in satin stitch, a sawtooth edge around their family information, a title, "Family Register," and generally, a pair of beautifully rendered satin stitch cornucopias. No advertisements for Lynn teachers have come to light. It is possible that the source of the samplers was the Lynn Academy that opened in 1805, but no female teachers are known to have been connected with that school. As Hannah noted on her sampler, she was born April 8, 1797, to Micajah and Joanna Newhall, the tenth of their thirteen closely spaced children. Two, Ellis and William, passed away on June 10, although a decade apart. Micajah was a soldier in the Revolutionary War, serving at Concord as a private with a company from Lynn. He continued to serve with other regiments in 1778 and 1780, moving up to the rank of corporal. Although unrecorded on Hannah's sampler, a year after his wife's death in 1826, Micajah remarried, to Hannah Coombs, but died not long afterward. Hannah Newhall never married. She lived at least part of her life alone, appearing as head of household in the 1850 and 1855 censuses. By 1860, at age sixty-three, she was living with the widowed daughter of her brother Paul, and her niece's two children. Later censuses show her living with Paul. Only a few of Hannah's many siblings achieved old age. Five of them died between 1821 and 1830—two in 1823. Hannah died August 12, 1878, aged eighty-one, the last of her family to pass away. She is buried in Pine Grove Cemetery in Lynn.

Betsy Attwill (1804-1882), Lynn, Massachusetts, 1814. Silk thread on linen, 16 1/2 x 16 1/2".
Stitches: cross over one and two, satin, straight, split, lazy daisy, Italian hem. Lynn Museum and
Historical Society, Lynn, Massachusetts.

Betsy Atwill was born February 4, 1804, in Lynn to John Daget Atwill and Martha Ingalls, the fifth of their thirteen children, some separated by only a little more than a year. Betsey's sampler provides a vivid illustration of the difficulties faced by eighteenth-century women, many of whom failed to survive their arduous childbearing years, as Martha did not. After the early death of her youngest son in 1816 and without the modest birth control that breastfeeding provided, only a few months went by before she conceived twins, one born on the second and one on the third of July. That may imply a long, hard labor—or it may just mean that they were born shortly before and after midnight. Martha died that day, a not uncommon outcome of a difficult delivery. Remarkably, both twins survived. Daughters Patty, Mary, and Betsy were all teenagers by the time of their mother's death; surely their tender ministrations must have helped save their new brothers' lives. Betsy married Benjamin Ward in Lynn on October 1, 1822. According to the 1850 census, Benjamin was a "cordwainer," or shoemaker. They were the parents of seven, three sons and four daughters, outliving all but one son. Benjamin died in 1879 at the age of eighty and is buried in Pine Grove Cemetery in Lynn alongside Betsy who died March 19, 1882, at age seventy-eight. Betsy's sampler is nearly identical to those made in Lynn of Content Hood (1810), Lydia Mudge (1813), and Hannah Newhall (1814). In 1817, this sampler style reappeared, unaltered, at the Pinkerton Academy in Londonderry, New Hampshire. Did either Sarah Fitz, daughter of innkeeper Samuel Currier Fitz and Sarah George, or Mary Knight—the first two preceptresses of Pinkerton—admire and copy a Lynn sampler, or did one of them either attend a female academy in Lynn, or teach there? Since Mary appeared on an 1816 list of Pinkerton Academy students, it seems unlikely that she had also attended a Lynn academy. A third possibility is that the sampler style was brought to Londonderry by one of the daughters of the Pinkerton family of whom two brothers, wealthy local merchants, were major benefactors of the school. So far, the answer has failed to come to light.

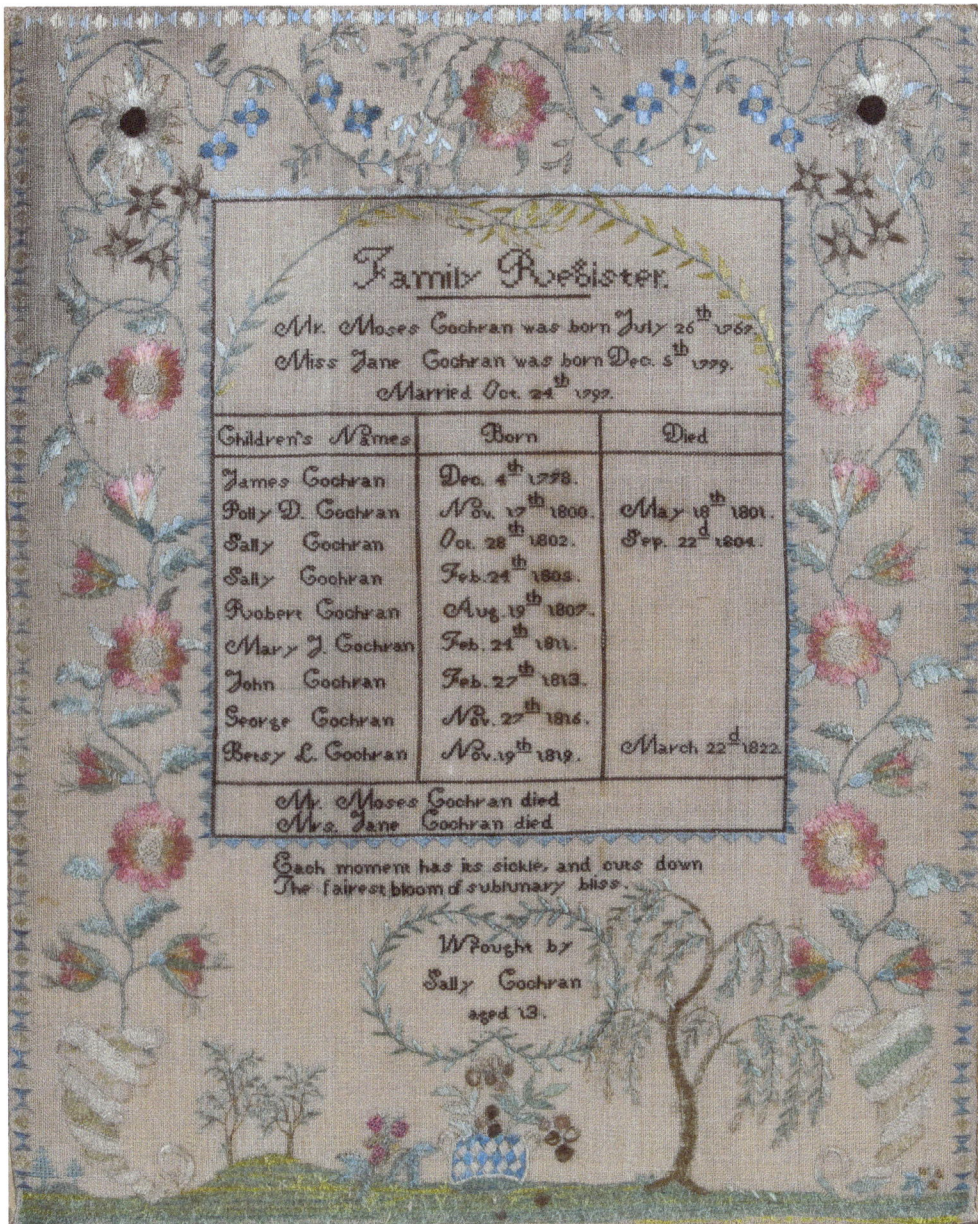

Sally Cochran (1805-1833), Londonderry, New Hampshire, 1818. Silk thread on linen, 23 x 18".
Stitches: cross over one and two, satin, straight. Saco Museum.

The sampler text reads:

Family Register.

Mr. Moses Cochran was born July 26th 1769.
Miss Jane Cochran was born Dec. 5th 1779.
Married Oct. 24th 1797.

Children's Names	Born	Died
James Cochran	Dec. 4th 1798.	
Polly D. Cochran	Nov. 17th 1800.	May 18th 1801.
Sally Cochran	Oct. 28th 1802.	Sep. 22d 1804.
Sally Cochran	Feb. 24th 1805.	
Robert Cochran	Aug. 19th 1807.	
Mary J. Cochran	Feb. 21 1811.	
John Cochran	Feb. 27th 1813.	
George Cochran	Nov. 27th 1816.	
Betsy L. Cochran	Nov. 19th 1818.	March 22d 1822.

Mr. Moses Cochran died
Mrs. Jane Cochran died

Each moment has its sickle, and cuts down
The fairest bloom of sublunary bliss.

Wrought by
Sally Cochran
aged 13.

Sally's lovely sampler is one of a group stitched at the Pinkerton Academy in Londonderry, New Hampshire, and the Adams Female Academy that continued the education of young women, and the iconic sampler style, after Pinkerton stopped accepting females in about 1821. Many of the group, which date from 1818 to about 1828, have elements that strongly link them to samplers made in Lynn, Massachusetts, a few years earlier, some of which are in the collection of the Lynn Historical Society. Mary Knight was the preceptress in the year Sally made her sampler. Some of the stories that accompany the samplers in this exhibit are sad—girls that died young, or women who lost most of their children to early deaths, or suffered early widowhood and poverty afterward—but Sally's is almost certainly one of the most unfortunate. Sally was the daughter of cousins Moses and Jenny Cochran. After growing up in Londonderry, she moved with her parents to Pembroke, New Hampshire, sometime between 1818-1820. There she wed her first cousin, Chauncey Cochran, on November 26, 1828. She moved into the Pembroke farmhouse of his widowed mother, where Chauncey ran the family farm. They hired a teen-aged boy, Abraham Prescott, to help out with farm chores. On June 23, 1833, Sally, by then the mother of two toddlers, went out to pick strawberries in the field behind the house with eighteen-year-old Abraham. For some unknown reason—perhaps in a fit of passion—he murdered her there. He was eventually executed for his brutal crime. Chauncey relocated to Corinth, Maine, and later remarried and raised a large family, one of whom eventually settled in Saco, bringing Sally's sampler with him. Sally's two children both died in young adulthood.

Celenda Richardson (1809-1848), born in Litchfield, sampler worked in Londonderry, New Hamp-
shire, 1819. Silk thread on linen, 19 x 16 3/4". Stitches: cross over one and two, satin, feather,
lazy daisy, stem. Collection of Dr. Steven P. Calawa.

Celenda was just ten years old when she stitched her delicately designed and expertly rendered family register, on which she carefully noted the birthdates of her family members and the deaths of her two young sisters. Their names also appear on the tombstone. Like other samplers from Pinkerton Academy and then Adams Female Academy, it includes a satin stitched floral border, containers that are worked in checkerboard satin stitch patterns, and sprigs at the top corners. The Richardsons and Reeds were among the first settlers of Litchfield, New Hampshire. On December 28, 1823, Josiah was one of seven signers of a petition to the town of Litchfield's selectmen requesting that the limits of the current three school districts be better defined, but it is unclear whether these men were trying to increase support for education, or limit their tax bills. The Richardson land bordered the town of Londonderry, making it unnecessary for Josiah's daughter to board in town to attend Pinkerton Academy (which advertised that "board may be had with respectable families"). Since Celenda stitched her sampler in either 1819 or 1820, she must have added the births of her two youngest siblings (and the death of one) after the sampler had been completed. Around 1835, Celenda married Captain Simeon Harvell of Litchfield. She likely gave birth to two sons before her death on October 11, 1848, as they appear, unnamed, on the 1840 census. Her last illness must have been trying; her epitaph reads in part, "Her days and nights of distress/ And weeks of afflictions are over." Only their son, Gershom, born in 1837 and named for Simeon's father, survived. By 1850, Simeon was living with his sister, Phebe, and Gershom, but he died later that year. In 1860, Gershom was managing the family farm. He later married and lived on until about 1920. He named his first-born daughter after his mother.

Margaret Gregg (1811-1831), Londonderry, New Hampshire, 1825. Silk thread on linen, 17 3/8 x 16 3/8". Stitches: cross over one and two, satin, stem, French knot. Museum of Fine Arts, Boston. Gift of Mr. and Mrs. Berger in memory of Susan Jeannette Westfall. Photograph © 2015 Museum of Fine Arts, Boston.

When Margaret stitched her parents' names at the bottom of her sampler, carefully leaving room for their death dates, did she have some foreboding of the tragedies yet to come? Of the entire group of samplers attributed to Pinkerton Academy and Adams Female Academy only two are currently known to have this format: Margaret's and that of Sally Cochrane. Margaret's father, Ebenezer Gregg, was probably descended from one of the two original Gregg settlers of Nutfield, the name of the enormous town that originally included present day Windham, Hudson, Salem, Derry, and Manchester, New Hampshire. He was probably the son of James and Margaret Gregg. Sarah, Mehitable, Elizabeth, and John Gregg all married and had families. Mary Ann died in 1827 at the age of twenty-three, Margaret on November 22, 1831, at age twenty, and Hannah Jane in 1832 at age twenty-three. Margaret's father passed away in 1836 and her mother only seven months later. Clusters of family deaths in that period were often associated with the ravages of tuberculosis—"consumption." Nearly all of the family is buried in East Derry's Forest Hill Cemetery.

Julia Ann and/or Elizabeth Bixby (1814-1842) (1814-1845), both born in Litchfield, New Hampshire, worked in Londonderry, New Hampshire, circa 1828. Silk thread and paper on linen, 21 x 16 1/2". Stitches: cross over one, satin, lazy daisy, French knot, stem, Italian hem. Collection of Dr. Steven P. Calawa.

The family register that Litchfield twins Julia Ann and Elizabeth are named on could have been stitched by one or both of them. While it contains a great deal of genealogical information, other important details are not mentioned at all. Elizabeth Nahor was the second wife of Captain William Bixby. His first wife, Sarah Thompson, died on June 4, 1811. Sarah's daughter, Polly, aged about sixteen, died the following summer. Elizabeth Chase Nahor, too, had been previously married. She was born in Litchfield, New Hampshire, and married Hugh Nahor on December 18, 1802. They became parents to three daughters and two sons before Hugh's death on March 25, 1812. When Elizabeth and William married, she must surely have been already expecting the twins. Even if the twins were born early, only four months passed between the Bixby marriage and the birth. Lucretia, whose death is noted on the monument at the bottom of the sampler, was born in 1816. Julia Ann died unmarried on March 25, 1842, and her twin, Elizabeth, also unmarried, on January 20, 1845. Nahors and Bixbys are buried side by side in the family plot of Pinecrest Cemetery of Litchfield. This sampler was stitched several years after Pinkerton Academy stopped accepting females and was most likely completed at the Adams Female Academy. It is the only known sampler from the academy that includes a paper section.

Mary Ann "Maria" Reynolds (1818-1903), Derry, New Hampshire, 1830. Silk thread on linen, 16 1/4 x 8 5/8". Stitches: cross, long-arm cross, eyelet. Henry T. Callan Antiques.

Mary Ann "Maria" Reynolds was born in Derry, New Hampshire, on July 2, 1818. She was one of the eight children of Colonel Stephen Reynolds and his wife, Sally Ela, with one older sister, Eliza, and three younger ones, Sarah, Lucy, and Ellen. Mary Ann's sampler includes enormous cross stitch flowers and a unusual bird in flight. Her name appears on a list of students who attended Adams Female Academy in Derry in 1832, although her sampler bears no resemblance to ones stitched there previously and based on its date, was likely completed before she attended the school. According to a history of the Ela family, Mary Ann married Robert Taylor on December 12, 1842. They moved to Boston, where Robert became a police officer and later a captain of the police. They were parents to three sons. Unfortunately, Robert may have had a problem with alcoholism since he died in December of 1866 of cirrhosis. Around 1877, sons Frank and George moved to New York City where they worked as clerks. Frank died shortly after he was enumerated on the 1880 census. Mary Ann is recorded in city directories there beginning in 1879, living at 13 East 130th Street. She remained at that address for the rest of her long life, passing away in 1903. She is buried with Robert, George, and Frank in Forest Hill Cemetery in East Derry, New Hampshire.

Frances E. Litchfield (1823-1845), Merrimack, New Hampshire, 1833. Silk thread on linen, 16 1/8 x 17 1/8". Stitches: cross over one and two, satin, overcast, hem, stem. Strawbery Banke Museum.

Although Frances worked her sampler in Merrimack, New Hampshire, she was born in Kittery, Maine, where the Litchfield family originally lived. Her father, Joseph, was the son of the Reverend Joseph, a prominent local minister, and Hannah Litchfield of Kittery. Joseph Litchfield Jr. married Elizabeth B. Dame in April 1819 and the couple apparently remained in Kittery until the mid-1820s. Reverend Joseph died in early 1823, the same year that Frances was born. By 1830, Joseph Jr. had relocated to Merrimack, New Hampshire, with his wife, daughter, and mother. Frances's father died in 1839, leaving his wife to run the family farm. The 1840 census lists Elizabeth Litchfield as the head of household living with one teen-aged male engaged in agriculture, her daughter, and mother-in-law. In 1843, Elizabeth's mother-in-law, Hannah, died. Frances passed away just two years later at the young age of twenty-two. Elizabeth may have returned to Kittery after her family members in Merrimack passed away. No further records of Elizabeth were found in Merrimack, but an Elizabeth Litchfield (age sixty-six) was listed on the 1860 census in Kittery. Frances, Joseph, and Hannah Litchfield are all buried in the Reed Graveyard in Merrimack, New Hampshire.

Elizabeth Jewett (1829-1912), Hollis, New Hampshire, 1841. Silk thread on linen, 21 3/4 x 21 1/2". Stitches: hem, satin, cross over one and two, chain, outline, eyelet, half-cross. Henry T. Callan Antiques.

By the time Elizabeth Jewett worked her very attractive, well-balanced, and refined sampler in 1841, the art of sampler making was dying out. Many of the female academies had closed. College was now an option for young women who could afford to attend. Elizabeth Frances Jewett was born August 25, 1829. She was the daughter of Captain Nathaniel Jewett and his third wife, Mrs. Mary Davis Hall, who had been born two months before the date of Nathaniel's first marriage. Elizabeth had two younger sisters. On her birthday in 1852, she married Levi W. Barton, about ten years her senior, who was a lawyer and would become a probate judge. They settled in Newport, New Hampshire, where she gave birth to six sons and a daughter. Three of her sons died as very young children, including Ralph and L. Marr, toddlers who died just days apart in 1863. Levi died in 1899. Elizabeth lived on until May 19, 1912, in her large Park Street home facing onto the town green in Newport with her surviving offspring, Florence, who never married, and Jesse, also a lawyer and judge, who married later in life.

Eliza Kelso (1820-1899), New Boston, New Hampshire, 1831. Silk thread on linen, 15 7/8 x 15 1/4". Stitches: cross, satin, straight. New Boston Historical Society, New Boston, New Hampshire, gift of Jane and Phil Workman.

Eliza Kelso was born in 1820 to William Kelso, a farmer from New Boston, and Susannah Coggin of Mont Vernon. Eliza was the eldest of their four children, three daughters and one son. She married Levi Dodge, a tailor, also originally from New Boston, the son of a farmer turned tailor. When they were first married they lived in Francestown, but by 1860 had moved to Manchester, where they lived on Granite Street on the city's west side. Eliza and Levi had three children, Eliza, Levi, and Arthur. Levi became a veterinary surgeon and Arthur worked as a machinist. Neither son ever married. Daughter Eliza married Charles McKean, a cabinetmaker from Manchester. Eliza Kelso Dodge died October 29, 1899. She is buried in Piscataquay Cemetery in Manchester, along with her husband, Levi, who died in 1917 at the age of almost ninety-seven, and both of her sons.

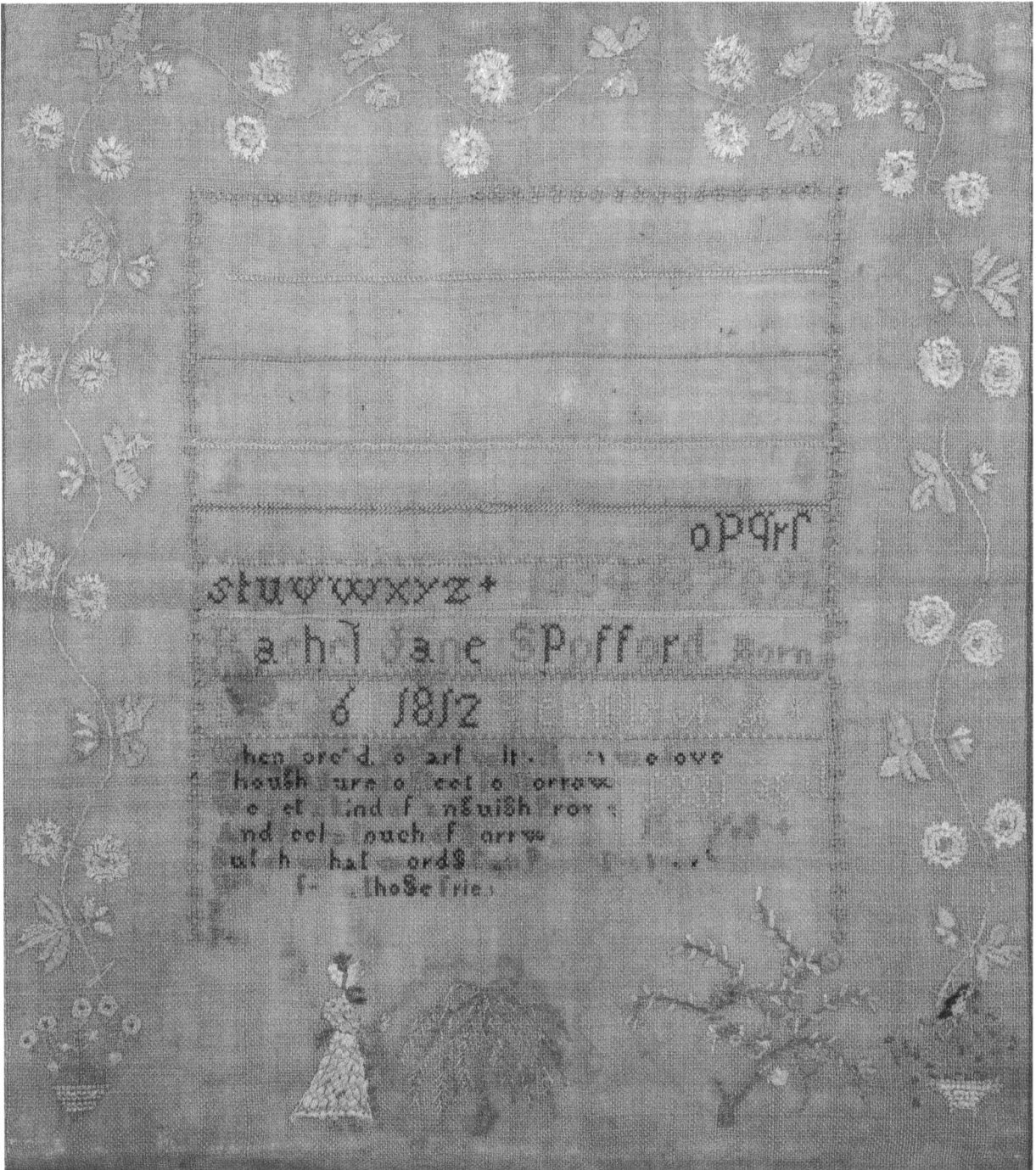

Rachel Jane Spofford (1812-1898), Temple, New Hampshire, circa 1822. Silk thread on linen, 16 3/4 x 15 1/2". Stitches: satin, outline, back, bullion, cross over one and two, long and short, seed, feather, long-arm cross. Collection of Glee Krueger.

Rachel Jane's sampler, with its blank areas, appears to have suffered significant stitch loss, rather than that it was never finished. Under raking light, the faint, shadowy remnants of her rows of alphabets are barely visible. She was the sixth of the one son and five daughters of Jesse Spofford and Sarah Tiddle who were married in Temple, New Hampshire, on July 21, 1796. On November 12, 1838, she married her first cousin, Artemas Spofford, in Boston, but the couple settled in Vermont where he was a farmer. Rachel gave birth to their only child, Daniel, on August 1, 1842. Artemas died in Temple on June 7, 1843. By 1850, Rachel was living with her parents again, although Daniel, just eight, was residing with an uncle in Massachusetts. On December 31, 1854, Rachel married Stephen C. Heald, a brewer who had been born in New Hampshire, but lived in Lynn, Massachusetts, with his four children. Daniel rejoined his mother in their new blended household. He would later serve for almost the full duration of the Civil War. Eventually, the Healds returned to New Hampshire. Rachel died March 11, 1898, in East Jaffrey.

Ruthy Davis (1774-1812), New Ipswich, New Hampshire, circa 1784. Silk thread on linen, 12 1/4 x 10 1/2". Stitches: cross over one and two, satin. Private collection.

Ruthy's relatively simple marking sampler incorporates a deeply arcaded border somewhat reminiscent of those associated with samplers from Middlesex County Boston suburbs, but the dates of those samplers are generally later than Ruthy's. A very similar border to Ruthy's was stitched by Elizabeth Jewett on her sampler from nearby Hollis, New Hampshire, but much later in 1841. Ruthy was the sixth of the nine children (of whom five may have died in early childhood) of Jonathan Davis of Ipswich, Massachusetts, and his wife, Sarah Melvin, who was born in Concord, Massachusetts. Jonathan relocated to New Ipswich in 1764 and farmed on the "old country road" near Temple. Ruth married Stephen Poor, a tanner, in Hancock, New Hampshire, on October 15, 1795. She gave birth to at least seven children between 1797 and 1812, including an infant that was born and died on the same day in 1804. Her daughter Mary and son Stephen both died in childhood, as well. On March 22, 1812, she and the infant she had given birth to that day both passed away. Ruth and all of those children are buried in Pine Ridge Cemetery in Hancock. Sometime after her death, Stephen moved to upstate New York with their remaining children, Melvin, Thomas, Olive, and possibly a daughter. A larger sampler that shares many elements with Ruthy's, including the wave and arcaded borders and oversized strawberries, has come to light. It was stitched by Mary Estabrook who, descendants believe, attended New Ipswich Academy, a co-educational academy that opened in 1789. Ruthy's undated sampler was almost certainly stitched under the instruction of the same teacher as Mary's.

Eliza Ann Wallingford (1809-1838), Dublin, New Hampshire, 1822. Silk thread on linen, 18 3/8 x 20 5/8". Stitches: cross, satin, stem, lazy daisy, hem. Courtesy of the Milford, New Hampshire, Historical Society.

Eliza Ann was born in June 1809, the eldest of the four children of Benjamin Wallingford and Hannah Needham. Benjamin was a farmer from Milford, New Hampshire, who moved to Dublin in 1805 and returned to Milford in 1835. Eliza Ann's life was a relatively short one. She died, unmarried, in Milford in 1838 at the age of twenty-nine, three years after her parents returned to the area. Both Eliza's sampler and that of her younger sister, Diana, were worked in the same year, and undoubtedly under the instruction of the same teacher. They share a similar border with an undulating vine surrounded by an inner sawtooth band. A scene with a centrally placed three-story house flanked by floral sprays occupies the bottom portion of both samplers, with the inscriptions of the makers located just below.

Diana Wallingford (1811-1881), Dublin, New Hampshire, 1822. Silk thread on linen, 16 7/8 x 17 3/8". Stitches: cross over one and two, satin, stem, lazy daisy, back. Courtesy of the Milford, New Hampshire, Historical Society.

Diana was born in 1811, the second of Benjamin Wallingford and Hannah Needham's children. After growing up in Dublin, New Hampshire, she moved to Milford with her parents. She was a successful teacher there for several years before marrying Moses Foster, a farmer and carpenter, in September 1842. Diana was Moses's second wife, his first wife having given birth to four boys before dying at the age of forty-three in May 1842. Diana and Moses had four children of their own, although all but one died young. Only their son Benjamin lived to adulthood. Moses died suddenly in April 1874, and Diana lived until 1881, when she died of breast cancer at the age of sixty-nine. Their son, Benjamin, lived a rather varied life, unlike his parents. When he was young, he worked as a photographer, but by the early 1900s, he had become an undertaker and embalmer. Benjamin married three times, divorcing his second wife, and marrying for a third time in 1913, by which time he had added auctioneering to his undertaking duties.

Mary Emmeline Holmes (?-1913), Antrim, New Hampshire, 1838. Silk thread on linen, 16 x 17 1/2". Stitches: cross over one and two. Private collection.

The design of Mary's artful sampler is a little unusual since she completely dispensed with the typical inclusion of numerous variations on the alphabet and made her verse the central focus of the work. A published local history reports Antrim schools in the first half of the nineteenth century operated by Miss Augusta Barber, Lizzie S. Tenney, and Miss Abby C. Morse, but does not provide dates for these. Mary's father, Thomas S. Holmes, a third son, inherited his father's homestead after his eldest brother relocated to Canada and his next eldest brother died of wounds he sustained in the War of 1812. Thomas married Sarah Dinsmore. She was the niece of the Mary Nichols who ran a female academy in Antrim from about 1818 to 1823 (as noted on page 11). A carpenter by trade, Thomas built a new house on the family land in 1812. Of their three sons and three daughters, only Mary and a single brother lived to marry. She married Hiram Fifield, a farmer about ten years her senior from Andover, New Hampshire, on April 20, 1867. Hiram died in 1899. Mary lived on alone in the family home until her death on February 1, 1913. They are buried together in Proctor Cemetery in Andover with their only child, Frank, who died at age eleven in 1884.

Sally R. Cressey (1806-1853), Bradford, New Hampshire, 1819. Silk thread on linen, 13 3/4 x 17 1/2". Stitches: cross over one and two, long-arm cross, satin, chain, eyelet. Courtesy of the Milford, New Hampshire Historical Society.

Sally's sampler is rather unusual. The meandering floral border growing out of checkered pots and the wide inner satin-stitched border resemble features found on samplers worked in Haverhill, Massachusetts, while the tree at the center bottom is unlike any found to date on other New Hampshire samplers. Sally's unknown teacher may well have been from the Haverhill area and brought the familiar style with her to rather-distant Bradford. Details about Sally Cressey's life are scarce. She was born in 1806 in Bradford, New Hampshire, and married merchant William Presbury Hoyt, probably sometime in the mid-1820s. Sally and William had at least two daughters: Georgianna, who was born in 1828 and died in 1844 at the age of sixteen, and Mary, born in 1832. Mary married Oliver Lull, with whom she had two daughters. The couple lived in Milford, and Sally's sampler descended in the Lull family until it was donated to the Milford Historical Society. Sally died in Milford, New Hampshire, on December 29, 1853, at the age of forty-seven. She is buried in the Presbury Cemetery in Bradford along with her daughter Georgianna.

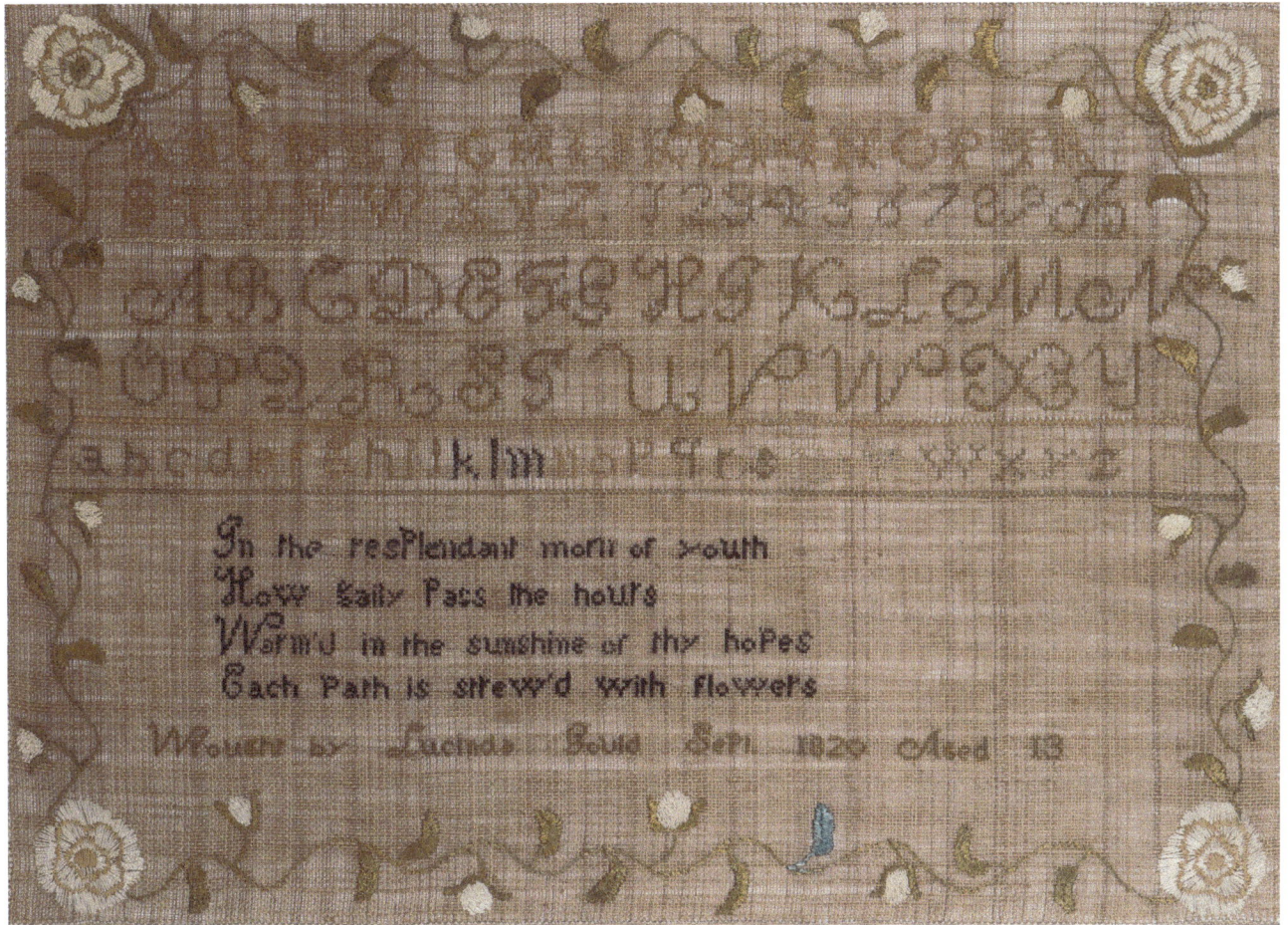

Lucinda Gould (1807-1900), Henniker, New Hampshire, 1807. Silk thread on linen, 12 x 17 3/8". Stitches: hem, satin, cross over one and two, stem, French knot. Henry T. Callan Antiques.

Lucinda Gould was born in Henniker, New Hampshire, on December 22, 1807, the daughter of Benjamin Gould and Abigail Clark. She probably had at least five siblings. Although official records are quite scarce, she appears, in around 1830, to have married Abel Willard Kent who may have been from Alstead, New Hampshire. They had become parents to two sons and two daughters by 1840, around the time that her husband disappeared from records. In 1850, she was operating a large boarding house serving female mill operatives in Nashua, New Hampshire, and on April 16, 1857, she married widower Amos Wood, a very successful farmer, and settled in Wilton, New Hampshire. He died in 1873. In 1880, she was living alone in the Wood homestead in Wilton. "Lucindy" Wood died there on April 18, 1900, at the age of ninety-two. Lucinda's nearly monochromatic sampler, likely stitched in rural Henniker, features an attractive leaf and rosebud border. Quite likely the green vegetable dyes that colored some of Lucinda's silk embroidery thread have proven to be "fugitive" and faded to more somber browns. No other samplers similar to Lucinda's have so far come to light. Like the most long-lived of her generation, Lucinda was born many years before railroads laced together the larger towns of New England. By the last years of her life, automobiles were braving New England's developing roadways—a remarkable change in just one lifetime.

Liva Connor (1811-1900), Henniker, New Hampshire, 1823. Silk thread on linen, 16 1/8 x 16 3/4". Stitches: cross over one and two, eyelet, satin, straight, stem, French knot. Collection of Carol Pesch.

Liva Connor's spectacular sampler was stitched in 1823 when she was twelve years old. It is an ambitious piece of needlework and has been carefully preserved by her family across five generations. Liva stitched four alphabets, including the unusual capital letters embellished with loops and tendrils like those on Sophronia Tucker's 1822 sampler. Other similarities include the decorative dividing lines separating the girls' alphabets, and their choice of verse, both beginning "I sigh not for beauty." Liva was born June 26, 1811, in Henniker. She was the third of the ten children of Abel Connor and Hannah Whitney who were married in Henniker on April 26, 1808. Abel was a successful farmer with a knack for grafting trees; he was one of the first in the Henniker area to grow apples for the purpose of marketing them to others. On December 10, 1839, Liva Connor became the second wife of Solomon Heath, a wealthy farmer from Bow, New Hampshire, and stepmother to his young son. By 1849, Solomon and Liva had four more children. On the 1870 federal census, Solomon Heath's real estate was valued at $23,000, making him one of the wealthiest farmers in the area. Three children were still at home, including their daughter Hannah, who was working as a teacher. She may be the "Miss Heath" listed as a teacher in the records of Henniker Academy. After Solomon's death in 1880, Liva and her son George continued to run the family farm, and daughter Emily kept the books. Liva died April 18, 1900, in Bow and is buried in Pages Corner Cemetery, Merrimack County, New Hampshire.

Sophronia Tucker (1812-1896), Henniker, New Hampshire, circa 1822. Silk thread on linen, 15 1/2 x 15 1/4".
Stitches: cross over one and two, satin, stem. Collection of Lynne Anderson.

At the age of ten, Sophronia Tucker stitched six different alphabets, each separated by a decorative dividing line. For her first alphabet, she stitched letters embellished with loops and tendrils. This style of fancy alphabet is usually associated with Scotland or the Netherlands, and may suggest the cultural background of Sophronia's teacher, whose initials may be the "MB" that appear at the end of the third line. Sophronia's four-line verse was a popular refrain from the play *In Search of Happiness* written in 1762 by British author and teacher Hannah More. Sophronia was born February 3, 1812, in Henniker, a small town about sixteen miles west of Concord. She was the second daughter of Ezra Tucker and Hannah Hardy, who was only fourteen when they married on April 25, 1804. They had five children, all of whom lived to adulthood and grew up in the substantial home built by their grandfather in 1772 that Ezra inherited in 1804. By 1830, Sophronia had gone to work in the textile mills in Nashua, New Hampshire. On November 17, 1836, she married Samuel Folsom of Henniker. They moved into a new home Samuel had built on land south of his parents' homestead. The couple had a son, Ezra, and a daughter, Julia Ann. Sophronia was widowed in 1859.   Ezra joined the Union army in June of 1864, at twenty-seven, older than most enlistees; he died from disease in Louisiana a year later. After his death, Sophronia sold her property and, along with her mother, moved to Hopkinton to live with Julia Ann and her family. Sophronia died there on March 12, 1896, of "apoplexy"—the term used for sudden death from a heart attack or stroke.

Sarah P. Adams (1814-1836), Henniker, New Hampshire, circa 1825. Silk thread on linen, 17 3/4 x 17 1/4". Stitches: cross over one and two, eyelet, satin, stem, lazy daisy. Collection of Lynne Anderson.

Sarah Adams stitched a delightful alphabet and verse sampler bordered on four sides by plants and sprays adorned with pink, blue, and yellow flowers. Unfortunately, the brilliant pink silks have faded to white, leaving her 190-year-old needle-work more neutral in appearance than she intended. Below her two alphabets, eleven-year-old Sarah stitched three verses, each by a different author. Her last verse is also her signature. This rhyming name pattern first appeared on seventeenth-century English samplers and undoubtedly crossed the Atlantic with the earliest New England colonists. Accenting her signature are two feathery, fernlike leaves—a motif that appears on later samplers from the area. Sarah Pool Adams was born February 18, 1814, in Henniker. Known as Sally, she was the third of five children born to Captain Stephen Adams and Abigail Alexander, and was named for her maternal grandmother, Sally Pool Alexander. Sarah's great grandparents, Captain Aaron and Betty Adams, and their three sons, were early settlers in Henniker, purchasing property in 1772. On May 10, 1832, Sarah married Jeremiah Morgan, son of Nathan and Mary (Emerson) Morgan of nearby Hopkinton. Four and a half years later, Sarah died of consumption on November 12, 1836. Her father died of the same disease in 1843.

Abigail F. Shute (circa 1802-after 1880), Hopkinton, New Hampshire, circa 1811. Silk thread on linen, 15 1/2 x 17 3/4". Stitches: hem, split, satin, lazy daisy, cross over one and two, eyelet. Henry T. Callan Antiques.

On June 12, 1799, Azubah Huse married Moses Shute in Hillsborough, New Hampshire. By 1810, they had relocated to Hopkinton, New Hampshire, and were the parents of a son and two daughters, all under the age of ten. One of the daughters was Abigail F. Shute who stitched her very attractive sampler, but most likely not under the instruction of Miss M. Hoyt (or Hoit), who taught Rebecca and Lucinda Huse, (Abigail's second cousins on her father's Huse side), in 1827. Abigail's sampler features a lovely naturalistic floral border that incorporates elongated satin stitches, and has a much more artistic design than the later Hoit works. By 1820, Azuba was listed as a widow on the Hopkinton census with a female child under the age of ten and another aged sixteen to twenty-five, most likely Abigail. Azuba appeared a few more times on records: living in Boston in the early 1830s and then in New York City where she likely died in 1865. Abigail married George T. Cook of Danvers, Massachusetts, a "trader," on September 30, 1824, in Hopkinton. On the 1850 census, they were residing in Boston, along with "Angela" Huse, age seventy-seven and born in New Hampshire, who might actually be Azuba. Abigail's age was listed as forty-eight, placing her birth date in about 1802, making the date of the sampler circa 1811. The final record that seems likely to be related to Abigail Shute Cook was that of a blind, New Hampshire-born widow, Abigail Cook, living in a rooming house in Gramercy Park, New York, recorded on the 1880 federal census.

Elisabeth Copps (1815-1887), Hopkinton, New Hampshire, 1827. Silk thread on linen, 10 3/4 x 14 3/4". Stitches: hem, cross over one and two, chain, satin, back, French knot. Collection of Glee Krueger.

Elisabeth C. Copps was born December 30, 1815, in Plaistow, New Hampshire, the seventh of the ten children born to Moses Copps and Mary (Polly) George. In 1820, Moses moved his family to Haverhill, Massachusetts, and then two years later they moved to Dunbarton, New Hampshire. By 1824, the Copps family had relocated—yet again—to Hopkinton, where Moses became a successful farmer who also made and sold shoes. In 1827, at the age of eleven, Elisabeth stitched a sampler in Hopkinton "under the inspection of Miss M. Hoit." Elisabeth embellished the corners of her sampler with large satin stitched flowers and short rainbow bands of contrasting colors. Grapes strung on vines fill in the borders on three sides. Within her multicolored sawtooth enclosure Elisabeth included two alphabets and a verse. On December 15, 1841, Elisabeth married Henry Dewey White (1815-1894), a dentist from Concord, New Hampshire, where they settled and raised a family. Between 1845 and 1850 Elisabeth and Henry had four daughters: Sarah, Ellen, Adelia, and Julia. Elisabeth Copps White died February 13, 1887, in Concord and is buried in the Woodlawn Cemetery in Penacook, New Hampshire.

Rebecca Huse (1810-1882), Hopkinton, New Hampshire, 1827. Silk thread on linen, 16 1/2 x 17 1/2". Stitches: hem, cross over one and two, satin, French knots, eyelet, chain. New Hampshire Historical Society.

In 1827, both Rebecca and her step-niece, Lucinda, stitched somewhat similar samplers "under the instruction of Miss M. Hoyt" in Rebecca's case, but "under the inspection of Miss M. Hoit" on Lucinda's sampler (which was sold by Carol and Stephen Huber). Rebecca Huse was the only child of Thomas Huse and his second wife, Annah Clough. Thomas's first wife was Sarah Story of Ipswich, Massachusetts, with whom he had ten children prior to her death in Hopkinton in 1808. Thomas and Annah were married February 22, 1810, in Hopkinton and Rebecca was born on Christmas Day of the same year. Rebecca's father died in 1814 at the age of sixty-seven when she was only three years old and her mother (who remarried to Benjamin Cressey by 1820) died in 1828, the year after she completed her sampler. Rebecca became the second wife of Sawyer Blanchard, an extremely wealthy carpenter from Concord, New Hampshire, on June 30, 1837. They were parents to three sons and a daughter. Rebecca died October 9, 1882. Lucinda's father, James Huse, was a son of Thomas Huse and Sarah Story. He first married Elizabeth Hoyt who died after giving birth to at least two daughters and a son. On July 8, 1812, James married Betsey Noyes in Henniker, New Hampshire, but relocated to Hopkinton, where Lucinda was born on September 10, 1814. Recent research by Dr. Lynne Anderson has identified Miss Mehitable Hoit as the most likely teacher of these well-designed samplers. Mehitable was born April 11, 1804, to Aaron Hoit/Hoyt and Betty Kilburn/Kilborn in Weare, New Hampshire, about nine miles south of Hopkinton. Mehitable was unmarried and aged twenty-three when the samplers naming "Miss M. Hoit" were stitched. Records indicate that she relocated to Hopkinton sometime prior to 1828. On October 16, 1828, she married Nathan Blanchard, Sawyer's elder brother, and the couple settled in nearby Henniker. There are no known samplers bearing the name M. Hoit stitched after their marriage. The couple became parents to at least a son and a daughter. Mehitable Hoit Blanchard died of consumption on July 27, 1854.

Maria F. Ridgway (1809-1836), Keene, New Hampshire, 1818. Silk thread on linen, 16 7/8 x 12 5/8". Stitches: cross over one and two, satin, straight. Private collection.

The births of the first seven of the children of James Ridgway and Faithey Stowell were recorded in Groton, Massachusetts, vital records, although the eldest two were born in Worcester and Boston. Maria Fiducia was born fourth, on April 16, 1809. When the Ridgways relocated to Keene, New Hampshire, around 1816, they left behind the graves of two tiny sons who had both been named after their father. James was both a silversmith and a jeweler and may have moved to Keene, a much larger town than Groton, because it presented better business opportunities. One more child was born to the Ridgways after they moved to Keene, Harriet Antionette, in 1818. A family bible indicates that Maria died on September 27, 1836. Harriet married, and passed her sister's sampler down to her descendants. Miss Catherine Fiske operated an academy in Keene with Miss Reed in 1815-1816, with Miss Sprague in 1817-1818, and by herself in 1819. She was the daughter of Luther and Azubah Fiske of Worcester, Massachusetts, born July 30, 1784, and died in Keene, May 20, 1837. She may have been Maria's teacher.

Louisa Cushing (1811-1871), Walpole, New Hampshire, 1821. Silk thread on linen, 19 3/4 x 18 1/2". Stitches: satin, long and short, bullion, cross over one and two, back, outline. Collection of Glee Krueger.

Louisa's family mobility, at least in her parents' generation, was not unusual for the time as land close to the coast of New England was being broken up into smaller and smaller parcels. Perhaps in response to the economic difficulties of small farms, David Cushing, who was born in the coastal Massachusetts town of Hingham, moved with his parents to Ashburnham, Massachusetts, near the New Hampshire border. He married Ashburnham native Polly Adams and that young couple set off up the Connecticut River to Walpole, New Hampshire, where they became parents to at least eight children from 1808-1829. Louisa was third from the youngest. Although her large, bold, floral-bordered sampler has suffered some stitch loss, it is still an eye-catching example of the sophisticated needlework that emerged from the Connecticut River Valley. It shares some design elements—similar flowers, a sawtooth border, and a diamond cross-border—with Caroline Emerson's Walpole sampler stitched three years later. Louisa named Eliza C. on her sampler; it is unclear if this was her teacher's name. On April 14, 1841, Louisa married Salem Towne, a successful farmer who had also relocated to Walpole, coming from Sturbridge, Massachusetts. Salem and Louisa were parents to seven children, but near Louisa's grave are stones marking the short lives of four of those offspring: William Elmer, who died at the age of four, Louisa, who was eleven, Elmer, just one, and Everett who lived until the age of twenty-seven. After Louisa's death, on March 30, 1871, Salem remarried and lived on for another couple of decades.

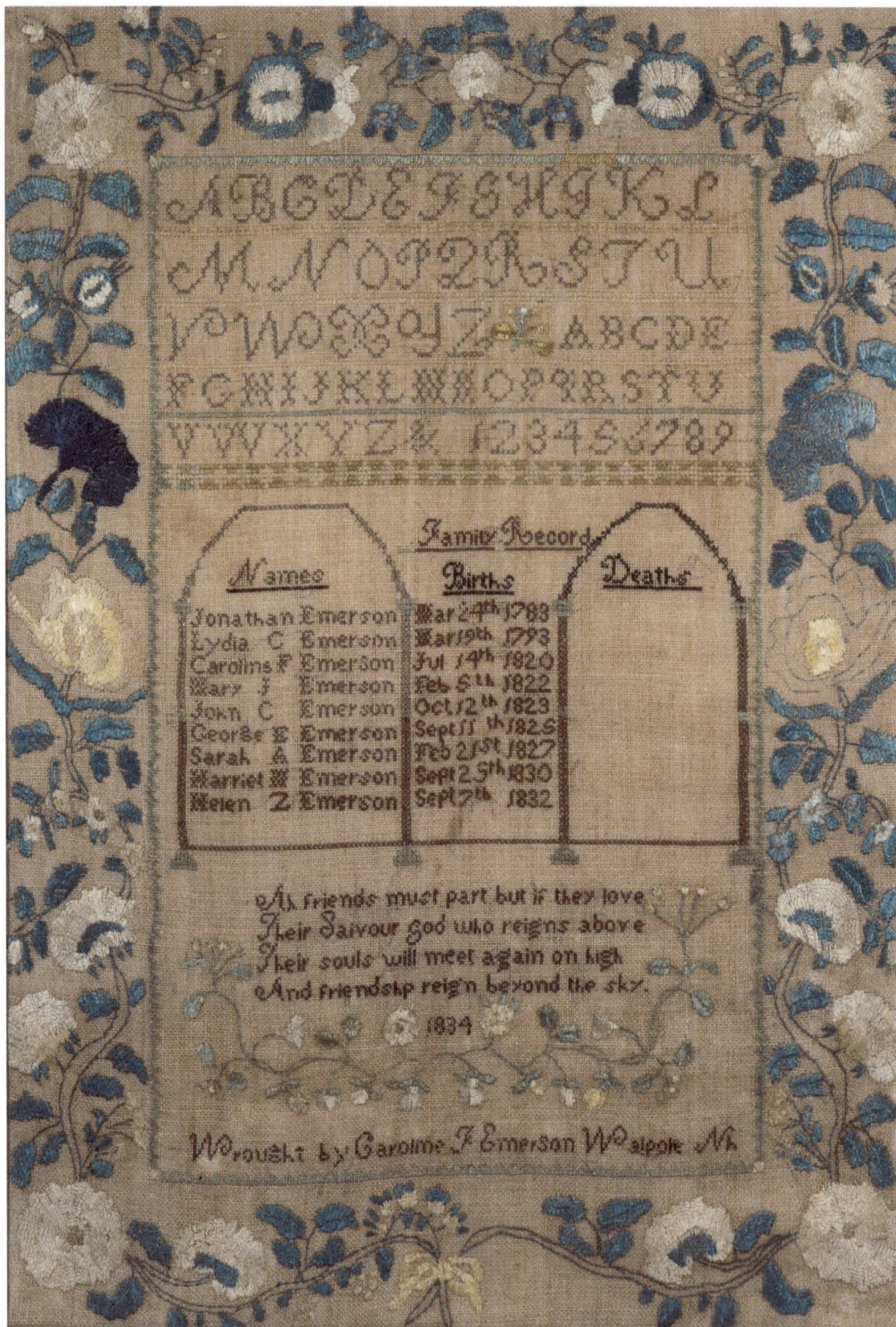

Caroline Emerson (1820-before 1859), Walpole, New Hampshire, 1834. Silk thread on linen, 24 3/8 x 16 3/4". Stitches: cross over one and two, satin, stem, straight. Private collection.

Like Ellen Hodskins, Caroline Emerson used her floral-bordered sampler to provide detailed information about her family. Her father, Jonathan, was the only son of Dr. Moses Emerson, who, (according to a local history), settled in Walpole in the last quarter of the eighteenth century, married Comfort Eastman, then, after she gave birth to their child, "disappeared suddenly from town and nothing more is known of him." Jonathan married Lydia Crosby of Dummerston, Vermont. Caroline grew up in Walpole and on November 8, 1838, married Silas Angier, a farmer from nearby Alstead, where the couple settled. They named their first-born child for Caroline's short-lived sister Helen. By the time of the 1850 census, they had two sons and two daughters. Although no death record could be found for Caroline, her husband remarried in 1859.

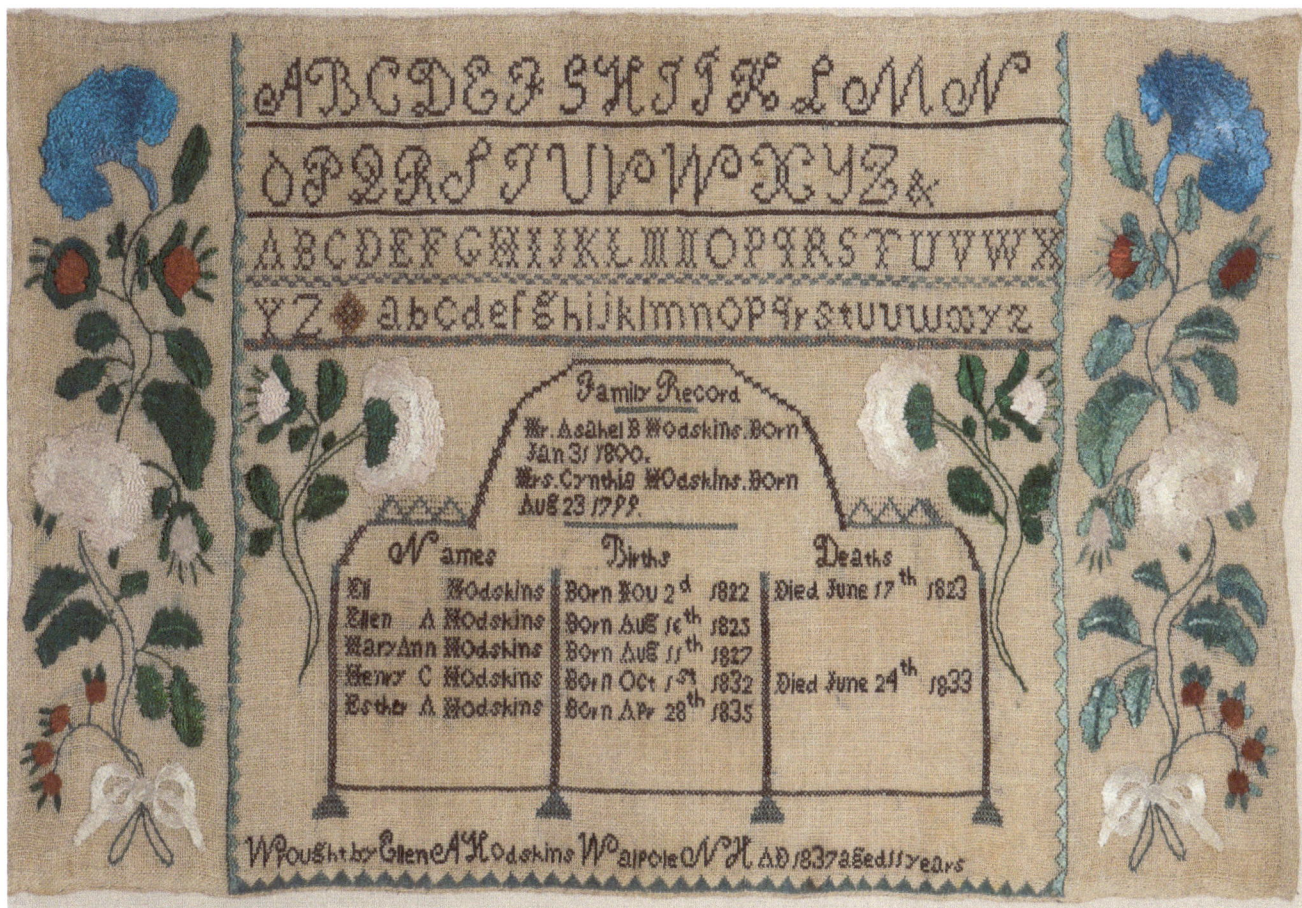

Ellen A. Hodskins (1825-1898), Walpole, New Hampshire, 1837. Silk thread on linen, 11 3/8 x 19 1/4". Stitches: cross over one and two, satin, stem. Private collection.

Ellen Amanda Hodskins was, as she noted on her family register sampler, the daughter of Asahel Hodskins (the brother of sampler maker Almira Hodskins whose work is in the collection of the New Hampshire Historical Society), and his wife, Cynthia Johnson. She also noted on her sampler the very short lives of two of her five siblings. Her sister Mary Ann also died young, passing away at the age of twenty-one. Ellen married Walpole farmer George D. Kingsbury on Christmas Eve, 1846. He was her next-door neighbor, but farmed on a much larger scale than her father. She and George were parents to two sons, Ashahel and George. Ellen outlived her husband by more than two decades and her eldest son by eight years. She died January 29, 1898, and is buried with many members of her family in Old Cemetery in Walpole. Ellen continued to make decorative needlework after completing her sampler. The New Hampshire Historical Society also has a lavishly embroidered red and white quilt in its collection that she completed in 1895. Ellen's sampler closely resembles the one stitched by Caroline Emerson. Given the dates they were made, they might have been completed at the Walpole Academy under the instruction of "Mrs. Burrill"; newspaper advertisements stated that she taught embroidery. If that was the case, then the resemblance of this sampler and the Emerson piece to Almira Hodskins' undated work is intriguing, since hers may have been completed at least ten years earlier, possibly under the instruction of Harriot Hayes (or sometimes Hays) who operated a female academy in Walpole from about 1808 until at least 1813 when her newspaper advertisement in the *Farmers' Museum* said "the well-known reputation of Miss Hayes as preceptress supersedes the necessity of any recommendation." In spite of three generations of Hodskins living and working in small Walpole, the author of a local history published in 1880 said, "No person is found in town who has any knowledge of this family."

Frances and Sophia Willard (1813-1897) (1815-1897), Charlestown, New Hampshire, circa 1827. Silk thread on linen, 16 1/2 x 16 1/4". Stitches: cross over one and two, satin, chain. Private collection.

Samplers stitched by more than one person are unusual. Frances and Sophia carefully noted their joint participation in theirs, but otherwise provided few clues to their identities. However, Charlestown, New Hampshire, was small town and their family was included in a local history. Frances "Fanny" was born April 7, 1813, and her next youngest sibling, Sophia, on December 19, 1815. They were the daughters of Abel Willard and Fanny Grout who were married on September 13, 1812, in Charlestown. The Willards were among the first settlers of the town. Fanny married Ebenezer Dunsmoor, a farmer in Charlestown, and had four children. She died May 15, 1897. Sophia married Newton Allen and also was the mother of four. Her husband, too, was a farmer in Charlestown, although he died while on a visit to Colorado in 1876. Sophia died February 2, 1897, only three months before her sister, and was buried in Claremont, New Hampshire. According to the published local history, seafaring Captain James Gilchrist moved to Charlestown in 1822 from Medford, Massachusetts. "Mrs. Gilchrist opened a select school for young ladies which was continued for a considerable time. She was a highly educated lady and previous to her marriage to Captain Gilchrist, had been a teacher in Medford in the celebrated school of Mrs. Rowson. Her school soon acquired a wide reputation and pupils were attracted to it from a great distance." Since Captain Gilchrist died in 1827, the income from the school was probably especially needed. Susanna closed the academy in about 1833 when her three eldest daughters married. She was most likely the daughter of Joseph and Mary Wyman, born March 18, 1784, in Woburn, Massachusetts. The mother of five daughters and four sons, one of her sons became a physician and another Chief Justice of New Hampshire. She died in Charlestown, March 20, 1858. If this connection to Mrs. Rowson is correct, then Susanna must have assisted Mrs. Rowson between the years of 1800-1803 when the academy was in Medford. Susanna was a resident there at the time of her marriage in 1805.

Malvina S. Huggins (1799-1876), Cornish, New Hampshire, 1818. Silk thread on linen, 16 x 17 1/2". Stitches: cross, satin, stem, chain, queen, couched. Collection of Sue and Dexter Pond.

The intricate sampler stitched by Malvina S. Huggins in 1818 provides many of the interesting details that help researchers better understand schoolgirl embroidery. She not only provided her age, the date when she completed it, the location where it was stitched, but also named her teacher, Miss Judith Chase. Malvina was the eldest of the six daughters of Jonathan Huggins and his wife, Abigail Spaulding, who were married on November 15, 1798. She was born September 13, 1799. The Huggins family lived in Cornish until about 1810, when they moved across the Connecticut River into central Vermont. Around 1816, the family returned to Cornish. Malvina never married. In 1850, she was residing with her younger sister, Caroline, and her husband, Benjamin Lewis. By 1860, Malvina had a small home of her own, but in 1870, she and now-widowed Caroline were sharing a home in Pittsfield, Vermont, where Malvina died on April 1, 1876, of a "liver complaint." Judith Chase, her teacher, may have been the sixth of the nine children of Caleb Chase and Tabitha Bemis who was born July 25, 1785. Her parents were married in Sutton, Massachusetts, and may have come to Cornish after passing a few years in Brookfield, Massachusetts.

Anonymous, Cornish, New Hampshire, circa 1818. Silk thread on linen, 20 1/4 x 16 7/8". Stitches: cross over one and two, eyelet, stem. New Hampshire Historical Society.

At some unknown time, but quite likely around 1818, an unknown girl stitched a sampler that closely matches that of Malvina S. Huggins. The sampler was donated to the New Hampshire Historical Society by Emma G. Carpenter. Emma, the daughter of John Gilman Gate and his wife, Anna Augusta Clark, married George A. Carpenter. A thorough investigation of the family trees of both Emma and her husband failed to identify anyone who had connections to western New Hampshire. It is unknown whether the sampler passed through Emma's family or if she may have purchased it. Given the many similarities of this sampler to that of Malvina, it is possible that it may have been stitched by one of her five sisters, only two of whom have been identified: Caroline, born in 1803, and Parthenia, born about 1810, who married Lyman Gibbs and settled in Vermont. The odd and very inaccurate date stitched on this sampler only increases the uncertainty regarding it. The sampler maker had no apparent trouble in working her alphabets or the long and neatly rendered verse. She seems to have written a variation of Aug. 8, and the year 1676, although her first 6 is unlike the way she stitched the number in two other places. Since this date is worked in thread that does not match any other on the sampler, it seems likely to have been a later addition by another less-skilled person.

Sarah Richardson (1815-1913), Cornish, New Hampshire, 1824. Silk thread on linen, 16 7/8 x 17 1/2". Stitches: cross over one and two, eyelet, satin. Private collection.

Sarah Richardson and her first cousin Martha Richardson likely stitched their samplers under the instruction of the same teacher in small Cornish, New Hampshire, located in the far western part of the state on the edge of the Connecticut River. Sarah was the eldest of the eight children of farmer Amos Richardson and his wife, Sophia Cummings, born in 1815. As an adult, Sarah taught school, a job that she may have found to be discouraging, as noted in an extant letter from her younger sister, Charlotte, who wrote to her from Florida in 1848. She said, "I do hope [this letter] will not find you so disconsolate as when you last wrote. I think you were unusualy [sic] depressed were you not—But I remember the teachers trials How many and arduous they are." Later in the letter, Charlotte's husband added a postscript: "Do not be afraid to get married even if they are widowers." Perhaps Sarah took his advice to heart. On April 30, 1853, she married widower Reverend Jonathan Symonds Herrick, and became a mother to her recently deceased cousin Martha's four children, aged one to six years old. Sarah lived on to the age of ninety-eight, spending the last years of her life in the care of her adopted children. Sarah listed her teacher on her sampler: Sukey Cumming. This may be Sally, (or in some records, Sarah) Cummings, her mother's eldest sister. A published 1903 genealogy states that Sukey Cummings was born July 7, 1767, and died December 17, 1842, although no other records could be found for her. Sarah's sister Sophia stitched a sampler in 1831 (current location unknown) that included similar columnar trees; she named Joann Cumings as her teacher. Joann was born in 1806 and taught school prior to her marriage to Cyrus Burge of Hollis, New Hampshire, in 1835.

Martha Richardson (1818-1852), Cornish, New Hampshire, 1829. Silk thread on linen, 15 1/2 x 17 1/4". Stitches: cross over one and two, eyelet, satin, stem, fishbone. Private collection.

Sampler maker Martha Richardson may have stitched her sampler under the instruction of Sukey Cummings, as her first cousin Sarah Richardson did, or perhaps Joann Cumings was her teacher. Martha was born September 8, 1818, less than a month after the death of her next eldest brother. She grew up in a farming family, one of seven surviving children, and later attended New Hampton Seminary, a large Baptist female academy under the supervision of Miss Martha Hazeltine. Prior to her marriage, Martha taught for six years in Wake Forest, North Carolina, eventually becoming principal of Pleasant Grove Female Academy. Extant advertisements indicate that no needlework was taught there. On March 4, 1846, she became the second wife of Reverend Jonathan Symonds Herrick of Warner, New Hampshire, the wedding coming just ten months after the birth of his first child and death of both mother and infant. Martha's first child, Maria, was named for Herrick's deceased first wife. Over the next five years, Martha would give birth to three more children, the last on January 10, 1852. She died of consumption just five months later on May 17, 1852, and is buried in Cornish, New Hampshire. According to her epitaph, "she manifested a great love for literature, was of beautiful spirit and unselfish in her life work."

Susan B. Kinsley (1815-1901), Grantham, New Hampshire, 1828. Silk thread on linen, 15 3/4 x 13 1/8". Stitches: cross over one and two, eyelet, satin. Private collection.

Susan Kinsley Bullard was photographed near the end of her life. The image shows an elderly woman gazing pensively off into the distance, but also captures a cheerful attitude. She was the second child of at least eleven of Zebediah Kinsley and Joanna Blodgett, born December 8, 1815. Zebediah was from Massachusetts, and although he and Joanna raised their older children in Grantham, they moved back to his home state by 1850, when he was working as a bricklayer in Somerville. On June 20, 1841, Susan married John Harris Bullard in Charlestown, but moved to Stoughton not long afterward. There she and John, a boot maker, became parents to five children, although most did not survive past young adulthood. Susan died on June 20, 1901, her sixtieth wedding anniversary, at the age of eighty-five in Stoughton of "senile debility." Her small, charming sampler includes a number of unique elements and names Grantham (in tiny faded letters) as the place where she stitched it.

Mary Ann Storrs (1818-1887), Lebanon, New Hampshire, 1830. Silk thread on linen, 17 x 19 3/4". Stitches: cross over one and two, satin, straight, chain. Private collection.

Mary Ann stitched her sampler, with its delicate, meandering leafy vines and realistic satin stitch roses, in Lebanon, New Hampshire. No other samplers from Lebanon have been identified. Her grandmother, a Lebanon native, was courted by two young men from nearby Dartmouth College. When she was unable to choose a husband between them, they drew lots! She married Elijah Lyman and went to Brookfield, Vermont, with him where he served as minster for the rest of his life. After his death, her other suitor traveled to Brookfield, hoping to marry her. She, comfortably settled, turned him down. Her daughter, Mary Lyman, married Dan Storrs, a farmer in Lebanon, in November, 1813. They were parents to three children; Mary Ann, born February 28, 1818, was the youngest. Neither she nor her elder sister Lucinda ever married. After their father died, Mary Ann, who had previously supported herself as a seamstress, moved in with her mother and took over the family farm. Lucinda also moved back in and worked as a "vest maker." Mary Ann died December 27, 1887.

Mary McClave (unknown), possibly Lyme, New Hampshire, 1835. Silk thread on linen, 16 3/4 x 17". Stitches: cross over one and two, stem, straight, lazy daisy. Collection of Mr. and Mrs. Dan Scheid.

Like quite a few other sampler makers in this exhibition, Mary provided only the barest of clues to her identity but her surname is an uncommon one. Since she completed her accomplished sampler on Christmas Eve of 1835, perhaps when she was around fifteen, she may have been born in about 1820. She included satin stitch flower pots that are reminiscent of the ones stitched at the Pinkerton Academy and Adams Female Academy in Londonderry, and her floral vines are quite similar to ones stitched in Jaffrey and Fitzwilliam, New Hampshire, all implying that she may have been from southwestern New Hampshire. The most likely candidate would be a daughter of John Stevenson McClave, born 1774, who married Hannah Patrick of Fitzwilliam in 1802. They settled in Lyme and, on the 1830 census, had a daughter aged ten to fifteen, who could be Mary; a number of family trees posted on Ancestry.com attribute a daughter by that name to John and Hannah. Unfortunately, all of Lyme's vital records from the first half of the nineteenth century were lost in a fire, making it very difficult to prove this is the correct McClave daughter. Mary's sampler makes excellent use of the lovely sheen of silk thread. By creating her scene with very long satin stitches, she added a beautiful luminescent effect to her stitchery.

Betsey Jenkins Morey (1801-1861), Orford, New Hampshire, circa 1812. Silk thread on linen, 8 5/8 x 11 1/4". Stitches: cross over one and two, satin. Collection of Lynne Anderson.

Betsey Jenkins Morey stitched her colorful marking sampler in the agricultural community of Orford, New Hampshire, along the Connecticut River. Unfortunately, someone—possibly Betsey herself—removed the stitches for the year when she worked her handsome sampler, that also, of course, hinted of her age. Betsey Jenkins Morey was the daughter of Israel Morey Jr. and his second wife, Margaret McHurd. She was born in October of 1801, the last of their four children and their only daughter. Her father was the eldest son of General Israel Morey, one of the first settlers and land grantees in Orford. He arrived with his wife and three young sons by wagon and ox sled in late 1765 from Hebron, Connecticut, one of numerous Connecticut settlers of the period to acquire land along the upper Connecticut River. General Morey operated Orford's first store and blacksmith shop, and his home became the town meeting place. In 1770, he gave the town a building that served as its first meetinghouse and school. Betsey Jenkins Morey never married and died of cancer across the Connecticut River in Fairlee, Vermont, on April 20, 1861, at the age of fifty-nine.

Almira Ann Hall (1804-1893), Bridgewater, New Hampshire, circa 1815. Silk thread on linen, 17 x 17". Stitches: cross, eyelet, satin, hem. Private collection.

Almira stitched a bright, appealing sampler that incorporates an oversized chicken, an attractive house, and a variety of spot motifs. She was the eldest of the three daughters of Reuben Hall and Sarah Davis, who were born in Rumney, New Hampshire, and married there on February 24, 1804. Although Acton, Massachusetts, records do not include her, New Hampshire vital records state that Almira was born there, and whenever she appeared on census records, her birthplace was listed as Massachusetts although there is no record of her parents residing there. By around 1812, her family had moved to Bridgewater, New Hampshire, where they remained until at least 1830. Almira married John Harran (or Hanan) on April 4, 1833, in Bristol, New Hampshire. On the 1850 census, John was farming there. Four children, a son and three daughters, were listed, but by their initials only. Almira's father was also living in the household. By 1860, the eldest child, Jonathan, and his sister Adelaide were both working in a factory and there was one more new addition to the family, Ida, eight months old. The final record that could be found for Almira, now a widow, was that of her death on April 25, 1893, in Plymouth. She may have been residing there with her son, John, prior to her death.

Mary Hall (1789-1868), Groton, New Hampshire, 1819. Silk thread on linen, 25 1/2 x 21 3/8".
Stitches: cross over one and two, buttonhole, eyelet, long-arm cross, satin, straight. Private collection.

Mary Hall's elaborate and very informative sampler is surely one of the most unusual in the exhibition. Sampler making, from the early years of the republic until it became less fashionable in the 1840s, was almost exclusively a schoolgirl art, and yet Mary, the eldest of the thirteen children of Benjamin and Mary Haines Hall, was thirty when she completed her work. It is possible that Mary worked her sampler to use as an example for students she may have taught, but so far no similar samplers nor evidence of her working as a teacher have come to light. Although Mary noted many other dates on her sampler, she did not record the date of her parents' marriage, which vital records indicate was June 5, 1789, perhaps because it was only five months before her birth on November 25, 1789. Mary resided with her parents until her father's death in 1835. After that time, as was typical for many unmarried women of her era, she lived with various family members. It is likely she is the Mary Hall recorded on the 1860 census living with her nephew, Charles Hall, and his family. Mary died on December 29, 1868, and was buried with many other members of the Hall family in the small, shady River Road Cemetery in Groton.

Eliza Ann Cummings (1811-1893), Plymouth, New Hampshire, 1823. Silk thread on linen, 16 5/8 x 17 3/4". Stitches: cross over one and two, satin, eyelet, straight, chain, French knot. Strawbery Banke Museum.

Eliza worked remarkably lifelike plants along the border of her sampler, along with very accurate versions of checked and banded mugs and wall pockets holding bunches of flowers. Eliza Ann Cummings was born August 26, 1811, in Plymouth, New Hampshire, the first child of Noah Cummings and Elizabeth "Betsey" Connor. Noah Cummings was a farmer and a substantial citizen of Plymouth, serving as a lieutenant in the militia and a selectman of the town for six years. In 1830, Eliza Ann married Dearborn Henry Hilton and shortly afterwards they moved to Chester, Vermont. Dearborn was a successful merchant who served as both state representative and senator, as well as a trustee of the Chester Academy. George Henry Hilton, their only child, was born in 1831; he too, became a merchant. Dearborn died in 1860; Eliza continued to live in the family home for a number of years afterwards. By 1880, Eliza had moved into her son's home and was living with his family; according to census records, Eliza's activities then were restricted by hip trouble. Eliza died August 10, 1893, in Londonderry, Vermont, at the age of eighty-three.

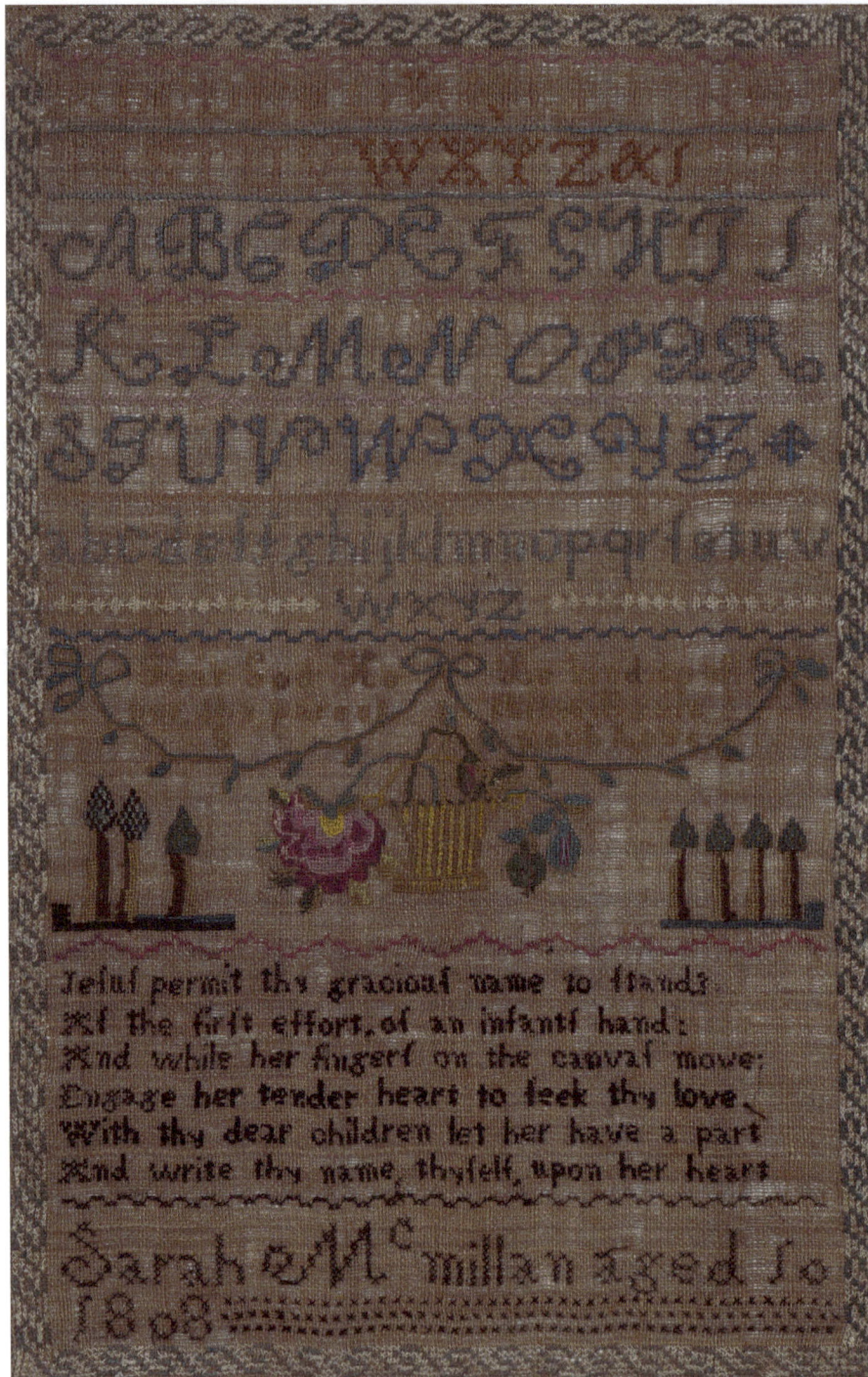

Sally McMillen (1797-?), Littleton, New Hampshire, 1808. Silk thread on linen, 17 3/4 x 11 5/8". Stitches: cross over one and two, hem. Private collection.

Although Sally McMillen was born in Washington, New Hampshire, she stitched her sampler in Littleton where her family had moved by 1800. Her father, Ananias, was from New Boston, New Hampshire, and her mother, Sarah White, from Hopkinton. They were married Christmas Day, 1792 in Henniker. Five months later, their first son was born in Washington, followed by a daughter born there in 1795. Sally was born September 26, 1797, in Washington. The remaining four children were all born in Littleton where a sister and a brother of Ananias also lived. Only four years after the birth of his youngest child, Ananias died in 1813. His widow and the children probably continued to live there since Sarah appeared on the Littleton census in 1850. On April 2, 1818, Sally married John Miller in Lyman, New Hampshire. The couple likely settled there, since a John Miller is recorded on the 1830 and 1840 censuses with a growing family that included two sons and three daughters by 1840. Their whereabouts after that census are unknown, however. No other records for the family could be located.

Eleanor H. Merrill (1818-1890), New Hampshire or Massachusetts, 1826. Silk thread on linen, 20 1/2 x 16 5/8". Stitches: cross over one and two, feather, queen, herringbone, eyelet, Smyrna cross. Henry T. Callan Antiques.

Eleanor, born January 7, 1818, was the third of the eight children of Joseph Merrill, the "first person born in Warren who received college honors" according to a local history, and Eleanor Haynes. After first teaching in Haverhill and Marblehead, Massachusetts, then studying to be a lawyer, Joseph took up the study of theology and began a career as a minister in about 1820. He served parishes in Dracut, Massachusetts, Ackworth, New Hampshire, and Wellfleet, Massachusetts, served a term in the Massachusetts Legislature, and finally retired to Lowell, Massachusetts. It seems likely that the entire family must have traveled with Joseph to those towns, making it uncertain whether Eleanor stitched this work in New Hampshire—or if she was even born there. Eleanor's tight, queen stitched diamond border and biblical verses forming a second border are especially distinctive and may, in the future, be found to resemble other samplers. On October 16, 1843, Eleanor married Ithiel Homer Silsby who had been born in Ackworth, New Hampshire. Harriet Merrill, Eleanor's sister, sometimes listed as an artist, joined them and lived with Eleanor for nearly the rest of her life. The newly married couple settled in Newton, Massachusetts, where they lived in the home of Ithiel's father. They were the parents of only one child, Homer, who lived to just the age of twenty. At the time of Ithiel's death in 1874, his occupation was listed as "gentleman." In 1878, Eleanor became the third wife of another wealthy merchant in Newton, Nathan P. Coburn. She died on December 12, 1890, in Newton and is buried in Mount Auburn Cemetery.

Frances Wilson (unknown), possibly Danvers, Massachusetts, 1814. Silk thread on linen, 12 1/2 x 11".
Stitches: cross, back, satin, eyelet, chain, outline, bullion. Henry T. Callan Antiques.

Frances Wilson incorporated a few tantalizing clues to her identity on her intriguing and charming sampler that had previously been attributed to a New Hampshire girl. It seems likely that the initials IW and MW may be those of her parents. Although the letters I and J were often interchanged, even as late as 1814 when Frances completed her work, she included both in her alphabet so it seems very probably that her letter I really does mean that. The parrot she included on her sampler may connect it to those stitched by a number of girls in Newburyport, Massachusetts, late in the eighteenth century. Frances's border, too, is very unusual, but it shares some similarities with that of Jane Herbert's 1796 Newburyport sampler (in the collection of the New Hampshire Historical Society). While Danvers and Newburyport are both in Essex County, about twenty-five miles apart, a Danvers teacher may have been familiar with and admired aspects of earlier samplers from Newburyport. On December 7, 1779, Isaac Wilson of Danvers married Dolly Dickinson of Rowley who was said to have been born in about 1756. The births of seven of their children are noted on Danvers vital records and include names that match up with most of the eleven sets of initials on Frances's work. Dolly, whose daughter Dolly was called Mary Dolly, may actually have been named Mary as well, which would account for the large MW initial. The only child whose birth is recorded, "Suckey" in 1785, but who does not have corresponding initials, died before Frances was born. Perhaps an additional clue is that Isaac's brother Jonathan named a daughter Frances in 1788, indicating that that relatively uncommon name was in use in the family. A thorough search of all 1800 and 1810 census records disclosed no other potential matches. No further records were found for a Frances born in Danvers in about 1804. Whether this sampler can be attributed to a daughter of Isaac and Dolly of Danvers remains uncertain

Female Academies and
Other Types of Schoolgirl Art

The Pink will fade the tulip wither
But a virtuous mind will bloom forever.

In the eighteenth and early nineteenth centuries, there were no colleges in America that accepted female students and yet there were many parents who attached great value to educating their daughters, as well as their sons. Female academies sprang up in profusion to fill this need. Some were boarding schools; others were day schools that served a local clientele. Girls, aged about ten to eighteen, were generally instructed in a wide range of academic topics: English, mathematics, sciences, French, geography, history, and arts, often including singing, dancing, instrumental music, painting, and various needle arts. For girls that boarded, the academies also offered a coming-of-age experience not unlike college does today. As public high schools opened and began accepting females, the first colleges for women were also established and expectations for females shifted; the academies lost their market dominance and gradually disappeared.

Martha Darling (1806-1883), mourning painting, Portland, Maine, circa 1826. Watercolor on paper, 16 1/4 x 22". Baxter House Museum, Gorham, Maine.

Martha's painted memorial lacks the winged cherub that appears on many silk mourning embroideries probably stitched at the academy of the Misses Mayo of Portland. However, the entire design of this schoolgirl painting is identical to other works from this academy. It was operated by Martha Merchant Mayo and her six daughters, beginning perhaps as early as 1810. Since Martha Darling was born September 4, 1806, she would have been at least twenty years old when she painted this memorial. She was the eighth of the ten children of John Darling, a very successful Gorham, Maine, hatter and his wife, Annah Lewis. Four of her siblings had died before she painted the memorial, including her sister Sarah (1799-1817). That raises the interesting question of why she painted a memorial to Henry Frost. Henry, born January 8, 1798, in Gorham, married Sophronia Irish in 1821. They were parents to two little girls, shown in the memorial, born in 1822 and 1824. Martha probably knew Henry well, since his home and her father's shop stood on opposite corners of the same intersection. Martha, like her sister Abigail, never married. By 1846, they were running a "fancy goods and millinery shop" in Portland. Martha died of "paralysis" on July 3, 1883.

Emeline or Eunice Wentworth (1817-?) (1818-?), painted memorial, Portland, Maine, circa 1830. Paint on velvet, 14 x 19". Collection of the Maine State Museum.

A lavishly embroidered family register sampler worked by either Sarah or Eunice Harding of Buxton, Maine, was included in the 2013 exhibition "I My Needle Ply with Skill." The death date of Sarah, "Sally," born July 4, 1793, was added after the sampler was finished. She died May 1, 1830. By about 1816, she had become the wife of Robert Wentworth, a Buxton clockmaker and later the operator of a foundry. Over the next twelve years, she gave birth to eight children. When her youngest child was just fourteen months old, Sally died. On June 27, 1832, Robert married again, to Sarah's younger sister, Eunice, born May 22, 1798. She gave birth to two sons and two daughters between 1833 and 1839. A son and a daughter died in childhood, and Eunice died, as well, on April 19, 1849. This mourning painting on velvet adds yet another aspect to the range of arts that were being taught, likely by the Misses Mayo of Portland. The scene is nearly identical to the watercolor on paper mourning painting of Martha Darling. While the figures in these mourning works are believed to represent surviving members of the family, Sarah probably left six daughters and a son when she died; all of these were enumerated on the 1830 census. The painting was likely done shortly after Sarah's death by one of the eldest of these, probably either Emeline, born August 2, 1817, or perhaps Eunice, born November 17, 1818.

Upper right:

Attributed to Thomas Dodds and Christian Claus (working 1791-1793), English Guitar, circa 1791-1793, New York City, 1791-1793. Spruce, maple, ebony, ivory. Saco Museum.

Eunice Cutts, the fifteen-year-old daughter of Saco merchant Thomas Cutts, attended the Boston female academy of Eleanor Druitt. While there, she purchased this guitar for $25, a substantial sum, from William Selby. For an additional $21.17, she received lessons from Selby for about six months in 1797. Music instruction was commonly offered at female academies. Refined young women were expected to be able to sing (at minimum), but instrumental accomplishment was even more desirable.

Lower right:

Nellie Lowe (unknown), knitting sampler, 1860, attributed to Deer Isle, Maine. Cotton. Private collection.

Knitting has long been a productive leisure time activity. The best knitters enjoy using complex stitches to decorate their work. Nellie Lowe proudly included her name and the date on her elongated swatch of varied and challenging stitches. Whereas early embroidered band samplers could be used to aide a woman in reproducing an attractive pattern, this would be far less true of a knitted sampler where the design would not necessarily reveal what needed to be done to create each pattern. A knitting sampler would then be more useful as a combination of practice work and proof of skill. A few other knitting samplers are known, along with some scrapbook-like collections of swatches of crocheted stitches, but the popularity of crochet dates to the second half of the nineteenth century so these are likely to be later compilations. Any of these, however, may represent either schoolgirl or adult accomplishments.

Lower left:

Pocketbooks, 1797 and circa 1770. Wool yarn on canvas. Collection of Sue and Dexter Pond.

The makers of these two wallets are unknown but daughters often stitched them for their fathers. "Hannah Leonard" is worked into the strip just below the flap of the right hand pocketbook. This may have been the mother of Nancy Leonard Smith (born 1785) who married Stephen Peabody. The papers found in the wallet indicate that this Bucksport, Maine, judge used it during at least the last years of his life. The left hand pocketbook belonged to John Burnham, identity unknown, but a slip of paper in that one states, "This was purchased from the 'two mad sisters of Stockton Springs' who settled their arguments by throwing firewood at each other."

Bibliography

Alexander, De Alva Stanwood. *The Alexanders of Maine*. Peter Paul Book Company, 1898.

Beatty, John D., Editor. *Vital Records of Biddeford, Maine Prior to 1856*. Camden, ME: Picton Press, 1998.

Bell, Charles H. *A History of the Town of Exeter, New Hampshire*. Boston, MA: Press of J.E. Farwell & Co., 1888.

Bolton, Ethel Stanwood and Eva Johnston Coe. *American Samplers*. Boston, MA: Thomas Todd Company, 1921.

Brewster, Charles W. *Rambles About Portsmouth, Sketches of Persons, Localities, and Incidents of Two Centuries*, Series I and II. Portsmouth, NH: C. W. Brewster & Son, 1859 and 1869.

Brown, Warren. *History of the Town of Hampton Falls, New Hampshire*. Manchester, NH: John B. Clarke Company, 1900.

Child, Hamilton. *Gazetteer of Grafton County, N.H., 1709-1886*. Syracuse, NY: H. Child, 1886.

Child, William H. *History of the Town of Cornish, New Hampshire with Genealogical Records 1763-1910*. Concord, NH: Rumford Press, 1910.

Cogswell, Leander. *History of the Town of Henniker, Merrimack County, New Hampshire, from the Date of the Canada Grant by the Province of Massachusetts, in 1735, to 1880; with a Genealogical Register of the Families of Henniker*. Concord, NH: Printed by the Republican Press Association, 1880.

Corliss, Augustus W. *Old Times North Yarmouth, Maine 1877-1884*. Somersworth, NH: New Hampshire Publishing Company, 1977.

Cross, Lucy R.H. *History of Northfield, New Hampshire, 1780-1905*. Concord, NH: Rumford Printing Co., 1905.

Cushing, James S. *The Genealogy of the Cushing Family*. Montreal, Quebec: The Perrault Printing Co., 1905.

Cutter, Dr. Benjamin. *A History of the Cutter Family of New England*. Boston, MA: David Clapp & Son, 1871.

Edmonds, Mary Jaene. *Samplers and Samplermakers: An American Schoolgirl Art 1700-1850*. New York: Rizzoli International Publications, 1991.

Ela, David Hough. *Genealogy of the Ela family, Descendants of Israel Ela of Haverhill, Massachusetts*. vManchester, CT: E. S. Ela, 1896.

Emery, William Morrell. *The Salters of Portsmouth, New Hampshire*. New Bedford, MA: New Bedford Printing, Co., 1936.

Fitts, James H. and Nathan Carter. *History of Newfield, New Hampshire, 1638-1911*. Concord, NH: The Rumford Press, 1912.

Folsom, Elizabeth Knowles Folsom. *Genealogy of the Folsom Family: A Revised Record and Extended Edition, Including English Records, 1638-1938*. Rutland, VT: Tuttle Publishing Co., 1938.

Garrett, Elisabeth, Theodore R. Mitchell, and Heather Caldwell. *Lessons Stitched in Silk: Samplers from the Canterbury Region of New Hampshire*. Hanover, NH: Dartmouth College, 1990.

Garvin, James. "St. John's Church in Portsmouth: An Architectural Study." *Historical New Hampshire*, Vol XXVIII, No.3, Fall 1973, pp. 153-175.

Howard, Cecil. *Genealogy of the Cutts Family in America*. Albany, NY: J. Munsell's Sons, 1892.

Huber, Stephen and Carol. *Samplers: How to Compare and Value*. London, England: Octopus Publishing Group, 2002.

Huber, Carol and Stephen, Susan Schoelwer, and Amy Kurtz Lansing. *With Needle and Brush: Schoolgirl Embroidery from the Connecticut River Valley, 1740-1840.* Middletown, CT: Wesleyan University Press, 2011.

Jameson, E. O. *The Cogswells in America.* Boston, MA: Alfred Mudge & Son, 1854.

Jordan, Tristam Frost. *Family Records of the Reverend Robert Jordan and his Descendants in America, complied by Tristam Frost Jordan.* Boston, MA: D. Clapp and Sons, 1882.

Kimball, Henry Ames. *The John Elliot Family of Boscawen, New Hampshire.* Concord, NH: The Rumford Press, 1918.

Krueger, Glee. *A Gallery of American Samplers.* New York: Bonanza Books, 1984.

————. *New England Samplers to 1840.* Sturbridge, MA: Old Sturbridge Village, 1978.

LaBranche John F. and Rita Conant. *In Female Worth and Elegance: Sampler and Needlework Students and Teachers in Portsmouth, New Hampshire 1741-1840.* Portsmouth, NH: Peter E. Randall Publisher, 1996.

Lewis, Alonzo and James R. Newhall. *History of Lynn, Essex County, Massachusetts.* Lynn, MA: Bookstore of George C. Herbert, 1890.

Little, William. *The History of Warren, a Mountain Hamlet Located Among the White Hills of New Hampshire.* Manchester, NH: W.E. Moore, 1870.

Lyford, James Otis. *History of the Town of Canterbury, New Hampshire 1727-1912.* Concord, NH: The Rumford Press, 1912.

Maine Cemetery Inscriptions, York County. Camden, ME: Picton Press, 1995.

McLellan, Hugh. *History of Gorham, Maine.* Portland, Maine: Smith and Sale, Printers, 1903.

A Memorial of the One Hundredth Anniversary of the Founding of Berwick Academy, South Berwick, Maine. Cambridge, MA: Riverside Press, 1892.

McDuffee, Franklin. *History of the Town of Rochester from 1722 to 1890.* Manchester, NH: The J. B. Clarke Co. Printers, 1892.

Mooar, Reverend George. *A Genealogical History of the Descendants of Isaac Cummings, An Early Settler of Topsfield, Massachusetts.* New York, NY: B. R. Cummings, 1903.

Morrison, Leonard. *The history of the Sinclair Family in Europe and America for Eleven Hundred Years: Giving a Genealogical and Biographical History of the Family in Normandy, France, a General Record of it in Scotland, England, Ireland, and a Full Biographical and Genealogical Record of Many Branches in Canada and the United States.* Boston, MA: Damrell and Upham, 1896.

Morrison, Leonard A. *The History of Windham, New Hampshire.* Boston, MA: Cupples, Upham & Co., 1883.

Moynahan, Frank, ed. *Danvers, Massachusetts: A Resume of Her Past History and Progress, Together with a Condensed Summary of Her Industrial Advantages and Development, Biographies of Prominent Danvers Men and a Series of Comprehensive Sketches of Her Representative Manufacturing and Commercial Enterprises.* Danvers, MA: Published in the interest of the Town by the Danvers Mirror, 1899.

Noyes, David. *The History of Norway [ME] Comprising a Minute Account of its First Settlement, Town Officers, Interspersed with Historical Sketches, Narrative and Anecdote.* Norway, ME: The author, 1852.

Parker, Reverend Edward L. *History of Londonderry, Comprising the Towns of Derry and Londonderry, N.H.* Boston, MA: Perkins and Whipple, 1851.

Parson, Langdon Brown. *The History of the Town of Rye From its Discovery and Settlement to December 31, 1903.* Concord, NH: The Rumford Press, 1905.

Pierce, Frederick Clifton. *Foster Genealogy*. Chicago, IL: Press of W. B. Conkey & Co., 1899.

Quinton, Rebecca. *Patterns of Childhood: Samplers from the Glasgow Museums*. London: The Herbert Press, 2005.

Ring Betty. *American Needlework Treasures: Samplers and Silk Embroideries from the Collection of Betty Ring*. New York: E.P. Dutton, 1987.

Ring, Betty. *Girlhood Embroidery: American Samplers & Pictorial Needlework 1650-1850*. New York: Alfred A. Knopf, 1993.

Rix, Guy S. *History and Genealogy of the Eastman Family of America*. Concord, NH: Press of Ira C. Evans, 1901.

Rounds, Leslie L. *"I My Needle Ply with Skill": Maine Schoolgirl Embroidery of the Federal Era*. College Station, Texas: Virtualbookworm Publishing, 2013.

Shelley, Hope, ed. *Vital Records of Wells, Maine 1619-1950*. Camden, ME: Picton Press, 2005.

Sleeper, Sarah. *Memoir of the Late Martha Hazeltine Smith*. Boston, MA: Freeman and Bolles, 1843.

Sprague, Laura Fecych, ed. *Agreeable Situations: Society, Commerce, and Art in Southern Maine, 1780-1830*. Boston, MA: Northeastern University Press, 1987.

————. "Schoolgirl Art From the Misses Martin's School for Young Ladies in Portland, Maine. Accessed at http://www.afanews.com/articles/item/851-schoolgirl-art-from-the-misses-martin%E2%80%99s-school-for-young-ladies-in-portland-maine.

Stackpole, Everett. *Old Kittery and Her Families*. Lewiston, ME: Press of the Lewiston Journal Company, 1903.

Stackpole, Everett, Lucien Thompson, and Winthrop Smith. *History of the Town of Durham, New Hampshire, with Genealogical Notes*. Durham, NH: Durham Historical Association, 1913.

Stickney, Matthew. *The Stickney Family: A Genealogical Memoir of the Descendants of William and Elizabeth Stickney, from 1637 to 1869*. Salem, MA: The Essex Institute Press, 1869.

Storrs, Charles. *The Storrs Family*. New York: privately printed, 1886.

Thompson, Patricia Dingwall. *Early McMillens of New Boston, New Hampshire*. Privately published. Accessed on April 27, 2015 at www.familysearch.org.

Webster, Henry. *Friends' Records at Vassalboro, Maine*. Gardiner, ME: 1915.

Wentworth, John. *The Wentworth Genealogy*. Boston, MA: Little, Brown, and Company, 1878.

Whiting, William. *Memoir of Reverend Samuel Whiting, D.D., and of his Wife, Elizabeth St. John*. Boston, MA: Press of Rand, Avery & Co., 1873.

Wiggin, Arthur C., Agnes Bartlett, and Alexander Lincoln. *The Wiggin Genealogy: A Combination of Manuscripts in the Library of the New Hampshire Historical Society*. Unpublished typescript, New Hampshire Historical Society.

Wiley, George F. *Wiley's Book of Nutfield*. Derry Depot, NH: George F. Willey, Publisher, 1895.

Index

Names of known teachers appear in bold-face type

Charlestown, New Hampshire, 136
Chase, Caleb, 137
Chase, Mary, 38
Chase, Judith, 137
Chase, Tabitha Bemis, 137
Chester Academy, 147
Chester, Vermont, 147
Chicago, Illinois, 47
Choate, Gertrude F., 40
Civil War, 79, 101, 119, 127
Claremont, New Hampshire, 136
Cleaves, Abigail Wingate Paul, 85
Cleaves, Martha, 85
Cleaves, Mary Ellen, 85
Cleaves, Samuel, 85
Clement, Betsey, 102
Cloudman, Alice M., 51
Cloudman, John, 51
Clough, Jonathan, 101
Clough, Rufus George, 101
Coburn, Nathan P., 149
Cochran, Chauncey, 111
Cochran, Jenny, 111
Cochran, Moses, 111
Cochran, Sally, 111, 113
Coe, Eva Johnston, 3
Cogswell, John Cleaveland, 95
Colcord, Miss Emily S., 16
Conant, Rita, 72
Concord Insane Asylum, 8
Concord, Massachusetts, 109
Concord, New Hampshire, 13, 104, 107, 127, 130
Connecticut River, 137, 144
Connor, Abel, 126
Connor, Hannah Whitney, 126
Connor, Liva, 126
Conway, New Hampshire, 103
Cony Female Academy, 35-38, 40
Cony, Judge Daniel, 36-37
Cony, Sarah L., 36
Cook, George T., 129
Copps, Elizabeth C., 130
Copps, Mary "Polly" George, 130
Copps, Moses, 130
Corinth, Maine, 111
Corning, Nathaniel, 13
Cornish, New Hampshire, 137-140
Couch, John, 107
Cressey, Sally R., 124
Crosby, Jonas, 56
Crosby, Lucy Tarbell Shed, 56

Crosby, Susan, 56
Cumings, Joann, 139-140
Cumming, Sukey (Sarah or Sally), 139-140
Cummings, Eliza Ann, 147
Cummings, Elizabeth "Betsey" Connor, 147
Cummings, Noah, 147
Currier, James, 104
Currier, Lucinda, 104
Currier, Nathan, 104
Cushing, David, 133
Cushing, Louisa, 133
Cushing, Madame, 43
Cushing, Polly Adams, 133
Cutter, George, 57
Cutter, Harriet, 31
Cutter, Levi, 31
Cutter, Lucretia Mitchell, 31
Cutter, Samuel Bucknam, 57
Cutter, Samuel, 57
Cutter, Sarah, 57

D
Dakin, Dr. Moses, 61
Dame, George, 64
Danvers, Massachusetts, 31, 74, 129, 150
Danville, Vermont, 10
Dartmouth College, 3, 33, 69, 142
Dartmouth, New Hampshire, 96
Daughters of the American Revolution, 40
Davis, Ruthy, 120
Davis, A., 84
Davis, Caleb, 100
Davis, E., 84
Davis, Hezekiah, 100
Davis, Jonathan, 120
Davis, Mary Ann, 83-84
Davis, Mary, 99-101
Davis, Sarah Melvin, 120
Davis, Stephen, 100
Dawes, Mrs. Elizabeth, 57
de Lafayette, General Marquis, 13, 34
Deerfield, New Hampshire, 20
Derry, New Hampshire, 95, 113, 115
Dillingham, Pitt, 37
Dixfield, Maine, 3, 4
Dockum, Harriet Ann, 74
Dodge, Arthur, 118
Dodge, Eliza, 118

Dodge, Levi, 118
Doiron, David, 28
Dorchester, Massachusetts, 75
Dore, Betsey, 80
Dore, Eliza, 80, 83
Dore, John Jr., 80
Dore, William, 80
Douglas, Eleanor, 25
Dover, New Hampshire, 43, 74, 89
Dracut, Massachusetts, 149
Dublin, New Hampshire, 121-122
Dummerston, Vermont, 134
Dunbarton, New Hampshire, 130
Dunlap, Abigail H., 22
Dunlap, Lois Gove, 22
Dunlap, Stephen, 22
Dunsmoor, Ebenezer, 136
Durham, New Hampshire, 74,89
Duxbury, Massachusetts, 58
Dyer, Alvira, 80
Dyer, Amelia, 50
Dyer, Ezekiel, 80
Dyer, Rebecca Horton Huston, 50
Dyer, Sophia, 41
Dyer, William, 50

E
Earl, Ichabod, 7
East Bridgewater, Massachusetts, 40
East Derry, New Hampshire, 115
East Jaffrey, New Hampshire, 119
East Kingston, New Hampshire, 3, 33
Eastern Argus, 25
Eastman, Octavia, 33
Eastman, Timothy, 3, 33
Eastmanville, Michigan, 33
Eastport, Maine, 34
Edmonds, Mary Jaene, 100
Eliot, Maine, 71, 77
Elliot, Edmund, 16
Elliot, Eliza S. Gilman, 16
Elliot, John, 18
Elliot, Martha Jane, 16, 17
Elliot, Nancy, 18
Elliot, Sarah Jane, 18
Emerson, Caroline, 133-135
Emerson, Comfort Eastman, 134
Emerson, Dr. Moses, 134
Emerson, Helen, 134
Emerson, Jonathan, 134
Emerson, Lydia Crosby, 134
Emerson, Reverend Joseph, 89

Walpole, New Hampshire, 133
Walton, Mary Ann, 82-83
War of 1812, 123
Ward, Benjamin, 110
Ward, Dorcas, 71
Ward, Elizabeth, 71
Ward, Margery Greenleaf, 71
Ward, Margery, 71
Ward, Mary Ann, 71
Ward, Miss, 71
Ward, Nahum, 71
Warner, New Hampshire, 107, 140
Warren, Charles, 27
Warren, Edward, 27
Warren, Elizabeth, 27
Warren, George, 27
Warren, John, 27
Warren, Pamela, 27
Washburn, Charles, 27
Washburn, Ichabod, 27
Washburn, Pamela Bradford, 27
Washburn, Rufus, 27
Washburn, Silvia Bradford, 27
Washington, General George, 40
Washington, New Hampshire, 148
Waterville, Maine, 58
Watson, Benjamin, 94
Watson, Clarence, 94
Watson, Effie, 94
Weare, New Hampshire, 131
Webster, Andrew J., 44
Wedgwood, Stephen, 13
Wellfleet, Massachusetts, 149
Wells, Maine, 42-47
Wentworth, Anne Tredick, 9
Wentworth, Joshua, 9
Wentworth, Sarah Jane, 9
Westbrook, Maine, 34, 51
Wheeler, Abner, 104
Wheeler, Sarah Stickney, 104
Wheler (Wheeler), Tryphena, 104
Whidden III, Samuel, 69
Whidden Jr., Joseph W., 75
Whidden, Elizabeth, 69
Whidden, Frances, 74-76
Whidden, Langdon, 69
Whidden, Mary Ann, 75-76
Whidden, Samuel, 69
Whidden, William, 69
White, Adelia, 130
White, Ellen, 130
White, Henry Dewey, 130
White, Julia, 130

White, Sarah, 130
Whiting, Henry, 61
Whiting, John Lake, 61
Whiting, Lucy, 61
Whiting, Mary, 61
Whiting, Olive Ross Wyman, 61
Whiting, Olive, 61
Whiting, Relief, 61
Whiting, Sarah, 61
Whiting, Seth, 61
Whitten, Priscilla, 46
Wiggin, Joseph, 79
Wiggin, Lucy Maria, 79
Wiggin, Rhoda Sinclair, 79
Wiley's Book of Nutfield, 12
Willard, Abel, 136
Willard, Fanny Grout, 136
Willard, Frances, 136
Willard, Reverend Joseph, 66
Willard, Sophia, 136
Willey, Elizabeth Fabyan, 78
Willey, Elizabeth Hoit, 78
Willey, John, 78
Willey, Stephen, 78
William, James Mason, 3, 4, 32
Williams, Eliza, 36
Williams, Frances, 3
Williams, Joshua, 3
Williams, Reuel, 36
Williams, Seth, 4
Williams, Virgil, 4
Wilmot, New Hampshire, 20
Wilson, Dolly Dickinson, 150
Wilson, Frances, 150
Wilson, Isaac, 150
Wilson, Jonathan, 150
Wilson, Mary Dolly, 150
Wilson, Suckey, 150
Wilton, New Hampshire, 125
Windham, Maine, 62
Winslow, Maine, 58
Winterport, Maine, 55
Winthrop, New Hampshire, 76
Wixson, George F., 40
Wixson, James, 40
Woburn, Massachusetts, 136
Wolfeboro, New Hampshire, 8
Woodbury, Josiah, 101
Woodbury, Mark, 11
Woodbury, Rufus, 101
Woodbury, Sophia, 101, 103
Worcester, Massachusetts, 32, 132
Wyman, Joseph, 136

Wyman, Mary, 136

Y
York, Maine, 6
Young, Eliza, 90
Young, John, 90

www.ingramcontent.com/pod-product-compliance
Lightning Source LLC
Chambersburg PA
CBHW060800270326

41926CB00002B/36